D1478637

The Search for Certainty

The Search for Certainty

A Philosophical Account of
Foundations of Mathematics

M. Giaquinto

CLARENDON PRESS · OXFORD

OXFORD
UNIVERSITY PRESS

Great Clarendon Street, Oxford OX2 6DP

Oxford University Press is a department of the University of Oxford.
It furthers the University's objective of excellence in research, scholarship,
and education by publishing worldwide in

Oxford New York

Auckland Bangkok Buenos Aires Cape Town Chennai
Dar es Salaam Delhi Hong Kong Istanbul Karachi Kolkata
Kuala Lumpur Madrid Melbourne Mexico City Mumbai Nairobi
São Paulo Shanghai Singapore Taipei Tokyo Toronto
with an associated company in Berlin

Oxford is a registered trade mark of Oxford University Press
in the UK and in certain other countries

Published in the United States
by Oxford University Press Inc., New York

© Marcus Giaquinto 2002

British Library Cataloguing in Publication Data
Data available

Library of Congress Cataloging in Publication Data
Giaquinto, M. (Marcus).
The search for certainty : a philosophical account of foundations of
mathematics / M. Giaquinto.
p. cm.
Includes bibliographical references and index.
1. Mathematics—Philosophy. 2. Logic, Symbolic and mathematical. I. Title.
QA8.4.G53 2002   511.3—dc21   2001052064
ISBN 0–19–875244–X

1 3 5 7 9 10 8 6 4 2

Typeset in Calisto MT by
Cambrian Typesetters, Frimley, Surrey

Printed in Great Britain
on acid-free paper by
Biddles Ltd
Guildford & Kings Lynn

I dedicate this book to the memory of my father Phil
and my mother Judith

Preface

This book is a philosophical examination of one of the most brilliant intellectual explorations ever, aimed at justifying mathematics in the wake of the class paradoxes. However one judges the success of that endeavour, its fruitfulness is undeniable. It stimulated a new era of debate in the philosophy of mathematics, vigorous, forward-looking, and mathematically well informed. It also produced mathematical logic, now a vast field with its own sub-fields, opening with a display of surprising and profound discoveries. Despite the importance and allure of the subject, there has been no synoptic philosophical account of it, as far as I am aware—something I missed when first approaching the subject as a student of mathematical logic. This book is intended to fill that gap.

Although I try to convey some sense of the unfolding story, this book is not a history. My aim instead is to set out and engage with the main philosophical ideas and arguments. For the same reason, the book is not a text in mathematical logic. But some theorems are the focus of important philosophical disputes, and so expositions of those theorems and aspects of their proofs are essential. I have done my best to make the account accessible, largely suppressing technical details or relegating them to the notes, except where I felt they would reduce puzzlement or serve my non-technical aims. I have also tried to present a big picture in a fairly short book. This has meant a constant struggle between scope and depth. There is scarcely a topic treated here that is not worthy of further investigation. In many cases I felt this keenly, and on no matter do I claim the last word, despite drawing definite conclusions. Again for brevity's sake, some 'foundational' research programmes have not been examined, notably Brouwer's intuitionist programme, though I do sketch the motivating ideas. This is justified partly by the fact that the aim of that programme was not to secure accepted mathematics but to replace it. It seemed to make no sense to say more about it, unless I was prepared to extend the book by several chapters and blur the focus. In any case, my omission of this and other programmes is not to be taken as a comment on their importance.

I am very grateful to Michael Potter and to Michael Resnik for reading the penultimate typescript and supplying copious comments that helped me to improve the book. I am indebted to Michael Detlefsen, Jeremy Gray, Moshé Machover, Jesse Norman, and two anonymous referees for comments on various parts of an earlier version of the book. Mic Detlefsen in particular forced me to revise my views and sharpen my arguments, although we still disagree about the survival of Hilbert's Programme. In this connection I should also thank David Auerbach; and I thank Paolo Mancosu for encouragement and his timely translation of papers by Bernays and Hilbert. My thinking in this area has been greatly influenced by teachers and colleagues: John Bell, Michael Dummett, Christopher Ferneau, Robin Gandy, Bill Hart, Wilfrid Hodges, Daniel Isaacson, Moshé Machover, Dana Scott, Crispin Wright, and no doubt others. I thank them all. Everyone working in this area will echo me in thanking Solomon Feferman, both for his foundational studies and for his edition of Gödel's collected works: I have found both extremely helpful. I owe a very special debt to Daniel Isaacson, whose approach to philosophical and foundational matters has guided me ever since he was my supervisor. I hope that this book does not fall too far below the standards Dan sets for himself. I would also like to thank Peter Momtchiloff for help and patience. Most of all, I am indebted to my wife Frances for her love and support.

M.G.
London

Contents

Contents

I wanted certainty in the kind of way in which people want religious faith. I thought that certainty is more likely to be found in mathematics than else-where. But I discovered that many mathematical demonstrations, which my teachers expected me to accept, were full of fallacies. . .

Bertrand Russell (1956*b*)

Let us admit that the situation in which we presently find ourselves with respect to the paradoxes is in the long run intolerable. Just think: in mathematics, this paragon of certainty and truth, the very notions and inferences, as everyone learns, teaches, and uses them, lead to absurdities. And where is certainty and truth to be found if even mathematical thinking fails?

David Hilbert (1926)

Part I
Setting

Clarifying Mathematical Analysis 1

In the early decades of the twentieth century, mathematicians showed an unprecedented concern for the foundations of their subject, not just in expressions of disquiet but also in attempts to find a secure basis. This search for certainty and the crisis that sparked it off is the subject of the central parts of this book. The aim of Part I of the book is to give the mathematical setting of this story, so that it is possible to see how the foundational endeavours grew out of the nineteenth-century quest for clarity and rigour in mathematics.

We should not assume that mathematical progress prior to the twentieth century had been untroubled. Advances in mathematics, especially the introduction of new kinds of entity and new methods, often produced puzzles and paradoxes. Sometimes these were easily solved, but not always; until solutions were found the new ideas were regarded with suspicion. But eventually ideas would be clarified and doubts dispelled. A case in point is the introduction of negative integers. In the seventeenth century the proponents of the new numbers treated ratios between negative and positive integers $-n$ and n as follows:

$$-n/n = -1 = n/-n.$$

Operating this way seems to work. But $-n$ is less than n, and so equating the right-hand and left-hand terms entails that a lesser stands to a greater as a greater to a lesser, which is impossible. This is Arnauld's paradox.[1] It can be solved by taking $-n$ (where n is a positive integer) to be not simply a quantity, but a quantity in the reverse direction. This seems natural when one considers applications of the integers, such as steps forward and steps backward, or money owed to you and money owed by you. It is then no longer correct to think of the terms '$-n/n$' and '$n/-n$' as denoting ratios of quantities. When the ratio notation is extended to the negative as well as the positive integers, a term b/c can be understood as denoting that number by which c must be multiplied to obtain b. Multiplication of a number k by a negative number $-j$ can be understood as multiplication by its absolute value j with the direction of the product $j.k$ reversed.

Problems of the infinite

The task of integrating new with old was rarely straightforward. Invention was accompanied by puzzles, followed by clarification and eventual acceptance. But with more sophisticated innovations came harder puzzles, and clarification took longer. By far the greatest source of puzzles was the infinitesimal calculus. Ever since its discovery in the seventeenth century there had been doubts and disputes about its epistemic acceptability.[2] An example of the kind of problem generated by the calculus concerns the idea of instantaneous velocity. In many natural cases of change over time, the calculus provides a way of working out the *rate* of change at any point when change is occurring. If a body is changing its distance from some place, the rate of that change is the body's velocity. The calculus enables us to work out the velocity of a moving object at a given instant. But this idea—instantaneous velocity—is puzzling. Velocity is distance travelled over duration of travel. An instant is a point of time and so has zero duration. But positive duration is required to travel a positive distance. So instantaneous velocity would seem to be zero distance over zero time, which is vacuous. Yet techniques for calculating instantaneous velocities and for incorporating the results into other calculations turned out to be very useful. So there must be some other way of explicating the idea. But what? Suppose we plot distance travelled by a moving body against time on a graph (Figure 1). It is easy to work out the body's average velocity between time t and a later time $t + h$: it is the distance travelled divided by the duration of travel. Representing the distance travelled by time x as $f(x)$, this amounts to $[f(t + h) - f(t)]/h$.

So average velocity over an interval of time is no problem. What about the velocity of the body at time t, its instantaneous velocity at t? The average velocity between t and $t + h$ is represented by the slope of the line PQ. So one could try to think of the instantaneous velocity at t as the slope of the line that PX would become as X moves back along the curve from Q to reach P. But this is bluff. Until X reaches P, the slope of line PX represents not an instantaneous velocity but average velocity over an interval; when X reaches P, it coincides with P and there is no such thing as the line PX. The idea we are considering can be put into symbols. The instantaneous velocity at t is what $[f(t + h) - f(t)]/h$ becomes as h becomes zero. As long as h is non-zero, this is not the instantaneous velocity of

4

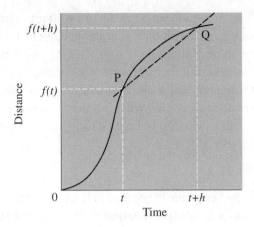

$f(t+h)$

Q

P

$f(t)$

Distance

0   t $t+h$

Time

Figure 1.1

the body at time t, but its average velocity over the interval from t to $t + h$; and when h is zero it has no value. We are back where we started.

What is needed is some way of singling out a straight line through the point P as *the tangent of the curve at* P; then we can define the instantaneous velocity of the body at t as the slope of that line. But how are we going to single out the relevant line? From the inception of calculus, accounts were given in terms of infinitesimal quantities. Leibniz, one of the inventors of calculus, thought of the tangent of the curve at P as the line through P that passes through two infinitesimally close points on the curve either side of P, and then the instantaneous velocity at t would be the slope of that line. Newton thought of instantaneous velocity as the ratio of an evanescent distance over an evanescent duration. This talk is suggestive but not illuminating. What is an infinitesimal quantity? What is an evanescent quantity? In a letter of 1687 Leibniz said that it was a non-zero quantity which is smaller than any assignable quantity.[3] This again is unclear, and he continued his attempts to elucidate, but without success. So mathematicians were left with the task of making sense of instantaneous velocity, something that was not really achieved for nigh on 150 years, when the concept of the derivative of a function was properly formulated. Although this clarification dispensed with the idea of infinitesimals, we will see that the infinite is still involved.

Other problems of this kind—that is, conceptual rather than technical problems—arose with the introduction of infinite sequences and operations on them. The infinite sum

$$1/2 + 1/4 + 1/8 + \ldots + 1/2^n + 1/2^{n+1} + \ldots$$

5

seems to make sense. As we add we get closer to 1 without overstepping it; but we do overstep each number less than 1, however close to 1 it is. So it seems right to say that the value of this infinite sum is 1. One can visualize the operation as the successive addition of fractions of a line segment of unit length. After the initial segment of half a unit has been drawn, adding a term in the sequence corresponds to extending what has been drawn so far by half the length of the previous extension. But now consider an example disputed in the eighteenth century:

$$1 - 1 + 1 - 1 + 1 - 1 + \ldots$$

(Here the + and – signs continue to alternate. Despite the 'minus' signs, this is an infinite sum, as $x - y$ is x plus the number $-y$.) By writing the infinite sum as

$$(1 - 1) + (1 - 1) + (1 - 1) + \ldots$$

it seems clear that the sum must be 0. However, recalling that $-1 + 1 = -(1 - 1)$, we can also represent it as 1 followed by an endless repetition of '$-(1 - 1)$' thus:

$$1 - (1 - 1) - (1 - 1) - (1 - 1) - \ldots$$

In this case it seems clear that the sum must be 1. Finally, if S is the whole sum, we get

$$-S = -1 + 1 - 1 + 1 - 1 + 1 - \ldots$$

since the negative of a sum is obtained by reversing the signs before the summands. Now adding 1 to the front of each side gives

$$1 - S = 1 - 1 + 1 - 1 + 1 - 1 + 1 - \ldots$$

But the right hand-side is the original sum and so denotes S. That is, $1 - S = S$. It follows that $S = 1/2$. Thus we have obtained three values for S: 0, 1, or 1/2. Which is right? The answer we would now give is that it has no value, because the series, as such infinite sums came to be called, does not converge. However, the convergence criterion, which will be explained shortly, was not settled on until the nineteenth century.[4]

   This example is not as frivolous as it looks. Leibniz obtained the result that $S = 1/2$ by a method of expanding an expression as a power series: $1/(1 + x) = 1 - x + x^2 - x^3 + x^4 - \ldots$ Then substituting 1 for x gives the result.[5] Leibniz had used the method of expanding an expression as a power series[6] for the purpose of finding a numerical expression for the ratio of the circumference of a circle to its diameter.[7] Several decades later Euler used the same method to obtain results that we would find absurd. For example, he expanded $1/(1 - x)$

to find that $1/(1 - x) = 1 + x + x^2 + x^3 + \ldots$ Then, by substituting 2 for x, he obtained the result that $-1 = 1 + 2 + 4 + 8 + \ldots$ Euler was aware that the terms in the expansion tend to zero only if $0 < x < 1$, but he defended the use of divergent series on the pragmatic grounds that they were useful for obtaining results about convergent series.

Euler was writing in the mid-eighteenth century. In the early decades of the nineteenth century the pragmatic balance shifted. In the eighteenth century there had been a big debate about the proper solutions to the wave equation for a vibrating string; d'Alembert, Euler, Daniel Bernouilli, and Lagrange were the major participants. That debate was already well under way when Daniel Bernouilli claimed that all motions of a vibrating string were representable as a trigonometric series, that is, an infinite sum whose terms involve trigonometric functions.[8] The matter was revived in the nineteenth century, when Fourier proclaimed that the class of functions representable as trigonometric series is very broad and that these representations are extremely useful for solving problems of physics. But just how broad is this class of functions? Does it exclude functions without an analytic expression or non-periodic functions or functions with discontinuities? These problems helped to motivate a concern for rigour, because it was clear that satisfying answers would require precise general definitions of the terms in which the questions are couched and of the notion at the heart of the subject, that of an infinite sum.

On top of this, the heavy use of infinite sums had made clear the unreliability of taking results proven for convergent series to hold also for divergent series. One of the foremost analysts of the early nineteenth century, Abel, complains in one letter of 'the tremendous obscurity which one unquestionably finds in analysis' and of 'this miserable way of concluding from the special to the general'; in another letter he writes 'By using [divergent series] one may draw any conclusion one pleases and that is why these series have produced so many fallacies and paradoxes . . . with the exception of geometric series, there does not exist in all of mathematics a single infinite series whose sum has been determined in a rigorous way. In other words, the things which are most important in mathematics are also those with least foundation.'[9]

The problems mentioned above were not isolated cases. Absurd results were matched by fallacious arguments. A prominent example of a belief that was wrongly thought to have been proved is that a continuous function has a derivative wherever it is defined except perhaps at isolated points. It is not hard to see why this was regarded as plausible. Suppose a function f is represented by a curve. If there is a unique line that serves as the tangent to the curve at the point $\langle t, f(t) \rangle$ on the curve, the function is said to be differentiable at t and to have a derivative at t, which is just the slope of the tangent at $\langle t, f(t) \rangle$. It is natural to assume that a curve fails to have a tangent at its sharp corners, while at every point on a locally smooth part of the curve the curve has a tangent. Thinking visually of a continuous function as one that can be represented as an uninterrupted curve, it is very plausible that a continuous function can have sharp corners only at isolated points, so that a continuous function is either locally smooth at all its points or composed of pieces that are locally smooth at all their points. This prompts the belief that a continuous function has a derivative everywhere except perhaps at isolated points. Several arguments were offered as proof of this belief, though it turns out to be false.[10] Here again, the problem was the lack of clear definitions of concepts basic to analysis, in this case concepts of function, continuity, and derivative. Other concepts too were sorely in need of precise definitions, if analysis was to be set on a sound footing.

The demise of visuo-spatial intuition

Some seventeenth-century mathematicians had hoped to make sense of the techniques of infinitesimal calculus in purely geometrical terms. But that hope faded in the nineteenth century, when it became clear how misleading spatial intuition could be in analysis. Moreover, geometry itself lost its reputation for certainty in the nineteenth century when it was discovered that Euclid's parallels postulate can be replaced by a contrary alternative without introducing inconsistency, thus raising the possibility that the geometry of physical space is not Euclidean.[11] But the most important factor was growing awareness of the unreliability of spatial intuition.

The divergence between intuition and reality in analysis was underlined by the discovery of counterexamples to the belief that a continuous function must have a derivative everywhere except isolated points. These are known as continuous but nowhere differentiable functions. The first example was given by Bolzano.[12] Here is the basic idea of a simplified version of Bolzano's example. The function is the limit of a sequence of functions, all defined on the interval from 0 to 1 inclusive. The first function in the sequence is the identity $f_1(x) = x$, whose graph is the ascending diagonal from the origin to $\langle 1, 1 \rangle$. The second function f_2 replaces the diagonal by three straight line segments, from the origin to the point $\langle 1/3, 3/4 \rangle$, thence to $\langle 2/3, 1/4 \rangle$, thence to $\langle 1, 1 \rangle$. Thus, the first piece of f_2 rises to three-quarters of the height of the diagonal and goes one-third of the way along, the second piece of f_2 falls to one quarter of the height of the diagonal and goes another third of the way along and the third rises to the total height and goes the final third of the way along. This is illustrated in Figure 2(a). The third function f_3 replaces each piece of f_2 by three new pieces; each ascending piece is replaced in the same way that f_1 was replaced by f_2, and the middle descending piece is replaced by three pieces, each going a third of its horizontal span, the first falling three quarters of its vertical span, the second rising by a half of its vertical span and the last falling to its endpoint. This is illustrated in Figure 2(b).

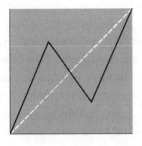
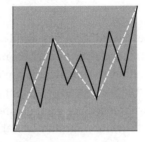

(a) Figure 1.2   (b) Figure 1.2

In general, f_{n+1} is constructed from f_n by replacing each piece of f_n by three new pieces in the same way. It is possible to prove that these functions approximate ever more closely to a single function which is continuous but at no point has a derivative.

If a continuous function does not have a derivative at a certain point, it has no tangent at that point, and so its curve forms a sharp peak or a sharp valley at that point. Intuitively, there must be parts of the curve either side of the sharp peak or valley that are smooth enough to have tangents; but a continuous, nowhere differentiable function has no tangent at any point, and so its 'curve' would have to consist of sharp peaks or sharp valleys at every point, a possibility that defies spatial intuition.

A related discovery reinforced the message. In 1890 Peano showed that it is possible to define a curve that completely fills a two-dimensional region. This appears to be impossible, as a curve with endpoints would seem to be a figure with length but not area. Since Peano's original example of a space-filling curve, many others have been found by considering the limit of an infinite sequence of ordinary curves. Hilbert explained the geometric idea underlying one way of generating a sequence of curves whose 'limit' curve fills a square. Figure 3 illustrates the first three steps of the generation of the Hilbert curve.[13]

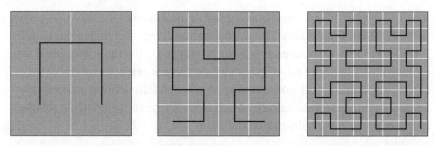

Figure 1.3

Of course, these discoveries could be properly established only when proper definitions of the relevant terms were in place. But they reinforced the belief that a rigorous account of the calculus could not be given in terms of a theory based on spatial intuition. Instead of looking for a geometrical account, then, analysts developed arithmetical ideas for clarification and reconstruction. By the end of the nineteenth century, substantial clarification had been achieved.

Clarification and quantifiers

To get an idea of this work, let us first see how the concept of convergence was defined. The key is the idea of the limit of an infinite sequence. An infinite sequence $p_1, p_2, p_3, \ldots$ of real numbers[14] is denoted '$\{p_n\}$'.

> A number c is the *limit* of a sequence $\{p_n\}$ if and only if, for any positive real number ε, there is a positive integer m such that, for all integers k greater than m, the difference between p_k and c is less than ε.

We can shorten this using familiar notation:

> $\text{Lim}_{n \to \infty} \{p_n\} = c$ if and only if for all $\varepsilon > 0$ there is an integer $m > 0$ such that for all integers $k > m$, $| p_k - c | < \varepsilon$.

The sequence $\{p_n\}$ is said to *converge* to c when $\lim_{n \to \infty} \{p_n\} = c$. A sequence that does not converge to any number is said to diverge. There are more general notions of limit, one of which we will come to shortly. But for present purposes this is the appropriate level of generality.

Now we can make precise the convergence criterion for infinite series $s_1 + s_2 + s_3 + \ldots$. First, we define its partial sums p_n as follows: $p_1 = s_1, p_2 = s_1 + s_2$, $p_3 = s_1 + s_2 + s_3$, and generally $p_{n+1} = p_n + s_{n+1}$. The infinite series satisfies the convergence criterion when the sequence $\{p_n\}$ converges, and if $\{p_n\}$ converges to c, $s_1 + s_2 + s_3 + \ldots = c$. In other words, the value of an infinite series is the limit of its partial sums. The definition of the limit of a sequence can also be used to define the limit function of a sequence of functions, which was used in the description of Bolzano's nowhere differentiable function. Let $\{f_n\}$ be a sequence of functions defined on the same set D, such as the unit interval [0, 1] or the set of all real numbers. Suppose that, for each x in D, the infinite sequence of values $f_1(x), f_2(x), f_3(x), \ldots$ converges. The *limit function f* of the sequence $\{f_n\}$ is then defined thus: for each x in D, $f(x) = \lim_{n \to \infty} f_n(x)$.

The concept of a limit can easily be extended to apply to entities other than sequences. Let f be any function defined on the real numbers.[15] For any point p, the limit of f as x approaches p is defined as follows:

$\lim_{x \to p} f(x) = c$ if and only if for every $\varepsilon > 0$ there is a $\delta > 0$ such that for any x, if $0 < |x - p| < \delta, 0 < |f(x) - c| < \varepsilon$.

If no number c satisfies this condition, f has no limit as x approaches p. It took the best minds many years to articulate this concept of a limit, freeing it of ideas of motion. The key is the arrangement of the quantifiers, which is not at all obvious from the experiential idea of a limit as the point that the process closes in on. Now we can define continuity, which was introduced earlier in a visual way as the property a function has when its curve is uninterrupted:

f is *continuous at p* if and only if $f(p)$ is defined and $\lim_{x \to p} f(x) = f(p)$.

A function is *continuous* on an interval $[a, b]$ if it is continuous at every point between a and b, and it is continuous without qualification if it is continuous at every point for which it is defined.

Precise definitions such as those just given were not in currency until late in the nineteenth century. Although we can draw some idea of limit and of convergence from experiential sources such as the perceptual image of a moving point homing in on a static destination, extracting from this image a general definition which is strictly and literally correct is no trivial task. A certain subtlety is required to get the right ordering of quantifier phrases, such as 'for any positive real number', 'there is a positive integer', 'for all integers greater than m' which occur in the definition of the limit of an infinite sequence.

Quantifiers, as we call the logical items expressed by these phrases, and the logic of quantifiers have a significant part in the story, so I will say a little about them now. If one removes a name from a simple sentence such as 'Sirius shines' one is left with a predicate '. . . shines'; a quantifier phrase in place of the name serves to specify a domain and the extent of the domain that satisfies the condition expressed by the predicate. Thus, 'Every star' in 'Every star shines' specifies the class of stars as the domain and the whole of that class as the extent of the domain that satisfies the predicate-condition. Here are some examples.

Quantifier phrase	*Domain*	*Extent*
Every star	the class of stars	all
No planet	the class of planets	none
Some galaxy	the class of galaxies	at least one

When the extent is *all*, the quantifier is said to be universal. When the extent is *at least one*, the quantifier is said to be existential. Sequences of quantifiers are used when dealing with relational conditions, such as '. . . succeeds . . .' If we want to use this predicate to say that every natural number[16] has a successor, we cannot just put quantifier phrases in the gaps: neither of the sentences 'Some natural number succeeds every natural number' and 'Every natural number succeeds some natural number' says what was intended. Instead, we put all quantifiers at the front and use letters for cross-referencing: 'For every natural number x, there is some natural number y such that y succeeds x.' If we reverse the quantifiers, we turn a truth into a falsehood: the sentence 'There is some natural number y such that for every natural number x, y succeeds x' says that some number succeeds all. So the order of quantifiers is significant.

The importance of quantifier order is underlined by a particular mistake of one of the great analysts. A large step in bringing clarity and rigour to analysis was made by Cauchy in his famous *Cours d'Analyse* of 1821. But his continued use of the language of infinitesimals prevented him from noticing the difference between pointwise convergence and uniform convergence for infinite sequences of functions, and this confusion led him into fallacy.[17] Attention to quantifier order reveals the difference between these two properties, as soon as one recognizes the logical difference between 'for every x there is a y such that . . .' and 'there is a y such that for every x . . .' Let $\{f_n\}$ be a sequence of functions defined on the same set D, and suppose that, for each x in D, $\lim_{n\to\infty} f_n(x)$ exists, i.e. that the sequence of values $\{f_n(x)\}$, that is, $f_1(x), f_2(x), f_3(x), f_4(x), \ldots$, converges. Then the sequence of functions $\{f_n\}$ is said to *converge pointwise* to f if and only if, for each x in D, $f(x) = \lim_{n\to\infty} f_n(x)$. Spelled out, this becomes:

> For every x in D and for every $\varepsilon > 0$ there is an integer $m > 0$ such that, for all integers $k \geqslant m$, $|f_k(x) - f(x)| < \varepsilon$.

In pointwise convergence, the integers m that can serve depend on both ε and x. In uniform convergence, the integers m that can serve depend only on ε. That is, if for a given ε the same integer m serves for all x in D, the sequence of functions $\{f_n\}$ *converges uniformly* to f:

For every $\varepsilon > 0$ there is an integer $m > 0$ such that, for every x in D and for all integers $k \geqslant m$, $|f_k(x) - f(x)| < \varepsilon$.

Applied to functions defined on real numbers with real number values, uniform convergence entails that, for each positive ε, if $k \geqslant m$ the entire graph of f_k lies within a horizontal distance of ε from the graph of the limit function f.[18]

Often in mathematical texts there are just two or three domains of interest, and some convention associating specific letters with domains is adopted. For example, one might reserve m, n for natural numbers and x, y, z for real numbers. So the Archimedean property for real numbers can be succinctly expressed thus:

For all x and all y, if $x > 0$, there is some n such that $n > 0$ and $nx > y$.

In such cases the quantifier letters not only serve to make cross-references, but also indicate the quantifier domain. Used in this way, a quantifier letter came to be thought of as a variable ranging over the domain it indicates. All occurrences in a given sentence of a given quantifier letter are linked or 'bound together' by the preceding quantifier phrase in which the letter occurs. Accordingly, quantifier letters are known as 'bound variables'.

Let us now see how the puzzle of instantaneous velocity was solved. The velocity of the body at instant t is the limit of the sequence of slopes of PX as X moves back along the curve to P, that is, the limit of $[f(t + h) - f(t)]/h$ as h tends to zero. Writing 'F(h)' for '$[f(t + h) - f(t)]/h$', we can make it literal and precise, by applying the definition of the limit of a function given earlier:

$\mathrm{Lim}_{h \to 0} \mathrm{F}(h) = c$ if and only if for every $\varepsilon > 0$ there is a $\delta > 0$ such that for any h, if $0 < h < \delta$, then $0 < |\mathrm{F}(h) - c| < \varepsilon$.

The *derivative* of the function f at a point t, written $f'(t)$, is just this limit:

$f'(t) = \mathrm{lim}_{h \to 0} \mathrm{F}(h)$, provided that there is a number fulfilling the condition for being the limit.

The instantaneous velocity of the body at t is just the derivative of f at t.

If a function has a derivative at all numbers for which it is defined, the function is said to be *differentiable*. Differentiability of a function is an analytic counterpart of the experiential property of local smoothness of a curve, in the sense of an absence of corners or sharp points. But the analytic property cannot be read off from the experiential property. One reason is that some differentiable functions are not wholly representable in experience as curves.[19] There are other reasons. Local smoothness, being an experiential property,

13

might vary as one zooms in or out; there might be degrees of local smoothness, and more than one analytic property might serve as a counterpart of local smoothness. Again, the analytic property of continuity is not the same as the experiential property of uninterruptedness of a curve. For the analytic property one has to attend to the definition. As we saw, unpacking the definition reveals nested quantifiers with bound variables ranging over the real numbers. Similar remarks apply to integrability of a function and to all other basic properties of analysis. Special credit goes initially to Bolzano and Cauchy, and later to Dirichlet and Weierstrass, for getting the definitions straight.

This chapter has been concerned with the clarification of basic properties and relations of analysis. The objects of analysis—real numbers and more generally points, classes of points, and functions on classes of points—have been taken for granted. But in the later decades of the nineteenth century mathematicians came to feel that an explicit account of real numbers was needed; so my sketch is incomplete. The next chapter fills in this gap and adds an account of the transfinite numbers discovered—or, some would say, invented—by Cantor.

Numbers and Classes 2

The conceptual clarification described in the previous chapter dispenses with infinitesimals. But that was not felt to be good enough: some account of the real numbers was also needed. This chapter first explains that need and presents the two best known accounts of real numbers. That is followed by a sketch of the way in which the ideas for the transfinite ordinal and cardinal number systems grew out of the study of classes of points, and the rudiments of those number systems are presented. Finally, we look at accounts of the natural numbers. This will complete an account of the nineteenth-century movement to clarify mathematical concepts and to place the accepted practices and theorems of mathematics on a sound footing.

Points and real numbers

Mathematical analysis in the late nineteenth century saw the early development of our understanding of spaces of points. But points are puzzling. Consider the following puzzle. If one removes a single point from a line, there must be a gap where the point was; so there must be a positive distance between the remaining two segments of the line; hence the point must have had positive breadth equal to the distance between the segments; yet points have no breadth. Where have we gone wrong? Here is another puzzle. A continuous line has no gaps at all and its component points are packed as closely together as possible; yet no point touches any other, for between any two there is an interval. Such puzzles show that the idea of points we have from experience is confusing if not incoherent. Analysis needed an account of points that dispensed with allusion to visuo-spatial elements, and for this purpose mathematicians turned to numbers. If we think of points in a three-dimensional space as located by means of a framework of coordinate axes (vertical, horizontal, ahead–behind) with a common origin, we can identify a point with an ordered triple $\langle x, y, z \rangle$ of real numbers, x signifying the point's horizontal position, y its vertical position, and z its position to the fore or rear. Generally, points in an n-dimensional space can be identified with ordered sequences of n real numbers. But what are real numbers?

It is natural to seek clarification in terms of the kinds of magnitude to which we apply real-number arithmetic. Spatial length is a magnitude of this kind, as are duration and mass. Taking a specific length (duration, mass, etc.) as unit, say a metre, any other length is specified as its ratio to the unit. Consider the following.

The length of d = r metres.

This is equivalent to

r = the ratio of the length of d to the length of the standard metre.

So we can approach the problem by saying that real numbers are ratios of magnitudes of a certain general kind. But what kind? Usually a contrast is made with discrete magnitudes, like the cardinal number of a collection of things. A system of magnitudes is discrete when every magnitude (except first and last) has an immediate predecessor and an immediate successor. We take length, duration, etc., to be dense rather than discrete: between any two lengths there is another, hence infinitely many others, and none has an immediate predecessor or an immediate successor. But density is not enough. The system of rational numbers, numbers of the form n/m, where n and m are integers and m is not 0, is dense. But we take rationals to be insufficient for lengths, because the ratio of the length of the diagonal of a square to the length of its side is $\sqrt{2}$, which we know is not a rational number.[1] This is not an isolated case. $\sqrt{3}$ is the length of the hypotenuse of a right-angled triangle with other sides of lengths 1 and $\sqrt{2}$ units, and $\sqrt{3}$ is irrational; in general, for any positive integer n, $\sqrt{n}$ units is the length of the hypotenuse of a right-angled triangle with other sides of lengths 1 and $\sqrt{(n-1)}$, and unless $\sqrt{n}$ is an integer it is irrational.[2] It was felt that the relevant kind of magnitude has to be in some sense continuous as well as dense, but it was not clear what continuity amounts to in this context. So, although it turned out to be true that a real number is a ratio of continuous magnitudes, further work was needed in order to get a clear concept of real number.

As with the clarification of concepts of properties of sequences and functions, the effective motivation to get clear about real numbers was pragmatic. Cauchy had offered a useful criterion for convergence of a sequence:

$\{s_n\}$ converges if for all $\varepsilon > 0$ there is an integer $m > 0$ such that, for all k

$> m,\ |\ s_m - s_k\ | < \varepsilon.$

This *seems* right: if we can find end-bits of the tail of the sequence whose span is as small as one pleases, the tail must end in a point. But proving that this is right requires some account of the real-number system. Another useful assumption is that, if all the members of an increasing sequence are less than some given number, that sequence converges. This also seems right: one imagines the members of the sequence getting more and more squeezed together as it approaches its upper bounds[3] from below, until it ends at a point, and that would be the least upper bound of the sequence, its limit. But again, proving this requires an account of the real numbers.

Accounts of the real numbers were given by a number of people: Weierstrass, Dedekind, Cantor, Méray, Heine, and possibly others. All accounts take the integers and the rational numbers (ratios of integers) for granted. They then fall into two groups. The approach of one group is to define real numbers in terms of sequences of rational numbers. Cantor, for example, used sequences $\{s_n\}$ of rational numbers that satisfy the condition: for every rational number $p > 0$ there is an integer $m > 0$ such that, for all $k > m$, $|\ s_m - s_k\ | < p$. Cantor called such sequences 'fundamental' and stipulated that each one represents a real number.[4] This is essentially what we are doing when we take an infinite decimal to represent a real number, for the sequence of rational numbers represented by the successively longer initial segments of an infinite decimal is a fundamental sequence. Cantor added that two fundamental sequences $\{s_n\}$ and $\{t_n\}$ represent the same real number if and only if the limit of $|\ s_n - t_n\ |$ as n increases is zero. This relation between fundamental sequences is known as Cauchy-equivalence; the fundamental sequences fall into mutually exclusive classes, all members of the same class being Cauchy-equivalent and no two members from different classes being Cauchy-equivalent. Thus, for each class of Cauchy-equivalent fundamental sequences Cantor posited a unique real number. Cantor supplied further definitions and the proofs needed to ensure that his account works. Cauchy's criterion for convergence falls out of Cantor's account.

The other approach is to define a real number in terms of a division of the rational numbers into a lower and an upper class, with no overlap. Such pairs of classes are known as cuts and every such pair is taken to represent a unique real number. This is Dedekind's approach.[5] We sometimes think of a point as the locus of intersection of two lines when one cuts the other. Dedekind's proposal is a counterpart of this. Since his account is used in later chapters, I will present a precise but slightly modified version of it here. Let A_1 and A_2 be classes of rational numbers. The ordered pair (A_1, A_2) is defined to be a *Dedekind cut* if and only if

(i)   both A_1 and A_2 are non-empty,
(ii) every rational is a member of exactly one of the two classes,
(iii) for any rationals p and q, if $p < q$ and q is in A_1, p is also in A_1,
(iv) A_1 has no greatest member.

If in addition A_2 has no least member, (A_1, A_2) is defined to be *irrational*. (A_1, A_2) is irrational if for example A_1 is the class containing all negative rationals and the positive rationals whose square is less than 2 while A_2 contains all others. If p is any rational and A_1 is the class of rationals less than p (so that p is least in A_2), I will put p^* for (A_1, A_2). The ordering of cuts is defined thus: $(A_1, A_2) < (B_1, B_2)$ if and only if there is a rational p in B_1 which is not in A_1. With this definition it is possible to prove the transitivity of the ordering and the law of trichotomy: for any cuts c and d, exactly one of the following holds: $c < d$, $c = d$ or $d < c$. A cut c is defined to be *negative* if and only if $c < 0^*$, and *positive* if and only if $0^* < c$.

   If cuts are to do duty as real numbers, we need definitions of the arithmetical operations on cuts and proofs that the operations obey the familiar laws of real-number arithmetic, such as commutativity and associativity of addition and of multiplication. I will only present the definition for addition, for the sake of illustration. Let (A_1, A_2) and (B_1, B_2) be cuts. Let C_1 be the class of all rationals equal to $p + q$ for some p in A_1 and some q in B_1 and let C_2 be the class of all other rationals. Then one can prove that (C_1, C_2) is a cut, and it is this cut that is defined to be the sum $(A_1, A_2) + (B_1, B_2)$. For fear of tiring readers, I will not give definitions of the other arithmetical operations nor of the inverse operations ($-x$ and x^{-1}); they can be found in a number of introductions to analysis.[6] From these definitions, it is possible to prove that the cuts with the defined operations and distinguished elements 0^* and 1^* form an ordered field.[7]

   The rational numbers with their operations already form an ordered field. So there must be some structural property not deducible from the conditions for being an ordered field which distinguishes the real numbers from the rationals. The crucial extra property is continuity, also known as completeness. This is a property about the ordering of cuts and is not the same as the property of functions that goes by the same name. Geometry has two laws about the ordering of points on the line that are relevant here. One is the law of *density*: between every two points on a line there is another. It follows from the fact that the cuts form an ordered field that they too are densely ordered.

The other law of geometry is that, for every division of a line into lower and upper classes of points, there is exactly one point that produces the division. Dedekind identified this property as the crucial extra ingredient (added to density) that makes a line continuous. Dedekind proved that the cuts have the corresponding property of *continuity*: for any division of the class of cuts into two non-empty classes C and D such that, for any c in C and d in D, $c < d$, there is exactly one cut that is greatest in C or least in D. This is equivalent to the principle that is now known as Dedekind's *Continuity* (or *Completeness*) *Axiom*:

> Every non-empty class S of cuts with an upper bound has a least upper bound.

It follows that the cuts form a continuous or complete ordered field, and that this suffices for the cuts to serve as the real numbers. In particular, it enabled Dedekind to prove unproven assumptions used in many analytic arguments, such as Cauchy's criterion for convergence.

Let us reflect a little on these accounts of the real numbers before turning to other matters. Points in the spaces studied in nineteenth-century analysis are defined in terms of real numbers, and real numbers are defined in terms of rational numbers. Putting it like this misses something important: both accounts of real numbers involve arbitrary infinite classes or sequences of elements drawn from an infinite stock. Cantor's account not only takes as given the infinite class of rationals but also presupposes that there is a class of all fundamental sequences of rationals, without restriction to sequences we can actually define—in that sense they are 'arbitrary' sequences. These sequences are infinite objects. Dedekind's account presupposes that there is a class of all divisions of rationals into upper and lower classes, again without restriction to those divisions for which we have a definition. In terms of lower classes (i.e. classes C such that if $p < q$ and q is in C so is p) what is taken as given is the existence of a totality of arbitrary lower classes, each of which is an infinite object. In fact, sequences can be represented as classes, infinite sequences as infinite classes.[8] So both accounts in effect assume the existence of a totality of arbitrary infinite classes of elements from an infinite stock. This is significant. Our intuitive notion of points on a line is insufficient to provide a proper conception of real number; we have no grasp of real numbers except as kinds of infinite classes. Real numbers, and therewith the points of classical analysis, are infinite objects, despite being the mathematical counterparts of what we loosely think of as the smallest things possible.

One further matter. I have canvassed not one but two definitions of the real numbers. On one the real numbers are identified with classes of

19

Cauchy-equivalent fundamental sequences of rationals. On the other the real numbers are identified with pairs of lower and upper classes of rationals, the cuts. But no cut is a class of Cauchy-equivalent fundamental sequences. So a real number cannot be both a cut and a class of Cauchy-equivalent fundamental sequences. It appears then that one or both of these definitions is wrong. In fact, neither definition is wrong. Neither Cantor nor Dedekind took himself to be giving metaphysical identity conditions for real numbers.[9] An alternative is to regard them as defining representatives of real numbers. Each approach contains not only a definition of the representatives, but also definitions of certain properties and operations on the representatives. The role of each system of definitions is to pick out a class of objects, plus some properties and operations on them, which can be proved to have the structural characteristics attributed to the putative system of real numbers. The problem facing late nineteenth-century mathematicians was to verify their belief that it was possible for one collection of things to have all these characteristics together. If we think of these characteristics as summed up in the defining conditions for being a complete ordered field, the task was to show that there could be such a thing as a complete ordered field, in other words that there is something exhibiting that structure. Each approach does this by defining a system of entities and proving that it satisfies all the conditions for being a complete ordered field. That was all that was done and all that needed to be done to solve the mathematical problem. There is a further question, but it is a question of metaphysics, not mathematics: what are the real numbers, if anything? It turns out that any two complete ordered fields are isomorphic, that is, each can be mapped 1-to-1 onto the other in a way that preserves all structural properties; in short, all of them have exactly the same structure, which we can therefore call *the* structure of a complete ordered field. One answer to the metaphysical question in currency today is that the real numbers are nothing more than the positions in that structure. Granted that answer, the important task, for metaphysics as well as mathematics, was to show that there is such a structure. That, effectively, was done (in their different ways) by Cantor and Dedekind.

Point classes and transfinite indices

The general study of point classes grew out of the study of classes of points on a line, that is, classes of real numbers. (Henceforth I may also call real numbers 'reals' and the class of real numbers 'the real line'. I will also drop the cut notation $n*$, $(p/q)*$ and use numerals in the normal way to denote integer reals and rational reals, and when talking about the real numbers I may drop the qualifier 'real'.) Cantor's early research investigated trigonometric series of real numbers of a form studied by the mathematician Riemann.[10] In the course of this research Cantor developed some completely new ideas that contained the germ of his theory of transfinite ordinal numbers. The new ideas are now standard in the theory of point classes. Cantor gave the definitions for points on the real line, but they can easily be generalized for spaces of more than one dimension. Here is one of the definitions:

> Let p be any point and C any class of points. p is a *limit point* of C if and only if every open[11] interval containing p contains infinitely many points of C.

The class of limit points of C is denoted C'. Then Cantor defined the nth *derived class* of a class C, denoted $C^{(n)}$, as follows:

$$C^{(1)} = C'; \quad C^{(n+1)} = C^{(n)'}.$$

Clearly, if a class of points is finite the class of its limit points is empty. If C is an infinite class, it is possible that its nth derived class $C^{(n)}$ is finite so that all $C^{(n+m)}$ are empty. C is defined to be a class of the *first species* if and only if, for some finite positive integer n, $C^{(n)}$ is finite. Otherwise it is of the second species.

Cantor's study of point classes led him to investigate classes of the second species. If C is a class of the second species it will have limit points, points in $C^{(1)}$ that occur in all the subsequent derived classes $C^{(n)}$ with finite index n. The class of those points Cantor denoted $C^{(\infty)}$. Extending the notation in a natural way, Cantor defined $C^{(\infty+1)}$ to be the first derived class of $C^{(\infty)}$, and in general $C^{(\infty+n)}$ is the nth derived class of $C^{(\infty)}$. Obviously this can be continued, with $C^{(\infty+\infty)}$ $(= C^{(2\infty)})$ being the class of points in every $C^{(\infty+n)}$ for finite positive integers n. Using the same two principles of definition, it is easy to see that one gets derived classes with indices of the form $n\infty + m$ for all finite positive integers n and m. The class of points in all those classes has index $\infty \cdot \infty$ or ∞^2. Continuing in this way, Cantor obtained classes with indices of the form

$$n_0 \infty^m + n_1 \infty^{m-1} + \ldots + n_m,$$

and then (with some large jumps)

$$\infty^\infty, \ n\infty^\infty, \ \infty^{\infty+1}, \ \infty^{\infty+n}, \ \infty^{n\infty}, \ \infty^{\infty^n}, \ \infty^{\infty^\infty}, \ \ldots$$

Cantor later came to regard this transfinite system as a system of numbers in their own right, extending the natural numbers. But his original interest was not in extensions of the natural numbers. His primary goal was to characterize the continuum, the real line, and he had developed his classification of derived classes of the second species with the aim of developing a tool for this primary goal.[12] In the course of his investigations into the continuum, he made some remarkable discoveries in comparing infinite classes of reals in respect of 'power' or cardinality. But he had not been able to find a natural and systematic account of the cardinal sizes of infinite classes. Eventually he realized that the key to this problem was the system of transfinite numbers which he had in effect discovered in his classification of derived classes of the second species. These numbers are the transfinite ordinal numbers. Since the ordinals are of recurring importance, a brief presentation of the basic ideas might be useful.

Ordinal numbers

First, we need to define a kind of ordering of a class.

> A class C is *well ordered* by a relation < if and only if < is a strict linear ordering[13] of C and every non-empty subclass of C has a <-least member.[14]

It follows from this definition that, if C is well ordered by < and B is an initial segment of C (other than the whole of C), there is a member of C that is first after all the members of B. An example of a well ordered class is the class of natural numbers ordered by the 'less-than' relation. By contrast, the class of rational numbers ordered by the 'less-than' relation is linear but not well ordered, as the subclass $\{1/2, 1/4, 1/8, \ldots, 1/2^n, 1/2^{n+1}, \ldots\}$ has no least member.

An infinite class can be well ordered in many different ways. For example, the natural numbers ordered by <

$$0, 1, 2, 3, 4, 5, \ldots$$

has a first but no last element, and the first element is the only initial element, that is, one without an immediate predecessor. The way in which a class is ordered is known as its order type. Two ordered classes $(A, <_A)$ and $(B, <_B)$ have the same order type if and only if there is a 1-to-1 correlation c of the members of A with the members of B such that $x <_A y$ if and only if $c(x) <_B c(y)$. In figurative terms this means that, given a parallel pair of lists of the members of A and B in their respective $<_A$ and $<_B$ orderings, they can be paired off 1-to-1 by lines between members of A and B without any crossing of lines. The order type of the natural numbers ordered by < is known as ω. If the first three are placed after all the others, with the order otherwise the same, the result is a well ordered class of order type $\omega + 3$:

$3, 4, 5, 6, 7, 8, \ldots 0, 1, 2.$

This has a first and last element, and two initial elements. If evens are placed after all odds, the order otherwise unchanged, we get a well ordered class of order type $\omega + \omega$:

$1, 3, 5, 7, 9, \ldots 0, 2, 4, 6, 8, \ldots$

Distinct orderings of the same class may have the same order type. For example, the result of placing all multiples of three after all the rest, order otherwise unchanged, is again of order type $\omega + \omega$:

$1, 2, 4, 5, 7, 8, \ldots 0, 3, 6, 9, \ldots$

In these examples, one and the same infinite class is well ordered in different ways. Let us turn from orderings of the natural numbers to orderings of the ordered pairs of natural numbers. Consider them arranged in rows and columns, with $\langle n, m \rangle$ placed in the nth row and mth column:

$$\begin{array}{cccc}
\langle 0, 0 \rangle & \langle 0, 1 \rangle & \langle 0, 2 \rangle & \ldots \\
\langle 1, 0 \rangle & \langle 1, 1 \rangle & \langle 1, 2 \rangle & \ldots \\
\langle 2, 0 \rangle & \langle 2, 1 \rangle & \langle 2, 2 \rangle & \ldots \\
\vdots & \vdots & \vdots &
\end{array}$$

Consider the following ordering on this class: the members of a row precede the members of all lower rows, and within a row each member precedes all other members to its right. Each row has order type ω and the class of rows has order type ω. Thus, the ordering of the whole array is of type $\omega \times \omega$.

An *ordinal number* is the order type of a well ordered class. There are three kinds of ordinal. (i) The very first ordinal is the order type of the empty class (with the empty ordering) and we call it '0'. (ii) If α is an ordinal, the next ordinal after α, $\alpha + 1$, is the order type of class of all the preceding ordinals up to and including α under their order of precedence. Thus, the ordinal 1 is the order type of $\langle 0 \rangle$, 2 of $\langle 0, 1 \rangle$, 3 of $\langle 0, 1, 2 \rangle$, and $\alpha + 1$ of $\langle 0, \ldots \alpha \rangle$. (iii) For any unending succession of consecutive ordinals there is a first ordinal after the succession; this ordinal is the order type of the class of all the ordinals up to and including all ordinals in the succession under their order of precedence. Such ordinals are known as limit ordinals. The first limit ordinal is ω, the order type of the class of finite ordinals $\langle 0, 1, 2, 3, \ldots \rangle$. Every ordinal other than 0 is a successor ordinal or a limit ordinal; thus there are two ways in which ordinals are generated: by proceeding to the successor of an ordinal, and by proceeding to the first ordinal after an endless succession. With these principles of generation, we quickly find ordinals whose structure is mirrored by the indices of derived point classes of the second species. Let 'm' and 'n' range over natural numbers. Then we obtain these ordinals:

$\omega + (n + 1)$ the successor of $\omega + n$

$\omega + \omega (= 2\omega)$ the limit of the sequence of ordinals of the form $\omega + n$

$n\omega + (m + 1)$ the successor of $n\omega + m$

$\omega\cdot\omega (= \omega^2)$ the limit of the sequence of ordinals of the form $n\omega + m$

Proceeding in these two ways, we get ordinals of the form

$$n_0 \omega^m + n_1 \omega^{m-1} + \ldots + n_m$$

whose limit is ω^ω. Eventually in this manner we reach the following:

$$\omega^\omega, \; \omega^{n\omega+m}, \; \omega^{\omega^n}, \; \omega^{\omega^\omega} \ldots$$

Cantor not only presented this theory of ordinal numbers but also went on to develop ordinal arithmetic.[15] In the course of this work the similarities and differences between the transfinite and the finite ordinals became clear. A striking similarity is that any ordinal α has a unique representation as a sum of powers of ω, just as any finite number has a unique representation as a sum of powers of ten. A striking difference is the non-commutativity of ordinal addition: $1 + \omega = \omega \neq \omega + 1$. This enabled Cantor to give a twofold rebuttal of an ancient and much repeated objection to the possibility of infinite numbers. The objection is that addition of a positive finite and an infinite number would 'annihilate' the finite number and would just return the infinite. First, Cantor pointed out that it is a mistake to hold that all laws of finite numbers must hold for non-finite numbers too. As with every other extension of the natural numbers, there will be some laws that hold in the extended system and some that break down. Secondly, Cantor pointed out that adding a positive finite ordinal to an infinite ordinal does not annihilate the finite, as $\omega < \omega + n$ for positive n, although there is annihilation when one adds an infinite ordinal to a finite ordinal.[16] This neatly illustrates that similarities are accompanied by differences.

Cardinal numbers

In studying the continuum, Cantor had found many infinite classes whose members could be enumerated by the natural numbers. None of those classes included a continuous segment, so it was natural to suspect that continuous classes of reals were beyond enumeration by the natural numbers. In putting the question to Dedekind,[17] Cantor wrote that 'At first glance one might say no, it is not possible' to put the class of natural numbers $\mathbb{N}$ and the class of real numbers $\mathbb{R}$ into 1-to-1 correspondence, 'for $\mathbb{N}$ consists of discrete parts while $\mathbb{R}$ builds a continuum; but nothing is won by this objection'. Cantor found that the class of rational numbers, which is not discretely ordered, *can* be enumerated (correlated 1-to-1 with $\mathbb{N}$). Here is one of Cantor's proofs of this fact.[18] It is enough to show that the positive rationals can be enumerated by the positive integers; for if we have such an enumeration we can correlate, for all positive integers n, the nth positive rational p/q with $2n$ and its negative $-(p/q)$ with $2n-1$, and $0/1$ can be correlated with 0. We set out the positive rationals in rows and columns, with all in the nth row having denominator n and all in the mth column having numerator m (Figure 2.1).

The enumeration is in the order indicated by the arrows, omitting any rational that has already appeared; thus we skip over '2/2', as the number this denotes has already occurred in the guise of '1/1'. So the enumeration begins as follows:

(1) 1/1,   (2) 2/1,   (3) 1/2,   (4) 1/3,   (5) 3/1,   (6) 4/1, . . .

Clearly, this is a 1-to-1 correlation of the positive rationals with the positive integers.

The discovery that there are no more rationals than natural numbers, despite the fact that between any two rationals there are infinitely many others, was a little surprising. Cantor proved that this is true also of the class of

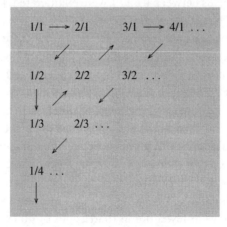

Figure 2.1

all algebraic real numbers, that is, the class of real number solutions of all equations of the form

$$a_0 x^n + a_1 x^{n-1} + \ldots + a_n = 0.$$

It was known that not all real numbers are algebraic.[19] What then of the continuum, $\mathbb{R}$? Cantor proved that $\mathbb{R}$ is not enumerable.[20] Here is a version of one of his proofs of this fact.[21] It clearly suffices to prove that the class of real numbers between 0 and 1 is not enumerable. Suppose that there is an enumeration of the reals between 0 and 1. Let the decimal expansion of each one be placed in the order in which they are enumerated, the $(n + 1)$th below the nth. If a real has two decimal expansions we choose the one with the recurring 9s, for example $0.2999\ldots$ rather than $0.3000\ldots$ Let $r_{k,n}$ be the nth digit after the decimal point of the kth decimal.

1	$r_{1,1}$	$r_{1,2}$	$r_{1,3}$	$r_{1,4}$	$\cdots$
2	$r_{2,1}$	$r_{2,2}$	$r_{2,3}$	$r_{2,4}$	$\cdots$
3	$r_{3,1}$	$r_{3,2}$	$r_{3,3}$	$r_{3,4}$	$\cdots$
4	$r_{4,1}$	$r_{4,2}$	$r_{4,3}$	$r_{4,4}$	$\cdots$

Now we can define a decimal that is not listed by running down the diagonal and putting 9s in place of 1s and 1s in place of any other digit: $c_n = 9$ if $r_{n,n} = 1$; $c_n = 1$ if $r_{n,n} \neq 1$. Then c is the real number whose decimal expansion is $0.c_1 c_2 c_3 c_4 \ldots$ with c_n in the nth position after the decimal point. The defined number c differs from each real number in the list: for each n the decimal expansion of c differs from that of the nth in the list at the nth position after the decimal point, and yet c lies between 0 and 1. This contradicts the supposition that all the reals between 0 and 1 were enumerated. Hence the assumption that they can be enumerated is false.

Two classes have the *same cardinality* if and only if there is a 1-to-1 correlation between the classes. The cardinality of a class B is *less than* that of a class C if and only if there is a 1-to-1 correlation between B and a subclass of C but no 1-to-1 correlation between B and C.[22] The cardinality of a class is just its cardinal number, the number of members of the class: to have fewer members is to have a lesser cardinal number. Cantor was the first to compare infinite classes by cardinal number. With his proof of the non-enumerability of the reals, he established that there were at least two infinite cardinal numbers.[23] He expected to find more by investigating higher-dimensional continua. A line segment of unit length surely has fewer points than a square of unit side, which in turn surely has fewer points than a cube of unit side. Not so, Cantor found, and he was sufficiently surprised to exclaim 'I see it, but I don't believe it.'[24] In fact a line segment, an interval in $\mathbb{R}$, however short, can be correlated 1-to-1 with the whole of n-dimensional space, $\mathbb{R}^n$, for any finite n.

Although Cantor did not find point classes of higher cardinality than the real line, he did show that there were classes of higher cardinality, in fact classes of ever higher cardinality. More specifically, he showed that for any class M the class of subclasses of M has greater cardinality than M itself, by showing the impossibility of a 1-to-1 correlation between them, a fact known as Cantor's theorem.[25] He did this by modifying the method of diagonalization he devised to establish the non-enumerability of the continuum. The idea of the proof is again to assume that there is a 1-to-1 correlation, this time between M and the class of its subclasses, and then to derive a contradiction from that assumption, thereby proving it false. So let M be any class and let c be a 1-to-1 correlation of M with the class of its subclasses, $\mathbb{P}$M:

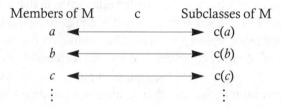

We can think of the members of any class M as listed in a row, each member standing at the top of a column. A subclass can be represented by a row of 0s and 1s: a 0 in the jth place in the row means that the member of M at the top of the jth column is *not* a member of the subclass represented by that row; a 1 in the jth place means that the member of M at the top of the jth column *is* a member of that subclass. Suppose also that the order in which the subclasses are represented is determined by the order in which the members of M are listed, so that, if the order is $a, b, c \ldots$ etc., then the row for $c(a)$ comes first, the row for $c(b)$ next below, the row for $c(c)$ just below that, and so on:

	a	b	c	d	e	$\ldots$
$c(a)$	**0**	1	1	1	0	$\ldots$
$c(b)$	0	**0**	0	0	0	$\ldots$
$c(c)$	1	0	**1**	0	0	$\ldots$
$c(d)$	0	1	0	**1**	0	$\ldots$
$c(e)$	1	1	0	0	**0**	$\ldots$
$\vdots$	$\vdots$	$\vdots$	$\vdots$	$\vdots$	$\vdots$	$\vdots$

The diagonal tells us which members of M are in the subclass with which they are correlated. Running down the diagonal, we see that a is not in its correlate $c(a)$, b is not in $c(b)$, but c is in $c(c)$, and so on. The diagonal, then, specifies the subclass of M containing just those x in M which belong to their correlated subclass $c(x)$. Using the notation '$\{x : \varphi(x)\}$' for the class of x that satisfy the condition φ, the diagonal represents $\{x : x \in M \ \& \ x \in c(x)\}$. Of the five members of M listed, only c and d belong to this class. If we go down the diagonal interchanging 0s and 1s, the result represents the subclass of M containing just those x in M that do *not* belong to their correlated subclass, that is, Cantor's class $\{x : x \in M \ \& \ x \notin c(x)\}$. Obtaining a class in this way is known as *diagonalization*. Since by assumption c is a 1-to-1 correlation between the members of M and the subclasses of M, there must be some member m of M whose correlate $c(m)$ is Cantor's class. But this impossible. For Cantor's class was constructed so that, for any member m of M, whichever value $c(m)$ has under the column headed by m, Cantor's class has the other value in that column. So for any member m of M, the sequence of 0s and 1s representing Cantor's class differs from the sequence representing $c(m)$. This contradicts the assumption that every subclass of M can be correlated 1-to-1 with a member of M.

A perfectly good objection to the argument put in this way is that, if M is non-enumerably infinite, the idea that its members can be set out in a row is dubious. But the core of the argument does not need this assumption. The visual idea of the rectangular array and its diagonal is dispensable, a cognitive route to the discovery of Cantor's class. The argument itself is simply this. Suppose there were a 1-to-1 correlation c of M with the class of its subclasses, $\mathbb{P}M$. Then define C thus: $C = \{x : x \in M \ \& \ x \notin c(x)\}$. Clearly C is a subclass of M. So there would have to be a member m of M with which it is correlated: $C = c(m)$. Now there are two cases to consider. (i) $m \in c(m)$. Then m does not fulfil the membership condition of C. So $m \notin$ C. But C $= c(m)$ by assumption. So $m \notin c(m)$. So in case (i) m both is and is not in $c(m)$, which is impossible. (ii) $m \notin c(m)$. Then m does fulfil the membership condition of C. So $m \in$ C. But C $= c(m)$ by assumption. So $m \in c(m)$. So in case (ii) m both is and is not in $c(m)$, which is impossible. Either way, then, we reach contradiction. Hence the supposition that there is a 1-to-1 correlation between M and $\mathbb{P}M$ is false.

However, there is a 1-to-1 correlation between M and a subclass of $\mathbb{P}M$: the correlate of each member m of M is the class whose sole member is m. So $\mathbb{P}M$ has at least as many members as M. Since they do not have just as many as each other, it is reasonable to think that $\mathbb{P}M$ has more than M. The argument does not make any assumptions about M and so applies to all classes. Thus, there are ever-greater transfinite cardinal numbers, those of $\mathbb{N}$, $\mathbb{P}\mathbb{N}$, $\mathbb{P}\mathbb{P}\mathbb{N}$, . . . However, Cantor could not use this series as a way of classifying the transfinite cardinalities, as he had not shown that the cardinality of $\mathbb{PN}$ is the first after the cardinality of $\mathbb{N}$. There might be some in between. Cantor knew that the cardinality of the continuum $\mathbb{P}$ is the same as the cardinality of $\mathbb{PN}$. So the question that confronted him was whether the cardinality of the continuum was the first after the cardinality of $\mathbb{N}$, which is the first transfinite cardinality. Cantor had found many infinite classes of points on the continuum with the cardinality of $\mathbb{N}$ and many with the cardinality of $\mathbb{R}$; but he had found none with cardinality in between. So it was reasonable to conjecture that there is no cardinality in between; equivalently, that the cardinality of the continuum is the second transfinite cardinality. This is Cantor's continuum hypothesis. Cantor struggled to prove the continuum hypothesis, but without success. He would have to look elsewhere for a systematic way of classifying infinite cardinal numbers.

The alephs

He found the key in the series of ordinal numbers. He called the class of finite ordinals the 1st number class; and the 2nd number class was the class of transfinite ordinals α such that the class of ordinals preceding α can be correlated 1-to-1 with the 1st number class. Cantor was able to show that the first transfinite cardinal number is the cardinality of the 1st number class and the second cardinal number is the cardinality of the 2nd number class. Generalizing this, Cantor defined the unending succession of transfinite cardinal numbers, the alephs:

$\aleph_0$ = the cardinality of $\mathbb{N}$;
$\aleph_{\alpha+1}$ = the cardinality of the class of all ordinals with $\aleph_\alpha$ predecessors;

if λ is a limit ordinal, then

$\aleph_\lambda$ = the cardinality of the class of all ordinals β such that, for some ordinal α preceding λ, β has $\aleph_\alpha$ predecessors.[26]

Cantor was able to show that every transfinite cardinal number was an aleph, that $\aleph_{\alpha+1}$ is the next cardinal after $\aleph_\alpha$, and that for limit ordinals λ, $\aleph_\lambda$ is the first cardinal after all $\aleph_\beta$ where β precedes λ. Thus, he defined a classification of transfinite cardinal numbers. Cantor also defined arithmetical operations for the cardinal numbers in a way that encompasses finite and transfinite cardinal arithmetic, and he developed the arithmetic of the alephs so as to reveal uniformities with and differences from the laws of finite arithmetic. Using this arithmetic, he could show that the cardinality of the continuum is $2^{\aleph_0}$. Thus, he found a purely arithmetical expression of his continuum hypothesis:

$2^{\aleph_0} = \aleph_1$. But he was never able to prove (or refute) it, and in 1900, when Cantor's career as an active mathematician had ended and David Hilbert was an ascendant star of the mathematical world, Hilbert presented the continuum problem as the first of twenty-three major unsolved problems in a now famous address to the Second International Congress of Mathematicians.[27]

Together with Cantor's discovery of the transfinite ordinals and his development of ordinal arithmetic, his theory of transfinite cardinals constituted a major intellectual achievement. Cantor quite reasonably felt justified in regarding transfinite cardinals as actually existing numbers rather than notational fictions, on a par with finite cardinal numbers. But Cantor's edifice had to face enormous resistance, or at least scepticism. Not only was there the inertial drag of time-honoured philosophical testimony against the possibility of knowable actual infinities from Aristotle on; there was also intense opposition from the influential mathematician Kronecker, one of Cantor's former professors and an admirer of his early research.[28] Kronecker's hostility was not confined to the theory of transfinite numbers. A much cited saying indicates the extent of his opposition to the direction of Cantor's work from his theory of real numbers onward: 'The dear lord made the integers; all else is the work of man'.[29]

The natural numbers

While few accepted Kronecker's view of the real numbers as fictions, almost everyone agreed that the integers, in particular the natural numbers, were genuine entities independent of human constructions. Yet some people still felt a need to define the natural numbers and arithmetical operations on them, so that the hitherto accepted laws of arithmetic could be proved. This was not merely the juggernaut of rigour rolling on. Dedekind and Frege, who both gave accounts of the natural numbers, had independent and rather different motivations.

Dedekind said that the theory of the natural numbers is part of logic. But he did not have in mind any positive conception of logic. In the preface to the first edition of his work on the natural numbers, he wrote: 'In speaking of arithmetic (algebra, analysis) as a part of logic I mean to imply that I consider the number concept entirely independent of the notions or intuitions of space and time. . .'[30] Dedekind had given an account of the real numbers in terms of classes of rational numbers, in order to free our understanding of them from reliance on geometrical or dynamical intuitions.[31] But rationals are understood in terms of integers, and integers in terms of the natural numbers. If, therefore, our understanding of the natural numbers depends on intuitions of space or time, the goal of his earlier work—the account of the real numbers—would not have been achieved.

Frege too claimed that the theory of natural numbers, and beyond that the theory of real numbers, is part of logic. Frege did have a positive conception of logic in mind, which, crudely summarized, is logic as a theory of predicate extensions, containing what we now think of as propositional and quantifier logic. His concern was to show that arithmetic is purely analytic, rather than synthetic as Kant had claimed, in the sense that arithmetic is derivable by purely logical means from definitions and purely logical laws.

Dedekind's account of the natural numbers follows an exposition of part of a general theory of classes.[32] The central notion is that of a simply infinite system. (Dedekind uses 'system' for class.) Let D be a class, let $s(x)$ be an operation defined for all members of D, and let b be a member of D. Then $\langle D, s, b \rangle$ is defined to be a *simply infinite system* if and only if the following conditions hold:

1. For all x in D, $s(x)$ is in D;
2. For all x in D, $b \neq s(x)$;
3. For all x and y in D, if $x \neq y$ then $s(x) \neq s(y)$;
4. D = the intersection of all classes containing b and closed under s.[33]

The operation s is intended to play the role of a successor function and the element b the role of a first element. Conditions 1, 2, and 3 are the axioms for the successor operation in Dedekind–Peano arithmetic (also known as Peano arithmetic). Condition 4 is equivalent to the axiom of induction of Dedekind–Peano arithmetic:

> For any K, if b is in K and for all x in K $s(x)$ is in K, then every x in D is in K.[34]

Dedekind went on to show that all simply infinite systems are isomorphic: if $\langle D_1, s_1, b_1 \rangle$ and $\langle D_2, s_2, b_2 \rangle$ are simply infinite systems, there is a 1-to-1 correlation c of D_1 with D_2 such that $c(b_1) = b_2$ and for all x, y in D_1, if $y = s_1(x)$ then $c(y) = s_2(c(x))$. This means that any two simply infinite systems have exactly the same structure.[35] On this basis Dedekind could give a purely structural characterization of the natural numbers. Here is how he put it:

If in the consideration of a simply infinite system N set in order by a transformation ϕ [$\langle N, \phi, b \rangle$] we entirely neglect the special character of the elements, simply retaining their distinguishability and taking into account only the relations they have to one another in which they are placed by the order-setting transformation ϕ, then these elements are called *natural numbers* . . .[36]

31

Later in the same paragraph he says that the theorems derivable from the defining laws (1–4) for simply infinite systems constitute the '*science of numbers* or *arithmetic*'.

There are two ways of construing this account of the natural numbers. One is that the members of every simply infinite system are natural numbers, but it is appropriate to call the elements of a simply infinite system $\langle N, \phi, b \rangle$ natural numbers only when we ignore the nature of the elements of N and pay attention just to their distinctness and the interrelations they have as a result of the ordering induced by ϕ. This is the most apt reading if the quoted passage alone is considered. But in chapter X, 'The Class of Simply Infinite Systems', Dedekind clearly implies that there is just one simply infinite system that constitutes the system of natural numbers. So if we are to assume that Dedekind had a consistent view, the quoted passage must be understood in a different way. This might be that, given any simply infinite system $\langle N, \phi, b \rangle$ of objects with individual characteristics, if we ignore these characteristics of the elements of N and pay attention only to their distinctness and their ϕ-induced relations, we achieve an awareness of another simply infinite system, one whose elements do not have individual characteristics, and that is the system of natural numbers. Lest this seems a far-fetched interpretation, it is worth noting that this is how Cantor thought of the structures or order types of linearly ordered classes. We arrive at our understanding of the order type of M, he said, 'if we only abstract from the nature of the elements m, and retain the order of precedence among them. Thus the ordinal type [of M] is itself an ordered aggregate whose elements are units which have the same order of precedence amongst one another as the corresponding elements of M, from which they are derived by abstraction.'[37]

Dedekind also defines addition and multiplication for the natural numbers and establishes the adequacy of those definitions. As he takes the first element to be 1 rather than 0, these definitions are not quite the familiar pairs of recursion equations, which are the remaining axioms of Dedekind–Peano arithmetic:

$$m + 0 = m; \quad m + s(n) = s(m + n).$$
$$m \times 0 = 0; \quad m \times s(n) = (m \times n) + m.\,^{38}$$

Here the variables are for natural numbers and 0 is the base element. Dedekind gives us just what is needed for natural number arithmetic and no more. The theory he is using as the basis, his metatheory, is a general theory of classes. His metatheory, however, included more than he realized. His account of the natural numbers assumes that there are simply infinite systems, which indeed there are if there are any infinite classes. Dedekind attempts to prove that there exist infinite classes, but the argument is fallacious. He argues that there can be infinitely many things 'which can be objects of my thought' and takes this to establish the claim. The objects are propositions, starting with some simple proposition p and proceeding from proposition x to the proposition of the form 'the proposition x can be an object of my thought'. One objection is that perhaps only a finite number of these can in fact be objects of one's thought; it is an empirical matter not capable of mathematical proof. But that is not the central objection. For one could instead choose other objects, for example strings of the letter type 'b', starting with a string having just one occurrence of the letter, and proceeding from any string x to the string that results from postfixing an occurrence of the letter to x. The central objection is that Dedekind assumes that, given a description, whether the description is 'possible objects of thought' or 'finite strings of 'b's' or something else, there is a class containing all things of the given description. So he is tacitly assuming some class existence principle.

Frege's account of the natural numbers is very different. His view was that the number n is the class of classes with exactly n members (ignoring a small expository wrinkle).[39] Thus, a natural number is a class of equinumerous classes, where classes are *equinumerous* if and only if there is a 1-to-1 correlation between them; and *the number of* Ψs is the class of classes equinumerous with the class of Ψs. The natural number 0, which Frege was careful to distinguish from the real number of that name, is defined to be the class of classes equinumerous with the class of objects that are not self-identical. The natural number 1 is defined to be the class of classes equinumerous with the class whose sole member is 0. Frege defines a predicate form meaning 'belongs to the series of natural numbers ending with n'. The successor of n is then defined to be the class of classes equinumerous with the class of objects belonging to the series of natural numbers ending with n.[40]

It is clear that the numbers that Frege's account was concerned with are answers to questions of the form 'What is the number of Ψs?'—in other words, cardinal numbers. In this respect Frege and Dedekind were not giving accounts of the same subject matter. The finite cardinal numbers under their natural ordering constitute one particular simply infinite system; the finite ordinals under *their* natural ordering constitute another. Dedekind was giving an account of the structure common to these ordered classes. None the less, both Frege and Dedekind can be taken as providing interpretations of the numerals as they appear in pure arithmetic. Also, both take as their basis a theory of classes. But Frege was much more explicit about the axioms of his theory of classes, and he argued that his theory counts as logic, on the grounds that classes are nothing but extensions of predicates, which comprise part of the subject matter of logic.

Conclusion

Towards the end of the nineteenth century, the drive for clarity and rigour seemed to be reaching a successful conclusion. Among its fruits were precise accounts of the real and natural numbers, the first general theory of transfinite classes and numbers, and a first account of quantifier logic—no meagre harvest. But celebrations had barely begun when certain paradoxes were found in the general theory of classes, which was the basis for all supposedly rigorous accounts of the number systems. This defeat in the hour of triumph made foundational research a major area of concern for mathematicians. Deeper excavation was needed, and the younger mathematicians who took up the task intended to reach bedrock. So the drive to find sure foundations for mathematics issued largely from problems internal to mathematics,[41] together with the conviction that, if certainty is to be found anywhere, it is to be found in mathematics. In this way, the mathematical concern was tied to a philosophical one: how can we be certain that the theorems of mathematics are trustworthy? The rest of this book examines the attempts to meet this challenge. In the next few chapters the class paradoxes are set out and initial responses to them are examined.

APPENDIX: THE DEDEKIND CUTS AS AN ORDERED FIELD

Let $\mathbb{R}$ be the class of cuts. Let $\langle\mathbb{R}\rangle$ be $\mathbb{R}$ together with binary operations $+, \cdot, -,$ / defined on $\mathbb{R}$, with distinguished elements 0^* and 1^*, and unary operations $-x$ and x^{-1} defined on $\mathbb{R}$ and $\mathbb{R}$ less 0^* respectively.

The order axioms for $\langle\mathbb{R}\rangle$

For all a, b in $\mathbb{R}$, if $0^* < a$ and $0^* < b$, then $0^* < a + b$ and $0^* < a\cdot b$.
For all a in $\mathbb{R}$, exactly one of the following is true: $a < 0^*$, $a = 0^*$ or $0^* < a$.
Not $0^* < 0^*$.

The field axioms for $\langle\mathbb{R}\rangle$

For all a, b, c in $\mathbb{R}$
Commutativity: $a + b = b + a$ and $a\cdot b = b\cdot a$.
Associativity: $(a + b) + c = a + (b + c)$ and $(a\cdot b)\cdot c = a\cdot(b\cdot c)$.
Distributivity: $a\cdot(b + c) = a\cdot b + a\cdot c$.
Identities: $a + 0^* = a$ and $a\cdot 1^* = a$.
Inverses: $a + -a = 0^*$ and if $a \neq 0^*$, $a\cdot a^{-1} = 1^*$.
Others: $0^* \neq 1^*$ and if $a\cdot b = 0^*$ then $a = 0^*$ or $b = 0^*$.

Part II
The Class Paradoxes and Early Responses

The Class Paradoxes   1

A paradox in common parlance is an apparently absurd proposition supported by an argument. But I will shift the focus and say that a paradox is an argument from apparently true premises by apparently valid steps to an
apparently false conclusion. Paradoxes fall into three kinds.[1] First, there are
paradoxes consisting of a sound argument with a true but surprising conclusion, such as Cantor's argument that a line segment of unit length contains no
fewer points than a square whose sides have unit length. Secondly, there are
paradoxes consisting of an unsound argument with a false conclusion, where
investigation reveals a clear fallacy, such as the well known arguments that
$2 = 1$.[2] Finally, there are paradoxes consisting of an unsound argument with
a false conclusion, where investigation reveals no clear fallacy. These paradoxes are known as antinomies. Often their conclusions are clear logical
impossibilities, and solving them requires finding a principled reason for
rejecting some seemingly obvious premise or pattern of inference used in the
argument. The paradoxes that we shall be concerned with in this book all
belong to this third category. The paradoxes that caused the crisis of confidence in the nineteenth century drive to make infinitesimal analysis clear and
rigorous arise from the basic theory of classes. There are three major class
paradoxes, though many variants of them. These are the Burali-Forti paradox, Cantor's paradox, and Russell's paradox.

The Burali-Forti paradox

The Burali-Forti paradox was discovered by Cantor in 1895 and Burali-Forti
in 1897, but was not regarded by them as a paradox.[3] It arises out of Cantor's
theory of ordinal numbers in a natural way. As it depends on some background knowledge, a full exposition has been relegated to an optional

appendix. But the basic idea is simple. The ordinal numbers form a strict linear ordering, so none can precede itself. If we consider the class of all ordinals, transfinite as well as finite, we find that it gives rise to a new ordinal, following those in the original class; but that class is by definition the class of all ordinals, so the new ordinal must precede itself, contradicting the fact that no ordinal precedes itself.

Cantor's paradox

Cantor's paradox was formulated by Cantor in 1899.[4] It depends on a simple theorem which Cantor discovered some years before.[5] We say that B is a *subclass* of C if and only if all members of B are members of C, and we write $\mathbb{P}$C for the class of all subclasses of C. The *cardinal number* of a class is how many members it has. The simple theorem, known as Cantor's theorem, is just that, for any class C, $\mathbb{P}$C is greater in cardinal number than C. Here is the paradox.

Let U be the class of all classes.
The class of all subclasses of U, $\mathbb{P}$U, has only classes as members.
So every member of $\mathbb{P}$U is a member of U.
Hence $\mathbb{P}$U is no greater in number than U.
But Cantor's theorem entails that $\mathbb{P}$U is greater in number than U.
So $\mathbb{P}$U both is and is not greater in number than U.

Russell's paradox

Discovered by Zermelo probably in the years 1899 or 1900,[6] and independently by Russell in 1901, this is the least technical and most fundamental of the class paradoxes. We can ask whether a given class is a member of itself. For example, if there is a class of all classes, it would have to be a member of itself, whereas the class of green apples is not a member of itself, as no class is an apple. Russell's paradox arises by considering the class R of all things that are not members of themselves.

If R is a member of itself, it must satisfy the condition on members of R that they are *not* members of themselves. Hence
(a) If R is a member of itself, R is not a member of itself.
If it is not, that is if R is not a member of itself, R thereby satisfies the condition for membership of R, so that R is a member of itself. Hence

(b) If R is not a member of itself, it is a member of itself.

Putting (a) and (b) together, we get an absurdity: R is a member of itself if and only if it is not a member of itself.

For later discussion it will be helpful to set this out in a more formal way. Suppose we have a sentence expressing a truth or a falsehood containing a name, such as '4 is a square integer'. The result of replacing one or more occurrences of a name by a free variable is an open sentence, e.g. 'x is a square integer'. An open sentence gives us a condition things may or may not satisfy. Thus, 4 and 9 satisfy the condition 'x is a square integer', whereas 6 and 10 do not. Given any open sentence $F(x)$ expressing a condition, we use an expression of the form $\{x : F(x)\}$ for the class of things that satisfy $F(x)$. Thus, $\{x : x$ is a square integer$\}$ is the class of square integers. We follow custom in using '$\in$' for 'is a member of' and we write '$\notin$' for 'is not a member of'. Finally, we use '$\leftrightarrow$' as short for 'if and only if'. Now we can set out Russell's paradox as follows:

(1) For any condition $F(x)$ and any object y, $F(y) \leftrightarrow y \in \{x : F(x)\}$.

So for the particular condition $x \notin x$ and for any class y, we get

(2) $y \notin y \leftrightarrow y \in \{x : x \notin x\}$.

When y is the particular class $\{x : x \notin x\}$, we get

(3) $\{x : x \notin x\} \notin \{x : x \notin x\} \leftrightarrow \{x : x \notin x\} \in \{x : x \notin x\}$.

But this is impossible.

Russell's paradox is closer to Cantor's paradox than it appears. Russell got his idea for the paradox from Cantor's proof of Cantor's theorem.[7] The manoeuvre underlying both arguments is known as diagonalization, and it crops up at key points in logical investigation. The second appendix to this chapter explains this. The following three chapters present responses of some major figures to the class paradoxes, along with some critical assessment. The differing attitudes will help us to see the paradoxes in perspective and to understand later developments.

APPENDIX 1: THE BURALI-FORTI PARADOX

To state the paradox fully, we need some definitions and theorems. Definitions of 'well ordered' and 'ordinal' are given in the section on ordinal numbers in the preceding chapter. The other definition needed is this.

If x is any member of a class C well ordered by <, the class of <-predecessors of x in C is said to be a *section* of C.

The theorems are these:

(a) The class of all ordinals, Ω, is well ordered by a certain relation $<$.

(b) Every well ordered class C has a unique ordinal, denoted 'ord(C)'.

(c) Every section of a well ordered class is well ordered.

(d) Every ordinal α is the ordinal of the section of ordinals less than α.

(e) If C is a well ordered class and D is a section of C, ord(D) $<$ ord(C).

Here is the paradox. The class of all ordinals, Ω, well ordered by $<$, has an ordinal, ord(Ω) (by (a),(b)). Putting S for the section of ordinals less than ord(Ω), it follows that ord(Ω) = ord(S) (by (b),(c),(d)). But ord(S) $<$ ord(Ω) (by (e)). Hence ord(Ω) $<$ ord(Ω). But ord(Ω) $\not<$ ord(Ω), as $<$ is a strict linear ordering, hence irreflexive.

APPENDIX 2: CANTOR'S DIAGONAL ARGUMENT AND RUSSELL'S PARADOX

Diagonalization was introduced in the preceding chapter, but we recapitulate in order to show the connection with Russell's paradox. Cantor showed that, for any class A, the class of its subclasses, $\mathbb{P}(A)$, is always greater in number than A. Since for each member x of A there is a distinct subclass $\{x\}$ of A, namely the class whose sole member is x, it is easy to see that there are at least as many subclasses of A as members of A. So, given that of any two distinct cardinal numbers one is greater than the other, to prove the theorem one need only show that the subclasses of A are not equal in number to the members of A; that is, there is no one-to-one correlation between its members and its subclasses. Cantor's proof is a *reductio ad absurdum* of the assumption that there is such a correlation.

Let A be any class and suppose that there is a one-to-one correlation between its members and its subclasses. If x is a member of A, let f_x be the subclass of A correlated with x. Now consider the following subclass of A:

$$C = \{x : x \in A \ \& \ x \notin f_x\}.$$

This is the class of members of A that are not in the subclass with which they are correlated. Since C is a subclass of A, it will by assumption be correlated with exactly one member of A. Let us call this member z. Then $C = f_z$.

> Now we ask: is z a member of f_z?
> If so, z must satisfy the condition on members of C, as f_z is C, which entails that $z \notin f_z$.
> So if $z \in f_z$, $z \notin f_z$.
> If not, z is a member of A but not a member of f_z, and so z satisfies the

condition for membership of C, and so it is a member of C, that is, of f_z. So if $z \notin f_z$, $z \in f_z$.

Combining these gives absurdity: $z \in f_z \leftrightarrow z \notin f_z$. Hence there is no such correlation.

If A is the class of everything, and each thing is correlated with itself, C is $\{x: x \notin x\}$, which is Russell's class R. Thence Russell's paradox follows Cantor's proof, excluding the conclusion of course, as we cannot deny that identity gives a 1-to-1 correlation. A variant of Russell's paradox uses the class R' = $\{x: x$ is a class such that $x \notin x\}$ instead of $\{x: x \notin x\}$. In this case, let A be the class of classes and let each class be correlated with itself. Then C = R'. Russell (1906a) shows how Russell obtained his paradox through simplifying Cantor's paradox.

Cantor's Approach to the Class Paradoxes

Cantor was the first to discover class paradoxes, but they did not strike him as paradoxical. Rather, he took them to confirm a view he had come to years before, that some totalities cannot be treated as objects of mathematical study. In the course of developing the theory of infinite sets, in particular the theory of infinite ordinal and cardinal numbers that he had created,[1] he naturally reflected on the totality of ordinal numbers and the totality of cardinal numbers, and he came to view them as importantly unlike other infinite totalities. It had been traditional to distinguish between finite and infinite, the former being increasable by addition, the latter not. Cantor challenged this tradition. Instead of a simple division into finite and infinite, Cantor's theory led him to a tripartite classification: finite, transfinite, and absolutely infinite. A transfinite number is unlike a finite number in having infinitely many predecessors; but it is like a finite number in being increasable. The sequence of all ordinals is absolutely infinite because it is unincreasable; that is, it cannot be extended to get a new ordinal, whereas the sequence of ordinals up to and including a transfinite ordinal α can be extended to get a new ordinal $\alpha + 1$. Similar remarks apply to the cardinals. Cantor articulated this distinction between the transfinite and the absolutely infinite some seven years[2] before formulating the Burali-Forti argument in 1895. Still earlier he had claimed that the absolutely infinite cannot be comprehended and is not a knowable object.[3] The Burali-Forti argument was taken by Cantor to vindicate this view: it shows that inconsistency results when one treats the absolutely infinite totality of ordinals as an object of mathematical knowledge.

What is an absolutely infinite multiplicity?

Cantor generalized his distinction between the transfinite and the absolutely infinite to apply to all non-finite classes. In a famous letter to Dedekind, he formulated in general terms his distinction between *absolutely infinite multiplicities* (AIMs) and all other multiplicities, finite or infinite, called *sets*; and he held that the error leading to paradox was to treat absolutely infinite classes as sets. Cantor drew the distinction thus:

For on the one hand a multiplicity can be such that the assumption that *all* of its elements 'are together' leads to a contradiction, so that it is impossible to conceive of the multiplicity as a unity, as 'one finished thing'. Such multiplicities I call *absolutely infinite* or *inconsistent multiplicities*. . . .

When on the other hand the totality of elements of a multiplicity can be thought without contradiction as 'being together', so that their collection into '*one* thing' is possible, I call it a *consistent multiplicity* or *set*.[4]

Let us scrutinize Cantor's explanation. He offers three distinct conditions for being an AIM and it is not at all clear that they are equivalent. A multiplicity is said to be an AIM if and only if

1. it cannot be consistently conceived of as a *finished* thing;
2. the thought that all of its elements *are together* is inconsistent;
3. it cannot be consistently conceived of as *one* thing.

The first two criteria are somewhat mysterious. What is it to conceive of a multiplicity as finished or unfinished? Few would hold that classes of abstract objects, such as the class of classes, come into being in time like a building under construction; so we do not conceive of them as finished or unfinished. Moreover, nothing that can be construed as thinking of the class of classes as finished enters into Cantor's paradox. Even if we accept that the class of classes is unfinished, the reasoning that leads to the contradiction is undisturbed. The same goes for the Burali-Forti paradoxes. Nowhere in the argument is it assumed that the class of all ordinals is finished, whatever that comes to.

Again, we do not usually think of the members of a class as having location, except in certain special cases, such as classes of spatial points. As abstract objects such as ordinal numbers do not have location, we do not think of them as being together or as being apart. Moreover, the paradoxes do not involve assuming that the members of the relevant classes are together. Cantor's talk of being finished and of being together is merely metaphorical. Though suggestive, these metaphors neither illuminate Cantor's notion of absolute infinity nor reveal the error at the root of the class paradoxes.

What about the third criterion, according to which an AIM is a multiplicity which cannot be thought of as *one* thing? If a multiplicity, such as the class of ordinals, is not *one* thing, is it *more* than one thing? Had this been Cantor's thought, surely he would have made it clear. He could have said that expressions for AIMs, such as 'the class of all ordinals', are ambiguous, or denote different multiplicities in different contexts, or something similar. But nothing like this was said. On the contrary, Cantor's idea that AIMs are unfinished suggests that an AIM is *not even* one thing. But then, did he say that an AIM is nothing, a mere fiction, that there is no class of all ordinals? No. He not only held that there are two kinds of multiplicities—sets and AIMs—but also used special symbols as names for the class of cardinals and the class of ordinals, and his way of writing about them strongly suggests that he thought they exist. So it is simply unclear what Cantor had in mind by saying that an AIM is a multiplicity which cannot be consistently conceived of as *one* thing.

Cantor's account of the distinction between absolutely infinite multiplicities and others does not escape metaphor, and so it is reasonable to doubt that Cantor had a real distinction in mind. Certainly we cannot rest content with any proposed solution to the paradoxes that rests on a distinction that cannot be characterized in clear non-metaphorical terms. Until we have a proper characterization of this kind, appeal to the distinction appears to be an *ad hoc* manoeuvre to escape contradiction: we deem any class that we find cannot be taken to exist consistently with the theory of classes to be an entity that lies beyond the scope of the theory.

But even if that were in substance Cantor's position, it would be psychologically inaccurate to say that Cantor indulged in *ad hoc* manoeuvring to save his theory. Three points can be made in Cantor's defence in this matter. First, Cantor did have some positive notion of absolute infinity. He used the term 'Absolute' with a capital A to denote God, for something that cannot be numbered.[5] This gets transferred to Cantor's idea of absolutely infinite classes as classes that have no cardinal number. Something analogous can be found elsewhere in mathematics. Consider all line segments in a metric space, that is, all lines with one or two endpoints. Those with two endpoints have length, as the extent of such a segment has a definite ratio to the unit length. But those with only one endpoint have no length. There is nothing *ad hoc* in saying this. Why then should we regard it as *ad hoc* to characterize AIMs as classes with no cardinal size?

Secondly, given that the class of all ordinals is an AIM, he used the following positive mathematical criterion for being absolutely infinite:

A class C is an AIM if there is a 1-to-1 correspondence between the class of all ordinals and C or one of its subclasses.[6]

This actually follows from Cantor's conviction that the class of all ordinals is an AIM together with other Cantorian principles.[7] So it is not right to say that Cantor was merely attaching the grand title of 'absolutely infinite' to the relevant class whenever he stumbled upon inconsistency. On Cantor's view, every well-ordered set, even if infinite, has an ordinal; but no AIM has an ordinal. An ordinal is a species of number, so this flows naturally from Cantor's idea of absolute infinity as that which cannot be numbered, an idea that antedates the paradoxes by several years.

Thirdly, it should be noted that post-Cantorian developments in set theory provide a non-metaphorical account of his distinction, given that there is such a thing as a universe of sets. If the Axiom of Foundation is included in the axioms of set theory, the universe of sets forms a well ordered cumulative hierarchy of stages.[8] Now, for any given class C, we can ask: is there a stage to which every member of C belongs? If the answer is 'yes' C is a set; otherwise C is not a set but an absolutely infinite multiplicity. Thus, a multiplicity C is 'one finished thing' and its members 'are together', if and only if C is a subclass of some stage.

Finally, I would like to dispel one possible source of disquiet about Cantor's view, which arises from a common description of it as 'the limitation of size' theory. Though there is some justification for this description, it can be a little misleading. The justification is that any set is in a certain sense smaller than any AIM. We define this relation as follows: class x is *smaller than* class y if and only if there is a one-to-one correlation (a bijection) between x and a subclass of y but not vice versa. From Cantor's views, it follows that any set is smaller than any AIM. This is the sole justification for describing the Cantorian approach as the 'limitation of size' theory. But this description can be misleading, because on Cantor's view sets come in all sizes without limit, whereas absolutely infinite multiplicities have no size. A genuine 'limitation of size' theory, by contrast, would say that there is some cardinal number κ such that only classes of cardinality less than κ are sets. That kind of view is subject to the criticism that there is no principled way of choosing the cut-off cardinality κ. In fact Russell made this criticism of an approach he attributed to another logician in terms of ordinals.[9]

A great difficulty of this approach is that it does not tell us how far up the ordinals it is legitimate to go. It might happen that ω was already illegitimate: in that case all proper classes [i.e. sets—M.G.] would be finite . . . Or it might be happen that ω^2 was illegitimate or ω^ω or ω_1 or any other ordinal having no immediate predecessor. We need further axioms before we can tell where the series begins to be illegitimate.[10]

Applied to Cantor, a criticism of this kind would not be fair. In fact it would be irrelevant. On Cantor's approach, there is no point at which the series of ordinals becomes illegitimate. Similarly, there is no cardinal such that classes having that cardinality or greater fail to be sets; there is no cut-off cardinality, in Cantor's view. None the less, the 'limitation of size' sobriquet may promote the erroneous idea that Cantor's view has the arbitrary character of the view criticized in this quotation.

Does Cantor's distinction block the class paradoxes?

In order to see whether Cantor's distinction blocks the class paradoxes, we should be clear about terminology. The term 'class' can be used to include both sets and AIMs; alternatively, it can be used restrictively to mean just 'set'. So in each case there are two arguments to consider, depending on whether we are talking of classes inclusively or restricting attention to sets.

First, there is the Burali-Forti paradox. Suppose we take 'class' to mean 'set'. Then the argument falls at the first hurdle with the assumption that there is a class of all ordinals. For there is no set of all ordinals, as the multiplicity of ordinals is absolutely infinite. On the inclusive reading of 'class', there is a class of all ordinals, on Cantor's view. But the premiss that every well ordered class has a unique ordinal is not true when 'class' is read inclusively, since a well ordered AIM has no ordinal. So Cantor's distinction does block the Burali-Forti paradox.

Secondly, there is Cantor's paradox. If 'class' means 'set', the argument does not work because there is no set of all sets. On the unrestricted reading of 'class', the matter is slightly more complicated. Cantor says that an AIM is not a mathematical object. Does that entail that an AIM cannot be a member of a class? If AIMs can be members, we can take U in Cantor's paradox to be the class of all classes. Then every subclass of U is in U, so there is an injection from the class of subclasses of U into U.[11] The mapping $x \mapsto \{x\}$ on U that takes each class to the unit class containing it is an injection from U into the class of all subclasses of U. Hence, by the Schröder–Bernstein theorem,[12] the members of U can be correlated 1-to-1 with the subclasses of U. But this is ruled out by Cantor's theorem. So the paradox would persist if AIMs could be members. Let us take it then that AIMs cannot be members. Then there is no class of all classes, as AIMs are classes. In that case we could modify Cantor's paradox and take U to be the class of all sets. But then there could not be a class of all subclasses of U, as that would have to have U and other

AIMs among its members.[13] So the paradoxical argument does not go through, as it assumes the existence of a class of all subclasses of U in applying Cantor's theorem.[14]

Finally, there is Russell's paradox. If 'class' is used restrictively to mean 'set', the first premise is true only if the Comprehension Principle is true for sets:

> For any condition F(x) there is a set {x: F(x)} whose members are all and only those things that satisfy the condition F(x).

But on Cantor's approach this is wrong: there are some conditions for which there is no corresponding set, such as the condition 'x is an ordinal'. So it cannot be assumed that there is a set whose members are the things that satisfy the condition 'x is not a member of itself'. In fact, it can be proved from Cantor's premises that there is no set of all things that are not members of themselves.[15]

Suppose now that 'class' is taken inclusively to apply to both sets and AIMs. Cantor nowhere explicitly endorses or rejects the idea that for any condition there is a class of exactly the things that satisfy it, as far as I know. If it is not accepted, the argument of Russell's paradox is blocked. If it is accepted, the class of things that are not members of themselves exists; more precisely, there is a class R such that for any object y

$$y \notin y \leftrightarrow y \in R.$$

The final step in the argument involves applying this generalization to R: if it is true for any object y, it is true in particular for R. Now R would have to be an AIM on Cantor's principles,[16] and AIMs should not be treated as mathematical objects, according to Cantor. As applying the generalization to R amounts to treating R as a mathematical object, the final step is unacceptable.

Conclusion

It is clear that Cantor's explicit views, with minor elaboration, suffice to block the class paradoxes, and so it is fair to conclude that the paradoxes do not reveal any inconsistency in Cantor's views. Moreover, when construed as arguments about sets, each of the paradoxes contains a clear fallacy, given Cantor's views. So Cantor's theory of sets escapes the paradoxes.

None the less, Cantor did not *solve* the paradoxes. Solving the paradoxes requires having compelling reasons, independent of the paradoxes, for one or more principles that block the paradoxical arguments, together with some diagnosis of our failure to see the fallacy. Cantor had no principle that determines which classes are absolutely infinite; he merely assumes that the class of all ordinals is absolutely infinite and then uses that as a lever to show other classes to be absolutely infinite. The only solid ground that Cantor could offer for taking the class of ordinals to be absolutely infinite was that the Burali-Forti contradiction would result from taking it to be a set. In general, Cantor gave no compelling reasons independent of the paradoxes for his claims that this or that class is not a set. The point was made in 1906 by the mathematician Hessenberg in connection with the class of all ordinals:

As yet there has been no profound analysis of the concept of set . . . Hence when we have established that it is not permissible to put all the ordinals together as a set, we are in no position to *prove* this from the concept of 'set' and 'ordinal number'; we must be content solely with the fact of the contradiction.[17]

The Cantorian understanding of sets lacked what was required to provide a solution of the paradoxes. In this situation people quite reasonably felt less than sure that the theory of transfinite sets is consistent. As that theory was at the heart of the foundational work of the last decades of the nineteenth century, this unease cast a shadow over the foundations of mathematics.[18]

Frege's Logicism and his Response to Russell's Paradox

Frege's logicism

According to Kant, the basis of our knowledge of geometrical truths is spatial intuition. Frege agreed. But Kant also held that arithmetical knowledge has an inescapably intuitive basis, and here Frege disagreed. Instead, Frege held, arithmetical truths are logical truths and can be known by purely logical means. Frege's goal was to establish this. In the opening section of his foundational opus *Die Grundgesetze der Arithmetik*, he stated his task as follows:

In my *Grundlagen der Arithmetik* [1884], I sought to make it plausible that arithmetic is a branch of logic and need not borrow any ground of proof whatever from either experience or intuition. In the present book this shall now be confirmed, by the derivation of the simplest laws of Numbers by logical means alone.[1]

Why did Frege think that arithmetic is a branch of logic, prior to any demonstration of the claim? One reason was a certain difference between geometry and arithmetic:

For purposes of conceptual thought we can always assume the contrary of some one or other of the geometrical axioms, without involving ourselves in any self-contradictions when we proceed to our deductions, despite the conflict between our assumptions and our intuition. The fact that this is possible shows that the axioms of geometry are independent of one another and of the primitive laws of logic, and consequently are synthetic. Can the same be said of the fundamental propositions of the science of number? Here we have only to try denying any one of them, and complete confusion ensues. Even to think at all seems impossible.[2]

What exactly is the difference here? The negation of Euclid's parallels postulate is not self-contradictory and is consistent with the other Euclidean axioms. But does this really mark a difference? The negation of the induction axiom of Dedekind–Peano arithmetic is not self-contradictory and is consistent with the other Dedekind–Peano axioms. The difference Frege may have had in mind is this. Our concepts of geometrical entities and relations allow us to conceive of a (counterintuitive) situation in which lines do not conform to the parallels postulate, while our concept of a finite cardinal number does not allow us to conceive of a situation in which the finite cardinal numbers disobey the induction axiom or any of the other Dedekind–Peano axioms. But this fact about the axioms of arithmetic (interpreted as statements about finite cardinal numbers) does not suffice to make them logical truths. For the negations of some geometrical axioms are inconceivable (taken as statements about geometrical lines and points).[3] Yet a collection of geometrical axioms whose negations are inconceivable is not a body of logical truths.

In fact, Frege had another reason for thinking that cardinal arithmetic is a matter of logic, 'the all-embracing applicability of arithmetical theorems'. Frege continued:

Virtually everything that can be an object of thought may in fact be counted: the ideal as well as the real, concepts as well as things, the temporal as well as the spatial, events as well as bodies, methods as well as theorems; even the numbers themselves can in turn be counted. Nothing is really demanded save a certain sharpness of circumscription, a certain logical completeness. From that fact can be gathered this much, that the fundamental principles on which arithmetic is constructed cannot relate to a narrower domain whose peculiarities they express as the axioms of geometry express those of what is spatial. Rather, those fundamental principles must extend to everything thinkable; and a proposition that is in this way of the greatest generality is justifiably assigned to logic.[4]

Universal applicability of a theory may or may not be sufficient for its being a part of logic. But if both of Frege's conditions are combined, his ground for thinking that finite cardinal arithmetic is a branch of logic is stronger: its laws cannot be coherently denied, and it applies to everything.

However, Frege was fully aware that this was not conclusive ground for his conviction that arithmetic is logic. He would need to show that the laws of finite cardinal arithmetic are derivable from purely logical laws and definitions by purely logical inferences. But what is logic? At the time Frege was writing, there was no clear account of logic. Our current view of logic was to emerge only many years later from the work of Frege and others concerned with the foundations of mathematics. Frege, not unreasonably, held that logic was or at least included a theory of concept extensions. A concept is just a condition, and the extension of a concept, e.g. 'x is a prime number', is just the class of things satisfying the condition, the class of prime numbers:

'Logicians have long since spoken of the extension of a concept, and mathematicians have used the terms set, class, manifold; . . . we may well suppose that what mathematicians call a set (etc.) is nothing other than an extension of a concept . . .'[5] It was not just a matter of terminology. Many statements about classes seem to be equivalent to logical truths. Consider the law that, if the class of Fs is a subclass of the class of Gs and the class of Gs is a subclass of the class of Hs, then the class of Fs is a subclass of the class of Hs. Is not that just an expression of the logical truth that if every F is G and every G is H, then every F is H?

For Frege, the essential fact about concept extensions is that the extensions of two concepts are the same if and only if whatever falls under one concept falls under the other.[6] So, for example, since

for any object x, $x = \pm\sqrt{4}$ if and only if $3(x^2) = 12$,

we can assert

$$\{x : x = \pm\sqrt{4}\} = \{x : 3(x^2) = 12\}.\,[7]$$

Frege viewed this way of reaching an identity statement about concept extensions as a step of logic: 'This possibility must be regarded as a law of logic, a law that is invariably employed, even if tacitly, whenever discourse is carried on about the extension of concepts. The whole Leibniz–Boole calculus of logic rests upon it.'[8] Frege also regarded the reverse step (from the identity to the general equivalence) as a step of logic, and he combined the two in his Basic Law V:

$$\{x : F(x)\} = \{x : G(x)\} \leftrightarrow \text{For all } x, F(x) \leftrightarrow G(x).\,[9]$$

Summarizing, we can say that Frege took logic to be (or to include) the general theory of concept extensions, and that he thought that arithmetic is logically deducible from laws about concept extensions and abbreviatory definitions. His ground for this was that the laws of arithmetic have the characteristic of logical laws that their negations are not genuinely conceivable and they have universal applicability.

Frege's programme

Frege had gone some way to vindicating his logicist view of arithmetic in the informal exposition in the later sections of his philosophical monograph of 1884. But he wanted to establish his view in a way that leaves no room for doubt:

Of course the pronouncement is often made that arithmetic is merely more highly developed logic; yet that remains disputable so long as transitions occur in the proofs that are not made according to acknowledged laws of logic, but seem rather to be based on something known by intuition. Only if these transitions are split up into logically simple steps can we be persuaded that the root of the matter is logic alone.[10]

Frege's intended method was to demonstrate the deducibility of arithmetic laws from logical laws and definitions by actually carrying out the proofs. The quoted passage indicates how a proof is to be carried out if it is to serve his purpose: every step in a proof must be logically simple. Moreover, Frege stresses that the unproved premises, i.e. the axioms, and the rules of inference must be stated beforehand.[11] But even this is not enough. For anything offered as a proof it must be clear whether it really is a proof, i.e. a sequence of propositions each of which is an axiom or follows from earlier propositions in the sequence by application of the rules. To make it manifest that these strict conditions are met, Frege needed a 'logically perfect' language, that is, one in which (i) the logical character of each proposition expressible in the language is clear from the form of the sentence used to express it, and (ii) the interpretation of each expression is so clear and precise that no tacit assumption could be smuggled in.[12] So there were three tasks in Frege's programme:

1. to set out a logically perfect language L, including definitions of arithmetical terms.
2. to set out sentences in L which are clearly logically true, to be used as axioms; and to set out clearly logically valid rules of inference for L.
3. to set out fully and explicitly derivations of the laws of arithmetic from these axioms by these rules.

This may strike one as a programme of pedantic excess. But, given that Frege's aim is to establish beyond doubt that the laws of arithmetic are not merely truths but logical truths, the programme is not excessive. The explicit proof of each law of arithmetic will provide 'a basis on which to judge the epistemological nature of the law', Frege said, and, comparing his proofs to those typical of mathematical texts he wrote:

Generally people are satisfied if every step in the proof is evidently correct, and this is permissible if one merely wishes to be persuaded that the proposition to be proved is true. But if it is a matter of gaining insight into this 'being evident', this procedure does not suffice; we must put down all of the intermediate steps, so that the full light of consciousness may fall upon them.[13]

The contradiction in Frege's system

The first part of Frege's programme was carried out and published in 1893, before the paradoxes had been discovered. In 1902, on the eve of publication of the second volume of this work, Frege received a letter from Russell pointing out the contradiction derivable in his system. 'Hardly anything more unwelcome can befall a scientific writer', Frege wrote, 'than that one of the foundations of his edifice be shaken after the work is finished.'

Before examining Frege's response to Russell's paradox, it will be helpful to have some account of the way it crops up in Frege's system. In addition to the symbolism introduced in the exposition of Russell's paradox, I use:

$\exists x$ to abbreviate 'for some x', and

$\forall x$ to abbreviate 'for all x',

where 'x' is a variable for objects—and the same for 'y' and 'z' in place of 'x'. I will also use concept (or predicate) variables 'F', 'G', and 'H' in place of 'x'. The laws and definitions in play are Frege's Basic Law V and his definition of the membership relation. It will be convenient to split Basic Law V into two parts:

(Va) $\forall x\,[\,F(x) \leftrightarrow G(x)\,] \to \{x : F(x)\} = \{x : G(x)\}.$

(Vb) $\{x : F(x)\} = \{x : G(x)\} \to \forall x\,[\,F(x) \leftrightarrow G(x)\,].$

The membership relation is defined essentially as follows:[14]

$$x \in y \leftrightarrow \exists H\,[\,y = \{z : H(z)\}\ \&\ H(x)\,].$$

Frege assumed that, for every predicate $F(x)$ in a logically perfect language, there is a class $\{x : F(x)\}$ that is its extension. In fact, this is implicit in (Va).[15] So we can take it that there is such a class as $\{x : x \notin x\}$. The argument of Russell's paradox can be reproduced in the system once we have derived the formula

$$F(y) \leftrightarrow y \in \{x : F(x)\}.$$

A derivation of this general formula from Frege's (Vb) and his definition of the membership relation are given in the appendix to this chapter. As it holds for any predicate $F(z)$, it holds in particular for '$z \notin z$'. So we have as an instance

$$y \notin y \leftrightarrow y \in \{x : x \notin x\}.$$

Since this holds for any object y, and since classes in Frege's view are objects, we obtain the contradiction:[16]

$$\{x : x \notin x\} \notin \{x : x \notin x\} \leftrightarrow \{x : x \notin x\} \in \{x : x \notin x\}.$$

As membership is a defined relation in Frege's system, one might expect that a contradiction can be derived without use of the membership symbol in the system. That is right. Let us use the symbol '$\neg$' for negation and let us define 'R' as follows:

$$R(x) \leftrightarrow \exists H\, [\, x = \{z : H(z)\}\ \&\ \neg H(x)\,].$$

Then the following contradiction is derivable in Frege's system:[17]

$$\neg R(\{x : R(x)\}) \leftrightarrow R(\{x : R(x)\}).$$

The derivation again uses (Vb), and assumes that for any predicate there is a class that is the predicate's extension, and that every class is an object. The argument is clearly a version of Russell's paradox.

Frege's response

Frege was alerted to the contradiction by Russell just as the second volume of his foundational work, *Grundgesetze*, was in press. He gave his response in an appendix to that volume. There he mentions several possible diagnoses of the problem, and after a cursory survey selects the one that appears, initially at least, to cause least disruption to his published derivations.

One diagnosis is that some classes, including $\{x : x \notin x\}$, are not genuine objects, and so terms for those classes may not be substituted for object variables. On this diagnosis, the term '$\{x : x \notin x\}$' cannot be substituted for the object variable 'y' in

$$y \notin y \leftrightarrow y \in \{x : x \notin x\}.$$

Hence the final step in the argument is invalid.

Frege rejected this option on two grounds. First, he supposed that it would be necessary to distinguish not only between proper and improper objects, but also between predicates that could be applied to improper objects and those that could not, then between the extensions of those two types of predicate, then between the predicates that could be applied to those two types of extension, and so on. The result would be a multiplicity of types, and this would be unwieldy if not unworkable. It would be 'extraordinarily difficult' to set up general rules determining which predicates were applicable to which entities. This reason for rejecting the 'improper objects' option is not decisive. One could stipulate that no predicate of the language of the system can be applied to improper objects, thus avoiding the need for many types.

Alternatively, one could embrace a system of types and live with the extra complexity. Frege's second ground for rejecting the 'improper objects' option is stronger. He states it curtly: 'the justifiability of the improper objects may be doubted'. This is the same as the widely felt worry about Cantor's distinction between absolutely infinite multiplicities and sets. There seems to be no way of telling that a class is an improper object prior to finding that contradiction results from treating it as a proper object, and the absence of an independent principle for distinguishing between proper and improper objects suggests that the distinction may not be real.

A second diagnosis is that there are no such things as classes and that class terms are non-denoting expressions, pseudo-names like 'the average wage-earner'. It may be that no one earns exactly the average weekly wage of £x. In that case every wage earner has a weekly wage of either less or more than £x; but we could not validly infer that the average wage-earner has a weekly wage of either more or less than £x. The rule of *universal instantiation* cannot be validly applied with non-denoting terms; nor can the rule of *existential generalization*.[18] In this case the substitution of a class term for a variable in the final step of Russell's paradox would be invalid, as that would be a step of universal instantiation with a non-denoting term. Frege had no dormant nominalism that might have been awakened by the paradox. Classes were central to Frege's outlook, to his view of logic, and therefore to his logicist programme for arithmetic. That was his reason for rejecting this 'no-class' option. More pragmatically, in Frege's system a finite cardinal number n is the class of classes with exactly n members; hence in his system a term for a number is a class term. So if all class terms are non-denoting expressions, numerical terms would also be non-denoting expressions. That would destroy the link between general arithmetical formulas and particular numerical equations. The view that cardinal numbers are classes is disputable, of course. But it is so central to Frege's approach that it was clearly reasonable for him to prefer an option that leaves it in place. Moreover, other kinds of mathematical entity are under threat if there are no classes. What are sequences, lattices, and semi-groups, for example, if not classes with a certain structure?

A third possibility Frege mentions is that not every concept has an extension. But he does not give this option serious consideration. Clearly, the paradox is blocked if the concept expressed by the predicate '$x \notin x$' has no extension. One reason for rejecting this way out is the lack of any principle for determining which concepts have an extension and which do not. 'Is it always permissible', Frege asks, 'to speak of the extension of a concept, of a class? And if not, how do we recognise the exceptional cases?'[19]

The diagnosis that Frege favoured turned on a careful analysis of the derivations of the contradiction in his system. Both derivations (one using membership, the other not), have Basic Law V as a premiss. Of the explicit assumptions of the derivations (as opposed to the tacit assumptions considered above) Basic Law V does appear to be the least secure. In his response to the paradox, Frege says:

It is a matter of my Basic Law V. I have never concealed from myself its lack of self-evidence which the others possess, and which must be properly demanded of a law of logic, and in fact I pointed out this weakness in the Introduction to the first volume.[20]

The part of Law V operative in the derivations is part (Vb):

(Vb) $\{x : F(x)\} = \{x : G(x)\} \to \forall x [F(x) \leftrightarrow G(x)]$.

However, (Vb) is damaging only in conjunction with the assumption that for every concept F there exists a corresponding class, the extension of F. I regard this existential belief and not (Vb) as the root error. For if the class of things satisfying F is identical with the class of things satisfying G, it follows quite trivially that exactly the same things satisfy F and G. Obviously, the appearance of (Vb) in the derivations leading to contradiction is *some* reason to doubt it. But without an independent reason for doubting (Vb) we should have no great confidence that the root error lies with (Vb) rather than with any of the tacit assumptions discussed earlier.

To save as much as possible of what Frege called his edifice, he proposed that (Vb) be replaced with the following: if a pair of concepts have the same extension, then, with the possible exception of that extension, what falls under one concept falls under the other:

$$\{x : F(x)\} = \{x : G(x)\} \to \forall y [[y \neq \{x : F(x)\}] \to F(y) \leftrightarrow G(y)].$$

This change does block the derivations. But it was an *ad hoc* move that Frege had no great faith in, made under the pressure of a publication deadline.[21] Frege was aware that it would require modifying many of his proofs; although he expressed confidence that the required modifications could be made, he noted that the matter needed to be checked. As it turned out, the move does not work. Some of the crucial theorems cannot be proved by modifying his derivations. Worse still, his new system with the modified version of Basic Law V still leads to contradiction.[22] Frege's programme was in tatters. This became Frege's own verdict in later years. He came to believe that talk of extensions is illusory and that arithmetic is not based on logic alone, reverting instead to a Kantian view.[23]

APPENDIX: A DERIVATION OF THE COMPREHENSION PRINCIPLE FROM FREGE'S PREMISSES

Given Frege's assumption that for any predicate F there is a class $\{x : F(x)\}$ that is the extension of F, we only need to show that

$$F(y) \leftrightarrow y \in \{x : F(x)\}$$

follows from Fregean premisses. A full reproduction of the argument in Frege's system would be lengthy and tedious, and the details would detract from the essential ideas (see §§54, 55 in Frege 1893 for the details). So I will give a sketch (following Resnik 1980), using modern notation and some straightforward second-order logic. The argument uses two premisses: Frege's definition of the membership relation and part of Frege's Basic Law V:

(Df) $x \in y \leftrightarrow \exists H\,[\,y = \{z : H(z)\}\ \&\ H(x)\,]$.

(Vb) $\{x : F(x)\} = \{x : G(x)\} \rightarrow \forall x\,[\,F(x) \leftrightarrow G(x)\,]$.

The argument for the implication from left to right runs:

(1) $F(y)$ [assumption]

(2) $\{x : F(x)\} = \{x : F(x)\}$ [logic of '=']

(3) $\{x: F(x)\} = \{x: F(x)\}\ \&\ F(y)$ [from 1 and 2]

(4) $\exists H\,[\{x: F(x)\} = \{x: H(x)\}\ \&\ H(y)]$ [from 3 by existential generalization]

(5) $y \in \{x : F(x)\}$ [from 4 and Df]

(6) $F(y) \rightarrow y \in \{x : F(x)\}$ [from 5 discharging assumption 1].

The argument for the reverse implication runs:

(7) $y \in \{x : F(x)\}$ [assumption]

(8) $\exists H\,[\{x : F(x)\} = \{x : H(x)\}\ \&\ H(y)]$ [from (7) and (Df)]

(9) $\exists H\,[\forall x\,[\,F(x) \leftrightarrow H(x)\,]\ \&\ H(y)\,]$ [from (8) and (Vb)]

(10) $F(y)$ [from (9)]

(11) $y \in \{x : F(x)\} \rightarrow F(y)$ [from (10) discharging assumption (7)].

The desired formula follows from (6) and (11).

Type Theory as a Response to the Class Paradoxes

Before settling on the doctrine of *Principia Mathematica*, Russell entertained a variety of responses to the paradoxes. One response he increasingly favoured was the idea of logical types, which he elaborated in *Principia Mathematica*. Russell's aims were very similar to those of Frege. Frege had aimed to show that arithmetic is merely highly developed logic, where logic includes a general theory of classes. Russell aimed to show the same for mathematics as a whole. Faced with the class paradoxes, a logicist has very little room for manoeuvre. If the theory of classes is to count as logic, classes cannot be special mathematical objects, otherwise the theory would not have the topic-neutral character of logic. Classes must be nothing but concept-extensions[1] and the theory of classes must apply to all of them. That rules out Cantor's response to paradoxes, according to which the paradoxical classes (such as the class of all ordinals, the universal class, and the Russell class) lie beyond the scope of the general theory. Furthermore, a membership statement '$y \in \{x : F(x)\}$' must be equivalent, logically speaking, to the simple subject–predicate statement '$F(y)$', otherwise class membership statements would still be about special objects and would therefore lack the topic-neutral character of logical truths. That rules out any response such as Frege's that would abandon the equivalence '$y \in \{x : F(x)\} \leftrightarrow F(y)$'. And that in turn rules out the response that some concepts, such as '$x \notin x$', have no extension.[2] Consequently, logicists are constrained to accept, first, that the logical theory of classes is a general theory of concept-extensions, and, second, the Comprehension Principle:

> For any concept $F(x)$ there is a class $\{x : F(x)\}$ such that, for any object y, y is a member of $\{x : F(x)\}$ if and only if $F(y)$.

The merit of the theory of types from the logicist point of view is that it provides a response to the class paradoxes while respecting these constraints.

Logical types

The basic idea can be illustrated by means of a simple example. Consider the following sentences, taking 'belongs to' to mean 'is a member of':

(a) 'Д' belongs to the Cyrillic alphabet.
(b) The Cyrillic alphabet belongs to the Glagolitic alphabet.
(c) The Cyrillic alphabet belongs to the class of Slavonic alphabets.

Even if you know nothing about the alphabets mentioned, you will be able to tell that the second sentence does not say anything true, though the first and third may do. You know this because you know that an alphabet is a class of letters and not an individual letter, so one alphabet cannot be in another (or in itself). This rules out sentence (b), as it says of an alphabet that it is in another alphabet. Sentence (a) is not ruled out as it says of a letter that it is in an alphabet. Sentence (c) is not ruled out as it says of an alphabet that it is in a class of alphabets. As one can know that (b) is defective without knowing the alphabets mentioned, the defect must be in some way involved with its form. But it cannot be a matter of English grammar, as (b) has no fault of syntax. Russell viewed it as a matter of logical form. Without special training, we become aware of the difference between individuals, classes of individuals, and classes of classes of individuals, and we become aware of membership restrictions on them. Let us say that individuals are things of the lowest logical type, classes of individuals are things of the first type above the lowest, and classes of classes of individuals are things of the first type above that. Then we know that an entity of one type can be a member of an entity of the next type up, but it cannot be a member of anything of equal or lower type. This law of logical type is violated in sentence (b), and we sense that error in realizing that (b) cannot be right. In Russell's view, laws of logical type would be respected in a logically perfect language by being incorporated into the syntax of the language, ruling out any sentence with a defect of logical type as ill-formed.

According to the doctrine of types, each entity has exactly one logical type. The entities of type 0 are all individuals and nothing else. Classes of individuals have type 1, classes of those classes have type 2, and in general classes of entities of type n have type $n + 1$. It is an important part of the doctrine that an entity of type n may be a member of a class of type $n + 1$, but it may not be a member of a class of any other type. Thus, the domain of individuals and classes is divided into a hierarchy of mutually exclusive strata indexed by the natural numbers. That is the metaphysical framework of the doctrine of types.

The grammar of types

Russell intended to demonstrate logicism in much the same way as Frege, by setting out a logical axiom system and showing that established mathematics could be derived in the system. This was not just a matter of formulating axioms, rules, and definitions, and setting out proofs. Prior to this there is the specification of a logically perfect language. It is here that Russell's cunning finds an escape from the class paradoxes. By insisting that a logically perfect language incorporate the grammar of types, he manages to save the Comprehension Principle. Let us see how it works.

Some preliminaries are needed to see how the laws of logical type can be reflected in the grammar of a language. A condition can be expressed by an open sentence, i.e. the result of removing occurrences of one or more names from a sentence, such as 'x rotates'. When an open sentence has more than one gap, the gaps have to be marked if the open sentence is to express a unique condition. There is, for example, a clear difference between 'x admires y' and 'x admires x'. Henceforth I will follow custom among logicians and call an open sentence a *predicate*, and the letters marking the gaps in a predicate its *variables*. A predicate with n different variables is called an *n-place* predicate. Thus, 'x rotates' and 'x admires x' are one-place predicates, 'x admires y' is two-place, and 'x introduced y to z' is three-place. Noun phrases with singular denotation such as 'Jupiter' and 'the class of Jupiter's moons' are called *terms*.

In the language that Russell envisaged, every term and every variable has a type. The type of a term is determined by the logical type of the entity it denotes. So the term 'the class of Jupiter's moons' has type 1, because the class it denotes has type 1. The type of a variable in a predicate[3] determines the type of terms that can replace it. To illustrate, let us signify the type of a variable by a numerical subscript. The term 'the class of Jupiter's moons', having type 1, can replace the variable in 'x_1 has sixteen members', but it cannot replace the variable in 'x_2 has sixteen members'. The converse is true of the term 'the class of subclasses of {Mercury, Venus, Earth, Mars}', as that term denotes an entity of type 2.

In a logically perfect language, syntax and semantics correspond. The syntactic law just illustrated is that, if the variable in a one-place predicate has type n, it can be replaced by any term of type n but by no term of any other type. Corresponding to this is the semantic law that the condition expressed by that predicate is true or false of each entity of type n but is neither true nor false of entities of any other type. At first sight this semantic law appears to contravene the logical law that every proposition is true or false. Consider the claim that Jupiter satisfies 'x_1 has sixteen members'. That is neither true nor false, according to the semantic law, as Jupiter is of type 0 and the condition is true or false only of things of type 1. This, however, is consistent with the law that every proposition is true or false, because the claim 'Jupiter has sixteen members' is not a proposition, according to the doctrine of types. To paraphrase Russell, every condition $F(x)$ has a range of significance, i.e. a range within which an entity e must lie if $F(e)$ is to be a proposition at all, whether true or false; that range is a type.[4]

Here is a summary. The syntactic rule (for one-place predicates) is this:

> If the variable of a one-place predicate is of type n, that variable may be replaced by any term of type n and no term of any other type.

The semantic correlate of that rule is:

> The condition expressed by a one-place predicate with variable of type n is true or false of each entity of type n; it is neither true nor false of entities of any other type.

These rules can be extended to cover many-place predicates.[5]

A language that respects the doctrine of types also has an important rule in connection with the membership relation '$\in$'. According to the doctrine of types, only entities of type n can be considered for membership of a class of type $n + 1$: a claim of form '$e \in$ C' has a truth value (i.e. is true or false) if and only if the type of e is one below the type of C. This is incorporated into the language of types by the following syntactic rule:

> The type of the term or variable on the left of an occurrence of the membership symbol must be one below the type of the term or variable on its right.

Put schematically, this says that, for any well-formed terms or variables α and β, if α has type m and β has type n, '$\alpha \in \beta$' is well-formed if and only if $n = m + 1$. In fact, this rule is forced on us by the rules governing subject–predicate sentences. This is because it is essential to the theory of types that (i) any class is the extension of some condition, and (ii) for a condition F and entity e, the statement that e is a member of the class of Fs is equivalent to the statement that e satisfies F.[6]

How type grammar blocks the class paradoxes

With these rules of the grammar of types in mind, let us re-examine the class paradoxes. First, let us recall Russell's paradox.

1. For any condition F(x) and any object y, F(y) $\leftrightarrow$ $y \in \{x : F(x)\}$.

So for the particular condition $x \notin x$ and for any class y, we get

2. $y \notin y \leftrightarrow y \in \{x : x \notin x\}$.

When y is the particular class $\{x : x \notin x\}$, we get

3. $\{x : x \notin x\} \notin \{x : x \notin x\} \leftrightarrow \{x : x \notin x\} \in \{x : x \notin x\}$.

The argument as it stands cannot be reproduced in the language of types, simply because no types are indicated. But we can go through the argument supplying type subscripts, checking its legitimacy as we go. Let k be a fixed but arbitrary natural number. The first line becomes

For any condition F(x_k) and any y_k, F(y_k) $\leftrightarrow$ $y_k \in \{x_k : F(x_k)\}$.

This is fine according to type theory. It is implied by the Comprehension Principle for classes of type k + 1.

The first transgression occurs in the step from the first line to the second. To get to the second line, we must assume that there is a condition expressed by '$x_k \notin x_k$'. This expression abbreviates the negation of '$x_k \in x_k$'; in symbols, '$\neg(x_k \in x_k)$'. That cannot express a condition unless '$x_k \in x_k$' expresses a condition. But the latter violates the rule that the type of the expression on the left of an occurrence of '$\in$' must be one less than the type of the expression on its right. So it is ill-formed and cannot express a condition. Hence $\neg(x_k \in x_k)$ too is ill-formed and fails to express a condition.

There is a further way in which the argument is blocked by the grammar of types. Even if we ignore the fact that the expression '$x_k \notin x_k$' is ill-formed and treat it as if it were a well-formed predicate expressing a condition on entities of type k, the step from the second line to the third would still be illegitimate. For this treats the would-be class $\{x_k : x_k \notin x_k\}$ as if it were of type k, in substituting '$\{x_k : x_k \notin x_k\}$' for 'y_k'. But as the members of such a class would be of type k, the class itself would have to be of type k + 1; hence the substitution is illegitimate. For these two reasons, Russell's paradox cannot be reproduced in the language of types.

How do the type restrictions block the other class paradoxes? Cantor's paradox assumes that there is a class of all classes, U, and deduces that the class of U's subclasses, $\mathbb{P}(U)$, both is and is not greater in number than U. This argument is blocked as there can be no term for a class of all classes in the language of types, because the variable of a class term must belong to just one type. This is not just a dodge. According to the doctrine of types there can be no class of all classes, for a class of all classes would have to have members of all types, whereas the doctrine entails that a class can have members of only one type.

How is this consistent with the Comprehension Principle? That Principle says that for any condition there is a class whose members are exactly the satisfiers of that condition. Applying this to the condition of being a class entails that there is a class U of all classes. The Comprehension Principle, then, appears to entail that there is a class of all classes, contrary to the doctrine of types. In fact this is not so, because it is part of the doctrine that there is no condition that is true or false of everything regardless of type. Rather, every condition is true or false of things of just one type. So there is no condition of being a class. The general point is that the Comprehension Principle is compatible with the doctrine of types because the doctrine restricts what is to count as a condition.

Although there is no condition of being a class according to the doctrine of types, there is a condition of being a class of type n, for each positive integer n. So, by the Comprehension Principle, there is a class of all classes of type n, which I will call U_n. Can the paradoxical argument be reproduced within type theory for U_n in place of U? It cannot. For U_n and all its subclasses, which are the members of $\mathbb{P}(U_n)$, are of type $n + 1$, whereas the members of U_n are of type n. So no member of $\mathbb{P}(U_n)$ is a member of U_n. Hence one cannot infer from the fact that all members of $\mathbb{P}(U_n)$ are classes that all members of $\mathbb{P}(U_n)$ are members of U_n, as is required by the argument. Parallel considerations apply to the Burali-Forti paradox: there is no class of all ordinals; and if we try to recast the argument within type theory, the result is invalid.

Is the doctrine of types an acceptable solution?

The restrictions of type grammar suffice to block all three class paradoxes. As far as is known, they block the paradoxes without merely relocating contradiction, unlike Frege's proposal. However, solving a paradox requires more than adopting rules that invalidate the paradoxical argument. It requires in addition some plausible principles as a basis for the rules, and an explanation of the failure to recognize those principles. In this case the basis is the doctrine of types; our failure to recognize its principles may be explained by the habits of thought induced by the medium of a language in which type distinctions are not marked. But is the doctrine of types plausible?

Russell says that the idea of types has some consonance with common sense, which makes it credible.[7] It is true that we are sensitive to a difference between mistakes of type and other mistakes: the claim that the McDonald clan belongs to the Douglas family is recognizably defective, even to those ignorant of McDonald–Douglas kinship relations. Furthermore, in the language of informal mathematics it is customary to use different lettering—different portions of the alphabet, or different cases, or different alphabets, or different fonts—each reserved for a range of entities, with no overlap of ranges. So the idea of exclusive types represented in the syntax of mathematical talk is not totally artificial.

However, the doctrine of types is too strict for credibility. Consider the class whose members are just Plato and Aristotle, a class of type 1. The class of all its subclasses is of type 2. These two classes have many things in common. For example, they are both finite classes. This is hardly deniable. Yet it must be rejected if the doctrine of types is correct. For the claim in question cannot be right unless there is a condition, namely 'x is a finite class', which is satisfied by things of more than one type, contrary to the doctrine of types. According to that doctrine, there are conditions 'x_1 is a finite class' and 'x_2 is a finite class' satisfied by the first and second classes, respectively; but there is no condition satisfied by both of them, and no proposition is expressed by saying that they are both finite classes. Surely, on this point the doctrine of types is implausible.

A related point is that there are no mixed classes, according to the doctrine of types. But why not? Not only the Douglas family but also the Douglas individuals belong to the McDonald clan. A clan, then, is a class with elements of mixed type, individuals, and classes of individuals. So it unreasonable to insist that no condition can be satisfied by entities of more than one type, and that no class has members of more than one type.[8] But if there are mixed classes, the doctrine of types provides no ground for denying that there is a universal class, and so Cantor's paradox threatens.

A further objection is that applying the doctrine to some of its own principles leads to the conclusion that those principles are not propositions, hence not true propositions. The point was made by Gödel. One of the principles of types is this:

> Whenever an object x can replace an object y in one meaningful proposition it can do so in every meaningful proposition.[9]

Writing about this, Gödel says

What makes the principle particularly suspect, however, is that its very assumption makes its formulation as a meaningful proposition impossible, because x and y must then be confined to definite ranges of significance which are either the same or different, and in both cases the statement does not express the principle or even part of it.[10]

It is possible that a doctrine has among its principles some true propositions that can be indicated but not stated. But I do not see how this can be made to work against Gödel's objection, for we have the statement. Another defence might use the possibility that a principle may have some kind of correctness without being a true proposition. This presumably is what we should say about the Comprehension Principle, given the doctrine of types. A type-free statement of it must be *systematically ambiguous*, in Russell's terminology, in the sense that it stands for all the different principles that result from an appropriate distribution of type subscripts; the statement is correct in the sense that all these different type-specific principles are true. However, this cannot be used to work in response to Gödel's objection. This is because the intended thought is essentially about all entities of all types (and all propositions) taken simultaneously.

We must, of course, distinguish between this doctrine, which is a philosophical view intended to justify the restrictions of type grammar, and an axiomatic system expressed in a language that obeys those restrictions, intended as a foundation for accepted mathematics. If it can be demonstrated that the whole of accepted mathematics can be derived within such an axiomatic system, and if the truth of its axioms and the validity of its inference rules are beyond rational doubt, then confidence in the truth of accepted mathematics can be justified. It need not matter that type restrictions prevent the expression of other propositions within the language; it need not matter for foundational purposes that the type restrictions are too strict. Russell, however, felt that they are not strict enough. His reasons are considered in the next two chapters.

Part III
The Language Paradoxes and *Principia Mathematica*

The Definability Paradoxes and the Vicious Circle Principle

Although the type restrictions block the class paradoxes, Russell did not think that the source of those paradoxes was just ignorance about types. Why not? Russell learned of other apparently logical paradoxes that are not blocked by the type restrictions, known as paradoxes of definability. Preferring a univocal explanation, he concluded that both the class paradoxes and the paradoxes of definability have their source in the violation of a single principle, which he called the Vicious Circle Principle. Let us first look at three definability paradoxes, before turning to Russell's diagnosis.

The paradox of the least indefinable ordinal

Let L be any language that is *semantically closed*, in the sense that it has the expressive resources for talking about its own expressive resources.[1] Let z be the total number of defining[2] expressions in L.[3] There is no total number of ordinals, hence there are more than z ordinals. It follows that some ordinals are not definable in L. As the ordinals are well ordered, it follows that one ordinal is the least ordinal not definable in L. This may be defined in L by the translation into L of 'the least ordinal not definable in L', as L is semantically closed. Hence for any semantically closed language there is an ordinal that both is and is not definable in that language.[4]

Berry's paradox

The number of words in English expressions for finite positive integers tends to increase with the integers, and must increase beyond any finite number n, since only a finite number of expressions can be made with n words and there are infinitely many positive integers. Hence some of them are not definable in English in fewer than fourteen words, and among those there must be a least, which can be defined as 'the least positive integer not definable in English in fewer than fourteen words'. But this expression contains thirteen words. Hence that integer both is and is not definable in English in fewer than fourteen words.[5]

Richard's paradox

This paradox adapts Cantor's diagonal proof that the collection of real numbers between 0 and 1 cannot be enumerated.[6] Let L be any language with an enumerable totality of expressions[7] and the resources to express Cantor's proof. Then the collection of real numbers between 0 and 1 definable in L can be enumerated. Let d_n be an enumeration of the entire collection, and let $d_h(k)$ be the single-digit number in the kth place of the decimal expansion of the hth real number in the enumeration, where h and k are any positive integers. Then $d_n(n)$ is the number in the nth place of the decimal expansion of the nth real number in the enumeration. Now we can define in L the following real number between 0 and 1:

$$c(n) = \begin{cases} d_n(n) + 1, & \text{if } d_n(n) < 9 \\ 0, & \text{if } d_n(n) = 9 \end{cases}$$

This definition guarantees that, for each positive integer n, c differs from d_n at the nth place: $c(n) \neq d_n(n)$. So c differs from every real number between 0 and 1 definable in L. But we have just shown that it is definable in L. So there is a real number that both is and is not definable in L.[8]

Definability paradoxes and type grammar

The definability paradoxes cannot be diagnosed as arising from violations of type restrictions, and similar paradoxes can be found in languages that incorporate the grammar of types. This can be illustrated using the paradox of the least indefinable ordinal. First, supposing that there were a least L-indefinable ordinal for a given language L, there is no reason to think that it would have to belong to a class of type equal to or less than its own. Secondly, if L is a typed language that is semantically closed within each type, the paradox can be reproduced. We may assume that there is a type n containing an initial segment of the ordinals of cardinality greater than the number of expressions in the language L. In place of 'the least ordinal not definable in L', we consider 'the least ordinal not definable in L by an expression of type n'. Then the troublesome definition has the form

the y_n such that [y_n is an ordinal and for all x_n, x_n is not a definition in L of y_n] and [for all z_n, if z_n is an ordinal and for all x_n, x_n is not a definition in L of z_n, $y_n \leq z_n$].

This is a term for an entity of type n, and so it can be correctly substituted for the free variable x_n in

For some w_n, w_n is a definition in L of x_n.

That substitution results in the contradictory statement that the least L(n)-indefinable ordinal (of type n) is L(n)-definable. But it contains no transgression of type grammar.

The Vicious Circle Principle

It follows that some new idea is needed for a solution of the definability paradoxes. Russell believed there to be a common error at the root of all the known paradoxes of an apparently logical character, the class paradoxes, the definability paradoxes, as well as some others. Adopting a proposal of Poincaré, he claimed that the common fault was failure to respect the Vicious Circle Principle.[9]

But what is the Vicious Circle Principle? None of Russell's various statements of this principle is clear.[10] The section on the Vicious Circle Principle in the substantial introduction of *Principia Mathematica* opens as follows.

An analysis of the paradoxes to be avoided shows that they all result from a certain kind of vicious circle. The vicious circles in question arise from supposing that a collection of objects may contain members which can only be defined by means of the collection as a whole.[11]

From this we can filter out the following slogan:

No collection has members definable only in terms of that collection.

Later in the same section there is a somewhat addled statement of the principle, which can fairly be boiled down to this:

No collection has members which presuppose that collection.

In the following paragraph we find a third formulation:

> Whatever involves *all* of a collection must not be one of the collection.

Commentators have disagreed on the question whether there is one or more than one principle here,[12] but in my judgement these statements are not clear enough to determine the matter. What is it for something to be *defined in terms of* a collection? What is it for something to *presuppose* a class? What is it for something to *involve all of* a collection? Russell's use of these expressions does not lead us to any precise answers. In fact, Russell's responses to the paradoxes involve two distinct principles, even though he did not distinguish them. However, only one of these principles is relevant for the system of *Principia Mathematica* and that principle can be used to deal with a wider range of paradoxes. So that is the principle we should identify as the Vicious Circle Principle.

The first two formulations of the Vicious Circle Principle given above present it as a principle about collections. But equivalent formulations with a different emphasis are more convenient. The claim that no collection has members definable only in terms of that collection is equivalent to the following:

> No entity is definable only in terms of a collection to which it belongs.

Suitably understood, this is the Vicious Circle Principle. The problem is that the import of this dictum is sensitive to small differences in the explication of 'definable in terms of'. Russell gives us little explicit help here, and his vague formulations suggest that he had no very precise account in mind. I will aim for an account that best suits Russell's purposes.

When we define an entity, we do so by means of a predicate, which I will call the defining predicate. For example, if we define the class of even positive integers thus:

$$E = \{x : \text{For some positive integer } y, x = 2y\}$$

the defining predicate is 'For some positive integer y, $x = 2y$'. One circumstance in which an entity e is defined in terms of a collection c is when the defining predicate contains a term that refers to c. For example, we could define a class thus:

$$G = \{x : x \text{ is in E and for some prime numbers } y \text{ and } z, x = y + z\}.$$

As the defining predicate of G contains the term 'E' for the class of even positive integers, G here is defined in terms of that class. But there is a more basic way in which an entity can be defined in terms of a class. To explain this, it will help to recall the ways in which a variable can occur in a predicate. An occurrence of a variable in a predicate is *free* in that predicate when it marks a gap in the predicate that can be legitimately filled by a name; otherwise that occurrence of the variable is *bound*.[13] In natural languages, expressions often hide their bound variables, in the sense that bound variables are constituents of the expression's semantic structure that lack counterparts in its surface syntax. An example is 'the oldest visible galaxy'. The predicate here means the same as 'oldest among all visible galaxies' or, more formally, 'x is a visible galaxy such that for every visible galaxy y, x is at least as old as y'. So 'the oldest visible galaxy' has a hidden bound variable. The quantifier phrase 'every visible galaxy' in the logically explicit formulation, though not a name of the class of visible galaxies, is a means of alluding to that class. So, assuming that one visible galaxy is older than all others, the expression 'the oldest visible galaxy' defines it in terms of the class of visible galaxies. Thus, there are at least two ways in which an entity e can be defined in terms of a class c. One way, mentioned before, is that the class c is denoted by a name or other referring term in the predicate used to define e. The other is that the class c is the domain picked out by a quantifier phrase in the defining predicate. So we could say that an entity is defined by a definition d in terms of a class c if and only if the defining predicate in d involves c in either of these two ways.

This explication of 'defines in terms of' suffices for a usable version of the Vicious Circle Principle, and this is what recent proponents of a Vicious Circle Principle have in mind. However, Russell wanted something more general. In his view, a variable in a meaningful expression must have a definite range of variation, whether or not any (further) restriction is made explicit in the expression, and he took the range of a variable in a predicate, whether free or bound, to be among the classes involved in the predicate. This is reasonable in view of the fact that the condition expressed by a predicate may depend on the ranges of its variables.[14] A class alluded to by a quantifier phrase will obviously be a subclass of the range of its quantified variable. So ensuring that an entity does not fall in the range of a quantified variable in its definition guarantees that it does not belong to the class alluded to by a quantifier phrase in its definition; we do not need to make separate provision for quantifier phrases. So we can say that an expression d defines e in terms of a class c if and only if d defines e and c is denoted by a term in the defining predicate in d or is the range of a variable in the defining predicate in d.

In *Principia Mathematica* there are no primitive names; it is intended that all terms are defined and eliminable. Referring terms are often introduced for convenience. To reveal the logical structure of sentences in which they occur they should be eliminated. The same is true of predicates. Letting the variables range over the integers, we define

y is *prime* if and only if $y > 1$ and for any x, if $1 < x < y$, x does not divide y

and

x *divides* y if and only if $x \neq 0$ and for some integer z, $x.z = y$.

This shows that the expression 'y is prime' hides a couple of bound variables.[15] So, for the purpose of making explicit all the variables in a defining predicate, we need to eliminate defined terms and predicates. To take this into account we can say:

d defines e in terms of a class c if and only if d defines e and, when all defined expressions are eliminated, c is the range of a variable in the defining predicate in d.

This account is adequate when the definition in question uses the class abstraction operator to define a class as $\{x : F(x)\}$. It is also adequate for definitions of propositional functions, which are theoretical counterparts of what I have been calling conditions. To define a propositional function is simply to give a predicate that expresses it, using an operator that turns the predicate into a term denoting the propositional function expressed. Thus, $\lambda x[x$ is an integer] is the condition of being an integer.[16] There is, however, one final wrinkle to be ironed out. Once we prove that a unique entity satisfies a given condition, we can define that entity using the definite article, as in 'the even prime' or, more explicitly, 'the x such that x is an even prime'. In definitions of this sort, known as definite descriptions, the defined entity *must* belong to the range of the predicate's free variable, and we need be wary only if the entity falls within the range of one of the predicate's *bound* variables. Accordingly, we must make an exception for definitions by definite description and say that, if d is a definite description, d defines e in terms of class c if and only if d defines e and, once all defined expressions have been eliminated, c is the range of a bound variable in the defining predicate in d.

The Vicious Circle Principle rules that no entity is definable only in terms of a class to which it belongs. A class is definable by means of several different predicates, and those predicates may differ in respect of variable ranges. This is illustrated by the fact that $\{x : x > 0\}$, where the range of 'x' is the class of integers, is the same as $\{x : x > \lim_{r \to \infty} 1/2^r\}$, where the range of '$x$' is the class of integers and the range of 'r' is the class of real numbers. This class is definable in terms of the class of real numbers; but it would clearly be wrong to say that it is definable *only* in terms of the class of real numbers. Noting this, we are in a position to see the practical significance of the Vicious Circle Principle. Let us follow custom and say that a definition of an entity in terms of a class to which the entity belongs is an *impredicative* definition. The significance of the principle is that, when introducing an entity into discourse by means of a definition, we must be sure that the definition is not impredicative, unless we can show that there is some other definition of it that is not impredicative. As it is difficult to see how we could show this without being able to supply a definition that is not impredicative, the practical upshot, at least for a foundational system, is a complete ban on introducing an entity by means of an impredicative definition.

Russell's treatment of the definability paradoxes

Before proceeding to assess the Vicious Circle Principle, let us examine Russell's treatment of the definability paradoxes.[17] Russell gives his solution for Berry's paradox and says that the other definability paradoxes are to be solved in the same way. Here is a reminder of Berry's paradox. There are only finitely many English expressions with fewer than fourteen words, hence only finitely many positive integers defined by an English expression with fewer than fourteen words. Of the infinitely many other positive integers, there must be a smallest, which may therefore be defined as 'the least positive integer not definable in English in fewer than fourteen words'. This definition has thirteen words.

Russell deals with this paradox essentially as follows. The defining expression alludes to the class of English expressions, a class to which it belongs. So this attempt at definition involves a vicious circle fallacy. This response to the paradox can be made more explicit by logically parsing the defining expression. An initial step gives

> the least positive integer x such that [x is not definable in English in fewer than fourteen words].

The next step parses the part in square brackets thus:

> For all y, if y is an English expression of fewer than fourteen words, y does not define x.

Logical parsing need go no further. The range of the bound variable 'y' in the above must include all English expressions of fewer than fourteen words;

hence the original expression involves a class that includes all such expressions, and that class contains the original expression as a member.[18] Russell counts this as a vicious circle and says that similar vicious circles are involved in the other definability paradoxes. We can easily see how this would go for the paradox of the least indefinable ordinal. The term 'the least ordinal not definable in L' means 'the least ordinal x such that, for all L-expressions y, y does not define x'. The range of the bound variable is a class that includes all L-expressions. So the translation into L of 'the least ordinal not definable in L' would have to be a definition in terms of a class to which it belongs. This would be viciously circular, and so the expression is non-defining.

Despite appearances, the precept underlying these treatments is not the Vicious Circle Principle. That principle is that no entity is definable only in terms of a class that contains it. Slightly expanded, this says:

> No entity e is definable only by means of an expression that alludes to a class containing entity e.

What Russell highlights in the definability paradoxes is that the defining expression alludes to a class containing the expression itself, rather than any entity the expression might define. So in dealing with the definability paradoxes Russell relied not on the Vicious Circle Principle, but on this alternative:

> No entity is definable only by means of an expression x that alludes to a class containing expression x.

But Russell's treatment of his own paradox does use the Vicious Circle Principle. So there is some truth to the charge that Russell confuses distinct principles. Whatever the merits of Russell's treatment of the definability paradoxes, the principle he uses cannot also be used to handle all the class paradoxes. It is irrelevant to the Burali-Forti paradox because a logically explicit rendering of 'the ordinal of the class of all ordinals' need not allude to a class containing that expression (or any equivalent). Cantor's paradox and Russell's paradox have forms that are similarly immune to treatment with Russell's alternative definability principle: logically explicit renderings of 'the class of all classes' and 'the class of all non-self-membered classes' need not allude to a class containing those expressions (or any equivalent). As it is clear that Russell intended to deal with the class paradoxes and the definability paradoxes by means of a single principle, I will ignore his alternative definability principle, and go on to consider whether the Vicious Circle Principle proper can be used to solve both sets of paradoxes.

The Vicious Circle Principle as the key to the paradoxes

Berry's paradox and the paradox of the least indefinable ordinal are blocked by the Vicious Circle Principle in the same way. The troublesome expressions begin 'the least positive integer not definable in . . .' and 'the least ordinal not definable in . . .' Understandably, one focuses on the expression 'not definable' as a potential source of trouble in a definition. But the fact that these expressions begin 'the least . . .' already signals their impredicativity. Unpacking the expression form 'the least ordinal x such that $F(x)$' gives

the ordinal x such that $[F(x)$ and for every ordinal y, if $F(y)$ then $x \le y]$.

The same applies when 'ordinal' is replaced by 'positive integer'. It is clear that the reference (if any) of such an expression must fall within the range of the bound variable 'y'. So any definition beginning 'the least ordinal. . .' will be impredicative. The same applies to the positive integers or any other well-ordered class of entities.[19] As the putative definition in each of these paradoxes is impredicative, and as we lack a co-referring definition that is not impredicative, the Vicious Circle Principle bars assuming that the putative definition actually defines something. So these paradoxes are blocked by the Vicious Circle Principle.

However, it is implausible that these paradoxes arise solely from use of 'the least . . .'. No logical error was involved in defining a term for the least electrical charge, the original use of the word 'electron'. The problem is surely due, at least in part, to the definition's describing the definiendum as indefinable (in some way). But the Vicious Circle Principle cannot be applied at this point, because the class alluded to in describing something as indefinable is a class of expressions, whereas the entity to be defined is not an expression; hence the allusion to indefinability is not a source of impredicativity. For this reason it is not credible that the Vicious Circle Principle is the key to these paradoxes.

Richard's paradox takes as given a language L with certain unremarkable properties. The argument proceeds by supposing that there is a class D of all real numbers between 0 and 1 definable in L; it is then inferred that D can be enumerated and that some enumeration d of D is definable in L; it is then inferred that the diagonalization c of d is definable in L and from this one quickly reaches contradiction. The real number c is defined in terms of d and d is defined in terms of D. So c is defined in terms of D. Since c would have to be in D, it follows that its definition is impredicative. Lacking any definition of c that is not impredicative, the Vicious Circle Principle forbids assuming that the putative definition of c defines anything at all.

Granted that the Vicious Circle Principle can be deployed to block Richard's paradox, does the principle really provide its solution? Rather than answer this, I will just set out an alternative that I happen to favour and let the matter rest there. The alternative is that, in a semantically closed language L, various semantic predicates lack definite extension; among these is the translation into L of 'x is definable in L' and the translations into L of predicates of the form 'x is a such-&-such definable in L'. Letting L be English, for example, there is no class of all satisfiers of the condition 'x is a real number between 0 and 1 definable in English'; as there is no such class there is no enumeration d of it; hence there is no such thing as the definition of d, from which to get a further definition by diagonalization. The same solution is available for the other definability paradoxes. The predicates 'x is an integer not definable in English in fewer than fourteen words' and 'x is an ordinal not definable in English' do not have extensions. Since no class is the extension of any of these predicates, they provide counterexamples to the Comprehension Principle for semantically closed languages.[20] Thus, the unrestricted Comprehension Principle can be seen as the real source of the definability paradoxes as well as the class paradoxes.

Does the Vicious Circle Principle fare better in dealing with the class paradoxes? Cantor's paradox assumes that there is a universal class or a class of all classes. If there were a universal class $\{x : x = x\}$, it would clearly have to fall within the range of the free variable in the defining predicate '$x = x$'; and as there is no way of defining a universal class that avoids this, the Vicious Circle Principle entails that there is no such entity as the universal class. Exactly parallel reasoning applies in the case of $\{x : x \text{ is a class}\}$, so Cantor's paradox is blocked by the Vicious Circle Principle.[21] Russell's paradox assumes the existence of $\{x : x \notin x\}$ or $\{x : x \text{ is a class such that } x \notin x\}$, and it assumes, in each case, that the class falls within the range of the free variable of the defining predicate. So again, in the absence of alternative definitions that avoid this, these class terms define nothing, according to the Vicious Circle Principle. Thus, both Cantor's paradox and Russell's paradox are blocked by the Vicious Circle Principle.

The Burali-Forti paradox is trickier. An ordinal is a property of a well-ordered class, its order type. For mathematical purposes, we may represent ordinals in a canonical way by identifying each ordinal with one of the well-ordered classes that have it. This can be done in such a way that a class of all ordinals would itself be an ordinal and would therefore fall in the range of the free variable of the predicate in '$\{x : x \text{ is an ordinal}\}$'.[22] But the Burali-Forti paradox does not depend on identifying ordinals with representative instances, and without such an identification we have no reason to think that

$\{x : x$ is an ordinal$\}$ is defined in terms of a class to which it belongs. So the Vicious Circle Principle gets no purchase here. But the principle does have effect if in place of '$\{x : x$ is an ordinal$\}$' we consider the expression 'the ordinal of $\{x : x$ is an ordinal$\}$'. For if the latter expression defined anything at all, the defined entity would belong to a class in terms of which it was defined; lacking any other definition of it that avoids this, we are forbidden by the Vicious Circle Principle to accept that the ordinal of the class of all ordinals exists. This, however, is not a way of avoiding paradox. For once we have accepted that there is a class of all ordinals, we are forced to recognize that it is a well-ordered class; hence its order type is an ordinal. Once we have got this far we are doomed, for the alternative, which is that a well ordered class lacks an order type, is again paradoxical. So it is mistaken to think that the Burali-Forti paradox is solved by the Vicious Circle Principle.

To summarize, the definability paradoxes can be blocked by the Vicious Circle Principle. But it is not plausible that violation of the Vicious Circle Principle is the error at the root of these paradoxes, and there is a more promising alternative: reject the Comprehension Principle for the semantic predicates of semantically closed languages. Turning to the class paradoxes, they can be blocked by the Vicious Circle Principle, but it is very clear that the Burali-Forti paradox cannot be *solved* this way. As all three class paradoxes are likely to have the same solution, it is improbable that the paradoxes of Cantor and Russell are solved by the Vicious Circle Principle. And again, there is an alternative to the Vicious Circle Principle, using Cantor's distinction between classes that are objects (sets) and classes that are not. But the Cantorian approach needs supplementation by plausible principles motivated independently of the paradoxes, and no such principles were on the horizon when Russell was working on the problem. Moreover, all the paradoxes of a seemingly logical character appear to harbour a circularity of some kind or other. So Russell's hunch that something like the Vicious Circle Principle is the key to all the paradoxes was quite sensible, if ultimately wrong.

Should we believe the Vicious Circle Principle?

The paradoxes aside, what reason is there for thinking that the Vicious Circle Principle is true? It is easiest to motivate the idea in terms of propositional functions. As mentioned before, a propositional function is Russell's theoretical counterpart of a condition. Let us adopt Russell's harmless expedient of identifying conditions with attributes: $\lambda x \, [x$ is bold$]$ = the condition of being bold = boldness. Here is an illustrative case.[23] If we try to the list the attributes required of a great general, we are likely to mention as well as boldness such attributes as decisiveness, strategic cunning, tactical flexibility, commanding presence, and others. Now consider the attribute G of having every attribute required of a great general:

(G) λx [for every y such that y is an attribute required of a great general, x has y].

G itself is an attribute required of a great general, because anyone who lacks G lacks some property required of a great general and so cannot be a great general. The range of the bound variable 'y' in the defining predicate of G must include the class of attributes required of a great general, and as G is one of those attributes G belongs to the range of 'y'. So G is here defined in terms of a class that contains it. In other words, the definition of G is impredicative. So the Vicious Circle Principle entails that, if this is our only definition of G, G is not a genuine attribute at all.

This conclusion is right. If there were such an attribute as G, possessing it would depend on having all the attributes on the list of attributes required of a great general; as G is itself on that list, having G depends on having G. But this is impossible. The relevant kind of dependency is constitutive. Being a father depends constitutively on being male and having offspring: those two attributes are the conditions that conjointly constitute being a father. It would be absurd to say that an additional condition for being a father is being a father. In general, possession of an attribute cannot be a constitutive condition for possessing that same attribute. It is natural to interpret the expression 'having all the attributes required of a great general' as meaning 'having all the *first-order* attributes required of a great general', where an attribute is first-order if it can be defined without allusion to attributes. This explains our initial feeling that the putative definition of G succeeds in defining an attribute. But if we do not interpret it that way, it is vacuous, and the reason seems to be that the putative definition is circular in just the way ruled out by the Vicious Circle Principle. Perhaps the simplest case of this kind of vacuity is the following. Let H be the attribute of possessing attribute H:

(H) λx [x has H].

It seems obvious that no real attribute has been defined, and this intuition is backed by a simple extension of the Vicious Circle Principle: no entity is definable only in terms of itself or a class that contains it.

For definitions of attributes (or conditions or propositional functions), the

Vicious Circle Principle often accords well with our intuitions. But sometimes it does not. Being round and being red are attributes, so being an attribute is one of their attributes. Hence being an attribute is an attribute. It follows that being an attribute must fall within the range of the free variable in its defining predicate:

λx [x is an attribute].

There seems to be nothing wrong here, even though the Vicious Circle Principle dictates that there is no such entity. One can also find apparently innocuous cases of attributes falling within the range of *bound* variables in their defining predicates. An instance is the attribute of having an attribute that one is unaware of having:

λx [For some attribute y, x has y but is unaware of having y].

There also appear to be attributes that fall in the ranges of both free and bound variables in their defining predicates, such as the attribute of being a conjunction of attributes:

λx [x is an attribute such that, for some attributes y and z, to have x is to have both y and z].

The free variable 'x' and the bound variables 'y' and 'z' have ranges that include the class of attributes; so the attribute here defined falls within those ranges.

However, our intuitions about attributes are not totally reliable. There seems to be attribute of being an attribute that is not an attribute of itself. An instance of it seems to be the attribute of being inexpressible. But we quickly get a Russell-style paradox by considering whether this attribute (λx [x is an attribute that is not an attribute of itself]) is an attribute of itself.[24] So some adjustment to our intuitions is necessary to avoid paradox, and it is quite possible that the optimum adjustment will rule against some harmless intuitions as well as those that beget paradox. If in addition we have some way of explaining why we had the intuitions now to be rejected, the remedy may even be palatable. Russell can explain the intuitions (about attributes) that conflict with the Vicious Circle Principle in terms of his theory of orders. Roughly, an attribute is first order if it does not allude to attributes of any order; for n greater than 1, an attribute is nth order if it alludes to attributes of order $n-1$ but none of higher order. Then for each positive integer n there is an attribute of order $n+1$ defined

λx [x is an nth order attribute].

Our intuition that λx [x is an attribute] is a *bona fide* attribute can now be explained as follows. As in almost all contexts our interest is restricted to first-order attributes, we overlook the order of attributes; not discerning the hidden indexical, we think that there is none, and therefore that 'x is an attribute' expresses a definite attribute.

Two ideas underlie the Vicious Circle Principle for attributes. One is that no attribute can depend constitutively on itself. This seems obviously right. The other underlying thought is that, if an attribute cannot but be defined in terms of some class c, that attribute constitutively depends on every member of c. This may be right but I do not know of a cogent argument for it. Attributes, i.e. propositional functions, are intensional: distinct propositional functions may have the same extension, and the constitution of a propositional function is tightly tied to its expression,[25] perhaps to the extent that the semantic values (or references) of the semantic constituents of a predicate are constituents of the propositional function expressed. Taking the range of a variable as its semantic value, it follows that a propositional function constitutively depends on the range of any variable in the predicate expressing it. That yields the conclusion that a propositional function depends on any class in terms of which it is defined.[26] But how do we reach the conclusion that it depends on all the *members* of a class in terms of which it is defined?

My tentative conclusion about the Vicious Circle Principle for attributes (or conditions or propositional functions) is that it may be right, despite the fact that it conflicts with some strong intuitions. Other intuitions confirm the principle, and those that conflict with it can be explained away. However, we lack any compelling argument for the Vicious Circle Principle for attributes and so the matter is very far from certain.

It is much harder to motivate the Vicious Circle Principle for classes. A class is constitutively dependent on its members and on the members of its members and anything lower still on its membership tree.[27] We standardly define a class as the extension of a given predicate. The entities alluded to in a predicate, however, often fall outside the membership tree of the predicate's extension. Consider, for example, the class of all stars beyond the light cones of every sentient being. As stars do not have members, the elements of the membership tree of this class are just the members of the class itself. So the class depends only on its members, certain stars. It does not depend on the Queen's corgis, though they fall within the range of 'every sentient being'. We are in principle unable to define this class without reference to sentient beings, yet the class is not dependent on sentient beings. Even if no predicates other than those alluding to all sentient beings were to have that class as its extension, the class would not depend on sentient beings.

Are mathematical classes different? If we set aside the representation of real numbers as classes and think of them as ratios of quantities of a continuous magnitude, a class of real numbers depends on its members and nothing else (as none of its members have members). Yet there are classes of real numbers that we can only define with reference to integers that are not members of those classes. An example is the Cantor set.[28] This is a class of numbers between 0 and 1 inclusive, but there is no way of defining it that avoids a bound variable with a range that includes an infinite class of positive integers. Any specification of the Cantor set depends on the positive integers; the class itself does not. It follows that a class, even a mathematical class, need not depend on everything that its specifications depend on. So the fact that a class cannot depend on itself is no ground for thinking that the specifications of a class cannot depend on that very class. The principle needed to rule out vicious circles with respect to classes is that no class can occur in its own membership tree, something that is vouchsafed by the theory of types.[29] Classes are extensional, and the Vicious Circle Principle is plausible only for intensional entities.

Why then did Russell, who was sensitive to the extension–intension distinction, believe the Vicious Circle Principle without restriction? The answer, I think, is that extensional entities are classes,[30] and classes are logical fictions, according to Russell. Apparent reference to classes, he held, is a convenient manner of speech replaceable by reference to propositional functions: '[A] proposition about a class is always to be reduced to a statement about a [propositional] function which defines it',[31] and 'classes, so far as we introduce them, are merely symbolic or linguistic conveniences, not genuine objects as their members are if they are individuals'.[32] On this view talk about classes is intensional, and so Russell could ward off the objection to the Vicious Circle Principle given above.

Conclusion

The Vicious Circle Principle has a practical entailment: do not try to introduce an entity into discourse by definition in terms of a class that would contain it. For the reasons given earlier, it is doubtful that the paradoxes are to be explained as resulting from violations of this practical entailment. The Vicious Circle Principle, or something close to it, may be right for intensional entities, but it is not at all plausible for extensional entities, and it is arguable that the ontology of much pure mathematics is extensional. This does not mean that a logical grammar devised to guarantee respect for the Vicious Circle Principle could not be a suitable framework for a foundational system of mathematics. What Russell sought was a framework strict enough to bar the paradoxes but not so strict as to bar the development of classical mathematics within it. What Russell came up with is now referred to as the ramified theory of types, the framework of *Principia Mathematica*.[33] This is examined in the next chapter.

Principia Mathematica 2

The universe of Principia Mathematica

Among the aims of *Principia Mathematica* (*PM*) is the reformulation of mathematical propositions in terms of a minimal number of undefined elements and the deduction of all established mathematics, thus reformulated, from a minimal number of unproved premisses.[1] Russell took the undefined elements to be logical and inferred that the success of the project would show that mathematical truths are truths of logical form:

Mathematics, therefore, is wholly composed of propositions which only contain variables and logical constants, that is to say, purely formal propositions—for the logical constants are those which constitute form.[2]

Despite this view of mathematics, *PM* has an ontology that contains individuals and propositional functions. A propositional function is what is expressed by a properly constructed predicate, though a propositional function may be inexpressible in a given language. A propositional function $\varphi(x)$ has a circumscribed range of inputs, and its output for any input c is a proposition $\varphi(c)$. Thus, the propositional function $\lambda x[x$ is a planet] has all and only individuals as inputs, and its outputs for the individuals Plato and Pluto are the propositions that Plato is a planet and that Pluto is a planet. *PM* is committed to the existence of individuals, propositional functions, perhaps propositions, but nothing of any other kind, not even classes.[3]

The use of class terms is ubiquitous in *PM* and there are sections devoted exclusively to classes; moreover, the objects of familiar mathematics are presented as classes[4] of this or that construction. Yet the official position of *PM* is studied neutrality on the question whether classes exist.[5] There is no tension here, as the formal theory provides the means to translate a sentence containing a class term into one that does not contain it.[6] So there is no need to posit classes, nor any need to deny them:

It is not necessary for our purposes, however, to assert dogmatically that there are no such things as classes. It is only necessary for us to show that the incomplete symbols which we introduce as representatives of classes yield all the propositions for the sake of which classes might be thought essential. When this has been shown, the mere principle of economy of primitive ideas leads to the non-introduction of classes except as incomplete symbols.[7]

The position then is that there may or may not be classes, but the propositions of *PM* are true even if there are none.

What is the source of this reluctance to admit classes? In chapter III of the Introduction to *PM* an ancient problem about the One and the Many is mentioned: if a class of things were admitted as an object it would have to be both one thing and many, which is impossible. This is not taken to be a decisive argument against the reality of classes, but it harks back to worries expressed by Russell in *The Principles of Mathematics*.[8] There he argues for a distinction between a class as many, such as the plurality of humans, and a class as one, such as the human species, and that resolves the ancient problem. But Russell thought that the distinction breaks down for unit classes (those with a single member) and empty classes (those with no members). In neither case is there a plurality, and in neither case, Russell felt, is there one object: a unit class considered as one object cannot be anything other than its sole member, and an empty class considered as one object is impossible, as a class of nothing cannot be a thing. Yet the formal theories of classes known to Russell at the time postulate an empty class and distinguish unit classes from their single members.[9]

Russell's concerns ran deeper than this, I suspect. Ordinary non-mathematical concepts of class fall into two: plurality, collection, or aggregate, as opposed to category, kind, or concept. In the first case a class is just the things collected, not something extra to them like a container. This is the class as many. But mathematics needs classes to be single entities, because we sometimes want to number them, as we do in saying that there are ^nC_r r-membered subclasses of an n-membered class. In the second case a class is unitary, but it is a way of thinking of many objects at once, hence a device of intellect, a 'class-concept' as Russell puts it. Yet mathematics postulates classes independent of thought and language, as in the theory of point classes. So a special mathematical concept of class must be in play. But why think that anything real answers to the special mathematical concept of class? Does it not offend a robust sense of reality to suppose that besides the aggregated objects there is some thought-independent entity over and above those objects, the aggregate itself? If we suppose that such things are real, we immediately run into scholastic puzzles about unit classes and the empty class.[10]

These puzzles can be answered, but the main question about mathematical classes—what are they?—is not so easy to answer. Russell knew of Frege's answer, that what conforms to the mathematical notion of a class is the logical notion of the extension of a concept (and he knew that Frege's answer verifies the existence of unit classes and the empty class: they are the extensions of such concepts as 'x = Euclid' and '$x \neq x$'). But this answer seems to assume that every concept has an extension, an assumption that Russell had shown leads to contradiction when conjoined with other assumptions seemingly as plausible.[11]

This I think is the serious motivation for Russell's 'no-class' view, but he also offers some weaker reasons. At certain points he uses Cantor's theorem (glossed as 'a class has fewer members than subclasses') as a basis for rejecting the existence of classes: as there are more classes than things, classes cannot be things.[12] This argument assumes that there is a class of all things; and, as the grammar of *PM* rules out as illegitimate any notion of 'all things', the argument cannot be taken as a serious motivation for refusing classes entry to the world of *PM*.[13] Yet in connection with the paradoxes, there is an advantage in holding this view of class talk. This stems from the fact that the Vicious Circle Principle is most implausible for classes but fairly plausible for propositional functions, as argued in the previous chapter. Moreover, the 'no-class' view augments the plausibility of the Vicious Circle Principle for propositional functions. For if a class is nothing over and above its members, the fact that a propositional function constitutively depends on any class in terms of which it is defined means that it constitutively depends on the *members* of any class in terms of which it is defined; the Vicious Circle Principle for propositional functions then follows from the fact that nothing constitutively depends on itself. So if classes, as distinct from their defining concepts and their members, are mere fictions, the Vicious Circle Principle is more likely to be a good guide in constructing a foundational system for mathematics.

Orders

The terms of *PM* (variables and terms for propositional functions and classes) are divided into orders, and there is a corresponding division of entities. Using this division, syntactic regulations ensure that the Vicious Circle Principle is respected. Every variable has a unique order indexed by a natural number. Using this, the hierarchy of orders[14] is then defined as follows:

A propositional function term or class term is of order $n + 1$ if and only if its defining predicate[15] has a free or bound variable of order n but no variable, free or bound, of order greater than n.

Terms of order 0 are just variables of order 0 (or individual constants). Terms of order $n + 1$ are variables of order $n + 1$ and propositional function terms of order $n + 1$ and class terms of order $n + 1$, and nothing else.[16]

This hierarchy transfers to entities as follows:

Every individual has order 0; the order of a propositional function or class denoted by a term of order n has order n.

For convenience, let me treat attributes and propositional functions as one and the same. To illustrate the hierarchy, here are propositional functions of individuals, of first, second, and third order, respectively:

(a) $\lambda x[x$ is an expert military strategist].
(b) $\lambda x[x$ has every first-order attribute required of a great general].
(c) $\lambda x[x$ has at least one second-order attribute required of a great general].

The quantifier phrases 'every first-order attribute' and 'at least one second-order attribute' in the expressions of (b) and (c) indicate the presence of bound variables of orders 1 and 2, respectively.[17] The inputs of these propositional functions are individuals. A point to note is that the order of a propositional function depends on the orders of both the free variable and the bound variable in its defining predicate. This means that the order of a propositional function depends on the order of its inputs and the orders of the members of the classes in terms of which it is defined.

For the sake of comparison, it may be helpful to recall the definition of types.[18] Individuals are entities of type 0; propositional functions with inputs of type n are of type $n + 1$ (as are classes with members of type n). The type of a propositional function depends only on the type of its inputs. In this respect types are unlike orders. Types are also attributed to terms. Each variable ranges over entities of a single type, and the type of a variable is the same as the type of the entities in its range; the type of a propositional function is one above the type of the free variable in its defining predicate—the bound variables are irrelevant. Hence the propositional functions (a), (b), and (c) are all of type 1, while having orders 1, 2, and 3 respectively. Examples of propositional functions of type 2 are:

(d) $\lambda \varphi[\varphi$ is a first-order attribute required of a great general].

(e) λφ[φ is a first-order attribute possessed by everyone who has some second order attribute required of a great general].

The inputs to these functions (d) and (e) are propositional functions of individuals, i.e. functions of type 1. Therefore (d) and (e) have type 2. What about their orders? Here the variable 'φ' is intended to be a variable of order 1; it ranges over first-order propositional functions of individuals. As that is the only variable involved in the expression of (d), (d) has order 2. The expression of (e) has not only the first-order variable 'φ' but also the variables indicated by the quantifier phrases 'everyone' and 'some second-order attribute', which will be variables of order 0 and 2 respectively. So (e) has order 3.[19]

It is not clear in *PM* exactly what the syntactic substitution rules are. The body of the text is totally devoid of indicators of type or order; it is supposed that the Introduction in *PM* makes it clear how to supply them. But details are missing. It is reasonable to take it that the free variable in a one-place predicate, if of order n, can be replaced just by terms of order n. But it is consistent with the explanations given in *PM* that a free variable of type t and order n ranges over all entities of type t that have order n or lower. In that case, a free variable of type t and order n would be replaceable by any term of type t and order less than or equal to n.[20] Everything I have said above about the type and order of a propositional function λx[x is/has such-&-such] applies *mutatis mutandis* to the corresponding class {x : x is/has such-&-such}.

It is easy to show that the order of a propositional function is never less than its type.[21] But for any type there are infinitely many orders of propositional functions of that type, as there may be an unending sequence of predicates with the same free variable but bound variables of increasing order. A common way of viewing the system of orders is as a superposition on the hierarchy of types. In fact, Russell's exposition encourages this, for he first argues that propositional functions must be divided into types and then argues that there can be no class of all propositional functions of a given type, so that propositional functions of a given type must be further divided into orders.[22] For this reason, the system of *PM* is sometimes known as the *ramified theory of types*, in contrast to the *simple theory of types*.

The theory of orders is complicated, more complicated even than it seems from this presentation, as I have not dealt with propositional functions defined by many-placed predicates.[23] But nothing of philosophical significance is to be gained by going into the further complexities. The important point for our purposes is that the Vicious Circle Principle cannot but be respected within the system of orders, as impredicative definitions are impossible. The order of a propositional function is higher than the order of any variable in its defining predicate, and a variable of order n ranges over things of order n (or lower). So a propositional function cannot fall in the range of any variable, free or bound, in its defining predicate, hence it cannot be defined in terms of a class to which it belongs. The same holds for classes in *PM*. Thus, the very definition of an entity in *PM* itself shows that it is definable without being definable *only* in terms of a class to which it belongs.

Impasse

Having constructed a language in which the known logical paradoxes cannot be reproduced, the task remained to translate mathematics into that language, thence to derive the principles of established mathematical theories. If the exclusion of impredicative definitions from the language increases security, it makes the translation task more difficult, impossible in fact. This is because normal mathematics, in particular real-number analysis, uses impredicative definitions in an essential way. For example, the constant e is defined to be the real number x for which

$$1 = \int_{1}^{x} \frac{1}{t}\, dt.$$

In this definition the letter 't', a variable bound by the operator 'dt', is intended to range over all positive real numbers. Nothing of this kind is possible in the language of orders, because the entity defined, which is supposed to be the positive real number e, cannot fall in the range of a bound variable in its definition; so 't' cannot range over all positive real numbers. In *PM* it can range over positive real numbers only up to a certain order; the defined entity would have higher order and would therefore be excluded.

This is not an isolated case. Concepts at the heart of classical real analysis[24] cannot be expressed in a language that excludes impredicative definitions, the concepts of *least upper bound* and *greatest lower bound*.[25] The words 'least' and 'greatest' signal impredicativity, since the least F must belong to the class of Fs, as must the greatest F. Eliminating class talk does not help: 'the least upper bound of a class of real numbers $\{r : \varphi(r)\}$' is short for 'the least real number not exceeded by any real number r such that $\varphi(r)$' and whatever these expressions denote must fall in the range of the bound variable 'r'. In the logicist systems of Frege and *PM*, integers, rational numbers, and real numbers are defined as classes, and so one might hope to define the least upper bound of a class *c* of reals in a way that avoids alluding to the class of upper bounds of *c*, by using features of the particular way that real numbers are defined in the system. In fact this can be done, but not in a way that avoids impredicativity.[26] Parallel remarks apply to the concept of greatest lower bound.

The concept of a least upper bound is central, as it figures in the standard version of an axiom of the theory of real numbers, Dedekind's Continuity Axiom:

> Every non-empty class of real numbers with an upper bound has a least upper bound.

Versions that do not use the concept of least upper bound use instead the impredicative concept of the greatest lower bound: every non-empty class of real numbers with a lower bound has a greatest lower bound. (This is provably equivalent to the standard version, given the other axioms of the theory of real numbers.)[27] Here was a serious obstacle for the programme of Whitehead and Russell. Classical mathematics needs Dedekind's Continuity Axiom, and this axiom needs an impredicative concept. A consistent theory of real analysis that excludes impredicative concepts will be significantly weaker than classical analysis.[28] Thus, one is forced to choose between classical analysis and the Vicious Circle Principle.

The authors of *PM* were well aware of this problem. But there was a yet more basic problem that they were not aware of. It has been shown by Myhill that the principle of mathematical induction over the natural numbers cannot be proved within ramified type theory.[29] Using '*m*' and '*n*' as variables for natural numbers, the principle of mathematical induction is this:

> If $\varphi(0)$ and $\varphi(n + 1)$ for every *n* such that $\varphi(n)$, then for every *m* $\varphi(m)$.

This is one of the axioms of Dedekind–Peano arithmetic. It turns out that there are some conditions $\lambda x \varphi(x)$ for which induction cannot be derived within a system of orders. Gödel pointed out that induction might be unprovable in ramified type theory even when $\varphi(x)$ is restricted to conditions of natural-number arithmetic.[30] So even natural-number arithmetic, let alone real-number analysis, might be beyond the scope of a logical theory within the framework of the hierarchy of orders.

The Axiom of Reducibility

To overcome these problems, Whitehead and Russell introduced an axiom that effectively allows us to ignore the bound variables in the defining predicate of a class or propositional function. To explain the axiom, it will help to have some abbreviating terminology. Let us say that two propositional functions are *co-extensive* if their defining predicates are true of exactly the same entities, and that a propositional function is *flat* when its order is just one above the order of its inputs.[31] To illustrate, among the following propositional functions only (a) and (d) are flat:

(a) $\lambda x[x$ is an expert military strategist].
(b) $\lambda x[x$ has every first-order attribute required of a great general].
(c) $\lambda x[x$ has at least one second-order attribute required of a great general].
(d) $\lambda \varphi[\varphi$ is a first-order attribute required of a great general].
(e) $\lambda \varphi[\varphi$ is a first-order attribute possessed by everyone who has some second-order attribute required of a great general].

The inputs of (a), (b), and (c) have order 0; their orders are 1, 2, and 3 respectively. The inputs of (d) and (e) have order 1; their orders are 2 and 3 respectively. Hence only (a) and (d) have orders one above the orders of their inputs; that is, only (a) and (d) are flat. The Axiom of Reducibility is this:

> Every propositional function is co-extensive with a flat propositional function.

Of course, this is really a schema with infinitely many instances, one for each order above the lowest. A version for binary relations (i.e. propositional functions of two free variables) is also stated.[32]

What is the practical significance of this axiom? It allows us to think in terms of classes, taking the order of a class to be just one above the order of its members, and to reason as we would in simple type theory.[33] This means that the theory can avoid splitting the real numbers into different orders, which is the bane of ramified type theory without the Axiom of Reducibility. For example, the definition of the constant *e* given earlier has a bound variable ranging over positive reals. To be admissible in the theory of orders, that variable must have a definite order, and so *e* would have to be a real number of yet higher order. Similarly, the definition of the least upper bound of a class *c*, on a reading that is admissible in ramified type theory, must define an entity of order higher than the order of members of the class *c*, as the definition must contain a bound variable ranging over members of *c*. But with the Axiom of Reducibility we can avoid this.[34] By the same token, Dedekind's Continuity Axiom can now be stated and proved in the system.

The advantages provided by the Axiom of Reducibility are not limited to the arena of real numbers. The axiom restores general constructions found throughout pure mathematics that are outlawed in unmoderated ramified type theory. For example, in algebra we often want to consider the smallest extension of a given class c closed under a certain operation f.[35] This is clearly an impredicative construction.[36] In the theory of orders, the nearest we can get is the f-closed extension of c that includes all nth-order f-closed extensions of c, which must have order greater than n. It can be seen that this is not what was intended from the fact that the class cannot be described as the smallest nth-order f-closed extension of c (as it is not nth-order). But the Axiom of Reducibility entails that there is a class fitting that description.[37] The point is more general than this, of course. It applies with any other property in place of 'f-closed extension of c', and it applies to the greatest as well as the smallest.

Reducibility and Russell's epistemology of axioms

How do we know that the Axiom of Reducibility is true? It is admitted that the axiom is not self-evident and that the reason for accepting it is inductive, in roughly the same way in which empirical sciences are inductive. But in the first edition of *PM* this is not regarded as a weakness. It is asserted, to the contrary, that any other axiom has the same kind of epistemic basis:

> The reason for accepting an axiom, as for accepting any other proposition, is always largely inductive, namely that many propositions which are nearly indubitable can be deduced from it, and that no equally plausible way is known by which these propositions could be true if the axiom were false, and nothing which is probably false can be deduced from it.[38]

An epistemology of this sort is clearly incompatible with the goal of endowing established mathematics with total certainty by deducing its principles from logical axioms. For this, the axioms would themselves have to be known with total certainty, and that can never be delivered by induction.[39] The impossibility of total certainty was not new. Frege's catastrophe had already showed that apparent self-evidence or intrinsic obviousness is not an absolute guarantee of correctness. As the only conceivable basis for total certainty about a general premiss is its intrinsic obviousness, it would no longer be rational to believe an axiom with total certainty:

> Infallibility is never attainable, and therefore some element of doubt should always attach to every axiom and all its consequences. In formal logic, the element of doubt is less than in most sciences, but it is not absent, as appears from the fact that

the paradoxes followed from premises which were not previously known to require limitations.[40]

None the less, intrinsic obviousness might be a defeasible ground for a high degree of confidence in a premiss. The goal of providing a high degree of rational certainty for established mathematics by deriving its principles from intrinsically obvious logical axioms was not ruled out. But Russell felt that the Axiom of Reducibility is not at all intrinsically obvious.[41] This prompted Russell to develop his inductive or 'regressive' epistemology for axioms.[42] In the light of this epistemology of axioms, the epistemological aspect of the project of *PM* can be viewed in the following way. The data of mathematics are the near certain propositions of basic mathematics, such as known equations and inequations of integer arithmetic. Such data can support a set of axioms by being derivable from those axioms, provided that the data are not known to be derivable from a rival set of axioms with no less intrinsic plausibility. By finding logical axioms that are extremely well supported by the data, one can provide those axioms with very great credibility, much higher than the initial credibility of the more troubled or amazing parts of mathematics, such as real-number analysis and transfinite-number theory. Then one can raise the credibility of those parts to practical certainty by rigorously deriving them from the axioms.

Let us ignore doubts about the inductive epistemology on offer.[43] The question to be settled is whether the Axiom of Reducibility is sufficiently well supported by its consequences to advance the project just described. For this, the axiom's consequences must include many nearly indubitable propositions that cannot be deduced without the axiom. We know that some instances of natural number induction not derivable in ramified type theory become derivable when the Axiom of Reducibility is added.[44] However, in those instances the induced property[45] has a fairly high level of complexity and so those instances do not count as 'nearly indubitable'. The real evidential data of number theory are its fairly simple unquantified equations and inequations involving the basic arithmetical operations, and these are derivable in ramified type theory without the Axiom of Reducibility.[46] So the axiom receives very little support from integer arithmetic. Where the axiom makes a big difference is in the theory of real numbers. The axiom can be credited with the theorems depending on Dedekind's Continuity Axiom, which are not derivable in ramified type theory. However, the theory of real numbers, in particular Dedekind's Continuity Axiom, cannot be regarded as nearly indubitable by anyone inclined to accept the Vicious Circle Principle. On top of the history of error in real-number analysis, the impredicativity in Dedekind's more rigorous presentation of the theory meant that the Axiom of Reducibility cannot gain support from this quarter. Indeed, one of the main purposes of the foundational project, when looked at in historical perspective, was to validate this theory. That is, the logical system was to provide a kind of justification for the theory of real numbers not obtainable inductively; hence the theory could not be used to justify the system. So, from the point of view of someone who believes the Vicious Circle Principle, the Axiom of Reducibility gets little epistemic support from its consequences. From the point of view of someone who does not believe the Vicious Circle Principle, but does believe the doctrine of types, the Axiom is again not supported, as there is an alternative at least as plausible that has all the mathematical consequences of ramified type theory with the Axiom of Reducibility, namely simple type theory.

All this is against the background of the 'no-class' doctrine. As is pointed out in *PM*, if one accepts that, for any propositional function $\lambda x \varphi(x)$, there is a class α of all its satisfiers, and classes are understood to be entities that are independent of the way they are defined, reducibility is ensured, as $\lambda x[x \in \alpha]$ would then be a flat propositional function co-extensive with $\lambda x \varphi(x)$. The paucity of inductive support for the Axiom of Reducibility and its lack of intrinsic plausibility (given the 'no-class' doctrine) presents a dilemma: accept the independent existence of classes, or abandon the Axiom of Reducibility.

The authors of *PM* themselves came to this view, and by the time of the second edition of *PM* they had given up the Axiom of Reducibility without having any alternative way round the problems that prompted them to adopt the axiom in the first place: 'irrationals and real numbers generally, can no longer be dealt with' they admitted ruefully.[47] Why did they abandon it?

This axiom has a purely pragmatic justification: it leads to the desired results, and no others. But clearly it is not the sort of axiom with which we can rest content. On this subject, however, it cannot be said that a satisfactory solution is as yet obtainable.[48]

This is all that is said by way of explanation. They may have felt that, however strong the inductive evidence in support of the Axiom of Reducibility, its lack of intrinsic plausibility made it untenable.[49] Alternatively, they may have felt that the inductive justification for the axiom is simply too weak.

The Multiplicative Axiom and the Axiom of Infinity

Two other axioms of *PM* should be mentioned at this point. One is the Multiplicative Axiom. This says that, given any (perhaps infinite) class c of pairwise disjoint non-empty classes, there is a class d that shares exactly one member with each member of c and has no member that is not in some member of c.[50] The class d can be thought of as the result of choosing exactly one member from each member of c, and for this reason this axiom is now known as the Axiom of Choice. It was called the Multiplicative Axiom apparently because it is equivalent to the proposition of generalized cardinal arithmetic that a product is zero only if one of its factors is zero. In the context of the 'no-class' stance, the Multiplicative Axiom says this. For any (perhaps infinite) plurality of propositional functions $\lambda x \psi_i(x)$, $\lambda x \psi_j(x)$, $\lambda x \psi_k(x)$, . . . no two being true of the same thing but each being true of at least one thing, there is a propositional function $\lambda x \varphi(x)$ that is (a) true of exactly one thing that $\lambda x \psi_h(x)$ is true of, for each function $\lambda x \psi_h(x)$ in the plurality, and (b) true of nothing that does not satisfy one of the functions in the plurality. As the phrase 'there is' signals, this is an existence claim. But why should we believe it? While there is an answer if there are classes that are independent of thought and language,[51] no answer is forthcoming on the no-class view. The authors of *PM*, perfectly aware of the difficulty, simply conditionalized all the theorems for whose proof it is needed, so that, in place of such a theorem T, they put 'If Mult ax, then T'.[52] They do not make it clear whether they regard the unconditional theorems T as true, but the conditionalizing move is an acknowledgement that these theorems have not been established to their satisfaction. This chiefly affects the theory of infinite cardinal arithmetic, but has consequences in all branches of mathematics involving infinite classes.

A greater embarrassment is the Axiom of Infinity, which postulates the existence of an infinity of entities. In modern terminology: for every natural number n there is a class with exactly n members.[53] Again, the authors choose to conditionalize:

This assumption, like the multiplicative axiom, will be adduced as a hypothesis whenever it is relevant. It seems plain that there is nothing in logic to necessitate its truth or falsehood, and that it can only be legitimately believed on empirical grounds.[54]

Elsewhere Russell goes further:

The axiom of infinity is true in some possible worlds and false in others; whether it is true or false in this world we cannot tell . . . [55]

The Axiom of Infinity is more of an embarrassment than the Multiplicative Axiom, not because there is less reason to believe it, but because it is needed for natural-number arithmetic. Specifically, it is needed to derive the Dedekind–Peano axiom that no two natural numbers have the same successor. In the system of *PM* all natural numbers after a certain one coalesce if the Axiom of Infinity is false.[56] Why did Russell not adduce his inductivist epistemology in support of the Axiom of Infinity at this point? As he believed that the Axiom of Infinity is false in some possible worlds, he may also have believed that in some possible worlds the numbers after some extremely large one do coalesce into one. In that case he would have wondered how we know that that possibility is not realised in the actual world. If there were a collapse at a sufficiently large number, he may have thought, the data of small number arithmetic would not reveal it.

Conclusion

As the work proceeded, Russell said in later years, he was reminded of the fable of the elephant and the tortoise: having constructed an elephant on which the mathematical world could rest, he constructed a tortoise on which the elephant could rest. 'But the tortoise was no more secure than the elephant, and after some twenty years of very arduous toil, I came to the conclusion that there was nothing more that *I* could do in the way of making mathematical knowledge indubitable.'[57]

This statement is in fact slightly misleading. Russell had come to the view that some element of doubt about axioms is inevitable soon after his discovery of the paradox. His goal was no longer unqualified indubitability, but the kind of security achieved by deriving mathematical beliefs that lie beyond the data of numerical computation in a logically rigorous way, from premises that one is well justified in believing. The project of *PM* was in no small part a response to the slovenly and sometimes fallacious practices of mathematics teaching at Cambridge University in the 1890s. 'The proofs that were offered of mathematical theorems were an insult to the logical intelligence', Russell wrote.[58] Given their epistemic standards, Russell and Whitehead had to settle for a system that fell short of securing for higher mathematics the degree of certainty they felt it proper and reasonable to demand. The Axiom of Reducibility robbed the first edition of *PM* of any certainty it might otherwise have had, and the second edition, without Reducibility, was too weak for the derivation of classical real-number analysis. On top of that, the Axiom of Infinity seems unjustified and at the same time indispensable for the theory of natural numbers.

So it is true that *PM* did not achieve its intended goal. But it was enormously influential in the development of mathematical logic and provided a springboard for further foundational work. It was, in particular, the basis of Ramsey's proposal. This will be examined after a brief look at the paradoxes of truth.

Paradoxes of Truth 3

This paradox was first discovered by Russell, who regarded it as variant of his class paradox.[1] The best known version of this paradox, known as Grelling's paradox, will be presented after Russell's original version, which is as follows. Some conditions seem true of themselves; others not. For example, the condition 'x is expressible' is expressible, but 'x is inexpressible' is not inexpressible. What of the condition 'x is not true of itself'? If, on the one hand, it is true of itself, it satisfies the condition 'x is not true of itself', which is just to say that it is not true of itself. If, on the other hand, it is not true of itself, it satisfies the condition 'x is not true of itself'; but this is the condition itself, and so it is true of itself. Hence, it is true of itself if and only if it is not true of itself.

Grelling's paradox is this. Some adjectives truly describe themselves; others do not. For example 'polysyllabic' is polysyllabic, but 'monosyllabic' is not monosyllabic. Those that truly describe themselves are *autological* adjectives; those that do not truly describe themselves are *heterological* adjectives. Schematically, for any adjective 'ξ',

'ξ' is autological if and only if 'ξ' is ξ;
'ξ' is heterological if and only if 'ξ' is not ξ.

By substituting 'heterological' for 'ξ' in the second schema, we obtain a contradiction.[2]

The parallel with Russell's class paradox should be obvious. In place of the relation 'x is a member of y', we have 'y is true of x' or 'y truly describes x'. In place of the class of things that are not members of themselves, we have the condition 'x is untrue of itself' or 'x does not truly describe itself'. These paradoxes are structurally identical.

Extended Russellian truth paradoxes

Russell's truth paradox has infinitely many extended versions. That paradox arises from asking whether the condition 'x is not true of x' is true of itself. A paradox also arises when we ask the same of the condition 'For no condition c is c true of x and x true of c'. The argument is a little more complicated than before, and it is easy to get lost without some symbolic abbreviations.[3] So let us call this condition 'r' and use 'xTy' for 'x is true of y'. Formally then r is the condition

(r) $\forall c \neg [xTc \ \& \ cTx]$.

The argument has two stages. First, suppose that r is true of r. Then, trivially, there is a c such that $rTc \ \& \ cTr$, namely r itself. So it is not the case that $\forall c \neg [rTc \ \& \ cTr]$. That is, r is not true of r. Hence if r is true of r, it is not true of r. Then, by the law of logic that $(P \rightarrow \neg P) \rightarrow \neg P$, we can infer that (i) r is not true of r. Secondly, suppose that r is not true of r. Then, by definition of r, there is a condition c such that $rTc \ \& \ cTr$. Let d be such a condition. Then $rTd \ \& \ dTr$. As r is true of d, $\forall c \neg [dTc \ \& \ cTd]$. But as this holds for all c, it holds in particular for r : $\neg [dTr \ \& \ rTd]$, which contradicts the earlier claim that $rTd \ \& \ dTr$. Thus, we have reduced to absurdity the supposition that r is not true of r. Hence it is not the case that r is not true of r; that is, (ii) r is true of r. Finally, the conjunction of (i) and (ii) is a contradiction.

Now define, for each positive integer n, the condition r_n as follows:

(r_n) $\forall c_1 \forall c_2 \ldots \forall c_{n-1} \forall c_n \neg [xTc_1 \ \& \ c_1Tc_2 \ \& \ldots \& \ c_{n-1}Tc_n \ \& \ c_nTx]$.

A straightforward generalization of the argument for r yields the contradiction that r_n is true of itself if and only if it is not true of itself.[4] So there are infinitely many Russellian truth paradoxes, and replacing 'x is true of y' by 'y is a member of x' gives infinitely many Russellian class paradoxes. The arguments are identical in form.

The Liar paradox

Here is a version. Consider the statement 'This statement is not true'. If it is true, it is as it says, namely, not true. If it is not true, it is as it says, hence true. Another version of the paradox uses a name for the offending statement:

[L]   L is not true.

Applying the schema " 'S' is true if and only if S", 'L is not true' is true if and only if L is not true. As 'L is not true' = L, it follows that L is true if and only if L is not true.

This paradox is thought to go back to ancient times. A version has been attributed to Eubulides of Miletus of the fourth century BC.[5] Aristotle's pupil and successor as head of the Lyceum, Theophrastus, is said to have written extensively on the Liar paradox, but the work does not survive in any form, as far as is known.[6] The paradox has been discussed by commentators on the New Testament. In the King James version of the Bible, Paul's epistle to Titus (1:12,13) says

One of themselves, even a prophet of their own, said, The Cretians are alway liars, evil beasts, slow bellies. This witness is true.

On reflection, it is easily seen that the testimony cannot be true, and no paradox arises from supposing it false. But this naturally prompts one to consider whether, if the Cretan had said 'I am now lying', he would have been truthtelling, thus resurrecting what was probably the original version of the Liar paradox, provided we ignore the fact that lying involves deceit, and assimilate it to saying an untruth.

The Liar paradox is surprisingly resilient: block one version of the paradox, and another version is liable to escape. For example, a sensible response to the first version given is that one cannot succeed in making a statement by means of the sentence 'This statement is not true.' Similarly, one might hold that no proposition is expressed by the sentence 'This proposition is not true.' But the following version is immune to that response. Consider the sentence 'This sentence does not express a true proposition.' If that sentence does not express a proposition, it does not express a true proposition; hence what it says is true; but if what it says is true, it says nothing true. So it does not express a true proposition if and only if it does express a true proposition.

There are a number of closely related paradoxes obtained by considering some condition on propositions other than 'x is not true'. I will canvass one relevant to mathematics. Consider the following proof of the statement 'This statement is unprovable.' Suppose it were provable. Then it would be true; hence, noting its content, it would be unprovable. So it would be both provable and unprovable. This reduces to absurdity the supposition that it is provable. Hence it is not provable. Hence it is true. Q. E. D. This situation is impossible. For we have just run through a proof of it, and so it is provable. But then it is true and therefore, noting its content, it is unprovable. So it is both provable and unprovable.

Extended Liar paradoxes

Just as there are infinitely many Russellian truth paradoxes, there are infinitely many Liar-style paradoxes. The Liar paradox arises from considering whether the following statement is true:

[A]   A is not true.

Now consider the three-element chain of statements:

[A]   B is not true.   [B]   C is not true.   [C]   A is not true.

Here B says that it is not true that C, and C says that A is not true; so B is equivalent to the statement that it is not true that A is not true, which is equivalent to the statement that A is true; hence B is equivalent to the statement that A is true. So the statement that B is not true is equivalent to the statement that A is not true. But A *is* the statement that B is not true, so A is equivalent to the statement that A is not true. Thus we have reduced the three-element chain to the single statement of the Liar paradox.

We can extend this to an argument by induction on the natural numbers that any circular chain of this kind with an odd number of elements is contradictory in the sense that there is no consistent assignment of truth-values to all its members. The argument is sufficiently simple to be set out here. The basis case is just the Liar paradox:

[A_1] A_1 is not true.

The inductive hypothesis is that the claim holds for the odd number $2n + 1$. In other words, the hypothesis is that the following chain is contradictory:

[A_1] A_2 is not true.   [A_2] A_3 is not true. . . .   [A_{2n}] A_{2n+1} is not true.   [A_{2n+1}] A_1 is not true.

Now we need to show that the corresponding chain with $2(n + 1)+1$ (or $2n + 3$) elements is also contradictory. This chain will be exactly the same up to and including A_{2n}, but then proceeds thus:

[A_{2n+1}] A_{2n+2} is not true.   [A_{2n+2}] A_{2n+3} is not true.   [A_{2n+3}] A_1 is not true.

Inspecting the final two elements reveals that A_{2n+2} is equivalent to the statement that it is not true that A_1 is not true, which is equivalent to the statement that A_1 is true. So A_{2n+2} is equivalent to the statement that A_1 is true. Hence the statement that A_{2n+2} is not true is equivalent to the statement that A_1 is not true. But A_{2n+1} *is* the statement that A_{2n+2} is not true. So A_{2n+1} is equivalent to the statement that A_1 is not true. Thus, the first $2n + 1$ elements of the chain with $2n + 3$ elements is equivalent to the chain with $2n + 1$ elements, which is contradictory by hypothesis. Hence the chain with $2n + 3$ elements is also contradictory. Let us regard the first element in a circular chain as the successor of the last element. Then we can conclude by mathematical induction that any circular chain with an odd number of elements, each saying of its successor that it is not true, is contradictory. In fact, this extends to circular chains each element of which says of its successor either that it is not true or that it is true: any such chain is contradictory, if it has an odd number of elements which say of their successors that they are not true.[7]

Logical types and paradoxes of truth

Every extended Russellian truth paradox involves a circular chain of propositional functions $\langle x, c_1, \ldots, c_n, x \rangle$, each allegedly true of its successor. (The chain is presented with the same element appearing at the start and end to indicate circularity, not double occurrence.) Russell's Truth paradox is just the special case when $n = 0$, the chain being $\langle x, x \rangle$. Every extended liar paradox involves a circular chain of propositions $\langle L, A_1, \ldots, A_n, L \rangle$, each endorsing or denying the truth of its successor, with an odd number of denials. The Liar paradox is just the special case when $n = 0$, the chain being $\langle L, L \rangle$.

It seems reasonable to require of a foundational system for mathematics not only that it avoid commitment to any of these circular chains, but also that we can have good reason to trust the system in this respect. This is achieved by the system of simple types. Circular chains of the kind involved in the Russellian truth paradoxes are ruled out by the fact that the type of a propositional function is higher than the type of any of the propositional function's inputs, hence anything it is true of. To deal with the liar-style paradoxes in simple type theory, its propositions must also be assigned types. But all that is required is that each proposition has a unique type and that its type is higher than the type of any proposition that it mentions by name, quotation, or definite description.[8, 9] Each element in a circular chain of propositional functions or propositions of the kinds involved in truth paradoxes would have to have a type higher than itself, which is impossible.

Although the truth paradoxes are blocked in the system of types, we should not regard the doctrine of types as solving them. Why not? First, any proposal that rules out all circular chains of propositional functions or propositions rules out too much of what seems to make sense. For example, the condition of being expressible in English is expressible in English; so this condition is the first and last of a one-element circular chain of propositional functions. Again, consider the following exchange.

Moore: The statement you are about to make mentions me.

Russell: The statement you have just made mentions me.

The doctrine of types entails that, despite appearances, these utterances do not express propositions. If one expresses a proposition then both do, and if both do, they constitute a two-element circular chain of propositions as each proposition mentions the other. But it seems right to say that in this exchange both speak truly, hence that their utterances express true propositions. This is not decisive. The intuition that these utterances express propositions can be overridden. But it is easy to construct parallel exchanges mentioning sentences instead of propositions—'the sentence you are about to utter . . .' etc. As a sentence must have higher type than any it mentions (if the system of types is to block certain versions of the Liar paradox), the doctrine of types entails that the sounds made would not have been utterances of sentences. This strains credibility too far.

The second reason for doubt depends on a point made by Kripke.[10] Liar-style paradoxes can arise contingently, when there is nothing intrinsically awry with what is said. Here is Kripke's example. Suppose Jones says

(A)   Most of Nixon's statements about Watergate are untrue.

Suppose in addition that Nixon's statements about Watergate are evenly balanced between the true and the false, leaving aside this statement by Nixon

(B)   Everything Jones says about Watergate is true.

Suppose finally that A is Jones's only statement about Watergate. It is not difficult to see that this situation produces paradox, even though the paradox arises not from transgression of a rule of logic or language, but from contingencies of the situation described. So this paradox is not solved by supposing that, owing to some mismatch of types, A and B make no sense. So we should not look to the doctrine of types for the solution. There are many solutions of Liar-style paradoxes on offer that are less restrictive than the doctrine of types, so there is no reason for despair.

The doctrine of types may be too restrictive, in that a system of types will not capture all permissible reasoning. But that does not mean that a system of types is too strict to capture all of established mathematics. A simple theory of types is more flexible and has more expressive power than its ramified counterpart, yet is still strict enough to block the paradoxes of truth and the class paradoxes by preventing the appearance of circular chains. This justifies giving serious consideration to a simple theory of types as a foundational system for mathematics. Ramsey proposed just that. His ideas for the foundations of mathematics are the topic of the next chapter.

Ramsey's Attempt to Rescue Logicism   4

Just when the first volume of the second edition of *Principia Mathematica* was published, Frank Ramsey, a Cambridge philosopher and mathematician then only 22 years old, published his own view of the foundations of mathematics.[1] Agreeing with Whitehead and Russell that the truths of pure mathematics are truths of logic, he proposed that a theory of simple types be taken as our foundational system, thereby avoiding the obstacles posed by the order restrictions. These views are elaborated and defended in one substantial paper on the topic, *The Foundations of Mathematics*.[2] In this chapter I consider first Ramsey's justification for his claim that a foundational system may ignore order distinctions, and then his defence of the claim that pure mathematics is logic, as realized in a system of simple types.

Ramsey's distinction between logical and linguistic paradoxes

Ramsey divided the paradoxes into two groups, logical and linguistic.[3] He specifically mentions eight paradoxes. In the group of logical paradoxes he included Russell's paradox, the Burali-Forti paradox, and a paradox not so far introduced, that of the relation which holds between relations when the first does not have itself to the second. We can take this group to include all the class paradoxes, for 'they involve only logical or mathematical terms such as class and number', in Ramsey's words, and so they must be due to faulty logic or mathematics. In the second group he put the definability paradoxes, Grelling's paradox,[4] and the Liar paradox. These paradoxes all contain some reference to thought or language, it was claimed. If they were due to faulty ideas about thought and language, Ramsey said, they would not be relevant to logic or mathematics, and he proceeded to argue that they depend on ambiguities of the terms 'means' or 'names' or 'defines', which would clearly be a fault of language.

Ramsey's division of paradoxes came to be widely accepted, but there is reason for caution. While some paradoxes depend on notions that are linguistic, it does not follow that those paradoxes are non-logical; for language has logical features, and it is not clear that only non-logical features are relevant in the linguistic paradoxes. Grelling's paradox, for example, essentially involves the notion of an expression's truly describing something. Granted that this notion is linguistic, it is unclear that it is not also a logical notion. If the paradox turns on this notion, it might be a logical paradox after all. In response, Ramsey warns against confusing distinct senses of 'logic'. The linguistic paradoxes do turn on matters of logic 'in the sense of analysis of thought', he concedes, but not in the sense in which mathematics is said to be part of logic, that is, logic as 'a symbolic system'.[5] Ramsey's idea seems to be that a paradox is logical in the relevant sense if it can be set out in a purely formal or symbolic way, and if the error can be located in the formalized argument. But if this is Ramsey's criterion, Grelling's paradox is a logical paradox, since it can be formalized in just the same way as Russell's paradox (about classes), and a common formal error can be located, viz. supposing that for a relation R there is an entity e such that

$$\forall y\, [\, y\mathrm{R}e \leftrightarrow \neg[y\mathrm{R}y]\,].$$

In Russell's paradox '$a\mathrm{R}b$' formalizes 'a is a member of b'; in Grelling's paradox it formalizes 'a is truly described by b'. Grelling's paradox is a version of Russell's truth paradox, and Russell's truth paradox is so similar to his class paradox that Russell regarded them as versions of the same paradox.[6] Since then, more than one person has treated the Liar paradox along with Russell's paradox in a common formal framework.[7] These connections can be found elsewhere. As was pointed out in the previous chapter, the extended truth paradoxes are formally identical to extended class paradoxes, and in each case it is possible to find a single formal feature that may be regarded as the locus of the basic error. These facts cast doubt on the adequacy of Ramsey's division of the paradoxes. However, this is not damaging to Ramsey's approach to the foundations of mathematics. As the Russellian truth paradoxes are formally identical to the Russellian class paradoxes, they too can be blocked by means of type restrictions. This applies also to the Liar paradox and its extensions, as was shown in the previous chapter. So, even if it must be conceded that the truth paradoxes are logical paradoxes, Ramsey's view that simple type theory can serve as a logical foundation for mathematics without the least attention to orders survives the concession.

There remain the definability paradoxes. Ramsey's proposal that orders be ignored is acceptable only if the theory of simple types that is to serve as the foundational system does not generate those paradoxes. An adequate foundational system does not have to incorporate features that block the very expression of a paradox; it is enough that any paradox that is expressible has a premiss or a step that is not validated by the system. On this matter there is reason for confidence. A definability paradox requires a predicate expressing definability in the language to which that predicate belongs. A foundational system for mathematics does not need a definability predicate; and even if there were a definability predicate, it need not be universal for the language. It is compatible with a system of types that definability predicates are stratified in such a way that a defining predicate which involves a predicate for definability of level n must itself be of higher level. So there is no reason to fear that a system of types without orders will generate definability paradoxes.

Is impredicativity acceptable?

Ramsey felt that the Axiom of Reducibility was unjustified, as eventually did Russell. But while Russell despaired, Ramsey argued that the axiom was not needed. It was designed to circumvent obstacles imposed by the system of orders, and the system of orders was introduced to exclude impredicative expressions. However, Ramsey argued, impredicative expressions are acceptable. The ban on impredicativity was an overreaction to the paradoxes. As just argued, the paradoxes that must be dealt with in a foundational system for mathematics are blocked by simple type restrictions, while the other paradoxes may be dealt with by special measures that need not affect the system.

However, it is possible that impredicative expressions are ultimately incoherent or unintelligible, even when their employment does not result in outright contradiction. Ramsey claimed that the circles involved in impredicative expressions are not in any way vicious. Let R be a relation that holds between propositional functions of individuals φ and individuals x, such as 'if having φ is required of a great general, x lacks φ'. In the absence of order restrictions, one can apply a universal quantifier to obtain a propositional function that applies to individuals thus: For every φ, φRx.[8] Applied to the example just used, this yields 'x lacks every φ required of a great general'. It is alleged that this is viciously circular because the propositional function so defined would be one of the totality of propositional functions φ mentioned in the definition. Ramsey argues that this is not vicious, in the following way. A quantifier is to be interpreted as one would interpret an operation of infinitary conjunction, in that 'For every φ, φRx' may be thought of as true (of an individual x) under the same conditions as a possibly endless array '$(\lambda yFy)Rx$ & $(\lambda yGy)Rx$ & $(\lambda yHy)Rx$ & . . .', with every term for a propositional function of individuals occurring to the left of 'R' in one of the conjuncts. If the propositional function expressed by the predicate 'For every φ, φRx' is thought of in that way, it would have to occur as the first relatum in one of its own conjuncts, as it is a propositional function of individuals. That of course is circular, but is no more vicious, Ramsey claims, than saying that 'Fx & Gx' is true of an individual under the same conditions as 'Fx & Gx & (Fx & Gx)'.

Ingenious though this defence may be, I doubt that it works where propositional functions are concerned. In assessing the Vicious Circle Principle in Chapter 1 of Part III, the putative attribute of having all the attributes required of a great general turned out to be chimerical, unless what one really has in mind is possession of all the *first-order* attributes required of a great general. With respect to classes, however, there is simply no problem with impredicative specifications. We can specify a class as the most populous insect species, and our ignorance prevents us from specifying it in any other way; yet this is an impredicative specification. The cause of our inability to avoid impredicativity is of no account: we can specify a class impredicatively even if we are in principle unable specify it in any other way, except perhaps in the special case that its members are or depend on our specifications.

Propositional functions and classes

For this reason, the acceptability of Ramsey's proposal to ignore order distinctions and allow impredicative definitions depends on whether the basic entities of his system other than individuals are classes or propositional functions. This matter is not straightforward. As classical mathematics is extensional, in the sense that it has no need to distinguish between co-extensive propositional functions (i.e. those true of the same things), it is very convenient to talk as if classes, rather than propositional functions, were the basic entities of mathematics. But logicism requires that mathematics is not about a special domain. Inasmuch as mathematics is about classes, the classes must be nothing over and above the extensions of propositional functions, so that class talk can be construed as a way of talking about propositional functions, which are items essential to any sort of reasoning whatsoever. This was the position of Whitehead and Russell. But here Ramsey discerned a problem. Calling a class 'definable' if it is the extension of a propositional function, he objected to the Whitehead–Russell view in the following words:

Whether there are indefinable classes or not is an empirical question; both possibilities are perfectly conceivable. But even if, in fact, all classes are definable, we cannot in our logic identify classes with definable classes without destroying the apriority and necessity which is the essence of logic.[9]

Ramsey went on to point out that 'class' does not mean 'definable class' and 'relation in extension' ('class of ordered pairs') does not mean 'definable relation in extension' ('definable class of ordered pairs'). He illustrated this using the partial definition: two classes have the same cardinal just when there is 1-to-1 correlation between them. Clearly, what is meant is not that there is some propositional function of two variables by which they are 1-to-1 correlated, but simply that their members can be paired off. In general, mathematics does not require that the members of a class have some common feature or satisfy some common condition. 'The possibility of indefinable classes and relations in extension is an essential part of the extensional attitude of modern mathematics', Ramsey added. He gave further support to this view in connection with the Multiplicative Axiom. This amounts to the claim that, for any (perhaps infinite) class c of pairwise disjoint non-empty classes, there is a class d that shares exactly one member with each member of c. While this seems obvious on reflection, it is highly dubious when restricted to definable classes. For then there would have to be a propositional function that is true of exactly one thing in each member of c, which is something we have no reason to believe.

Thus, Ramsey exposed an apparent incoherence at the heart of logicism. On the one hand, logicism requires that classes be nothing but extensions of propositional functions; on the other hand, it must accommodate the logical possibility that some classes are not the extension of any propositional function. Ramsey was aware of this tension, although he did not put it so starkly. In his exposition the matter gets entangled with considerations about identity that we do not need to go into at this point. But he also had what he thought was a solution. He proposed loosening the idea of a propositional function.[10] According to the Russellian conception, the values of a propositional function $\lambda x \varphi(x)$ for inputs a and b must be propositions $\varphi(a)$ and $\varphi(b)$ in which a and b are mentioned and ascribed the same condition: $\varphi(a)$ must say about a what $\varphi(b)$ says about b. Ramsey proposed that this condition for being a propositional function be dropped entirely. Any proposition-valued function whatsoever should be counted as a propositional function, if its domain of inputs consists of all the entities of a single type. On this conception, a propositional function can be a completely arbitrary assignment of propositions to the entities of a given type. A function whose inputs are individuals would be a propositional function provided only that to each individual it assigns a single proposition. So there will be a propositional function f such that

f(Fermat) = the proposition that species evolve, and
f(Gauss) = the proposition that Earth rotates.

A class, Ramsey stipulated, would be a function that assigns to each entity of a given type either a tautology or a contradiction; the members of the class would be those entities to which a tautology is assigned. As these class-determining functions can be completely arbitrary assignments of tautologies and contradictions to their inputs, the logicist requirement that classes be given by propositional functions places no constraint whatever on what a class is. A propositional function may be an indefinable entity, on Ramsey's conception; so classes may be indefinable too.

Thus, Ramsey appears to have escaped the logicist's dilemma. But this is illusory. If mathematics is not about special objects, its classes must be nothing but extensions of conditions; conditions belong to logic because any deductive reasoning that depends on quantifiers also depends on conditions, the items expressed by predicates. But on Ramsey's conception, a propositional function is no longer the theoretical counterpart of a condition, and a propositional function of two variables is no longer the counterpart of a relation. Taking arbitrary proposition-valued functions to be logical entities has no more justification than stipulating that arbitrary classes are logical entities: the link with logic is lost.

But if liberalizing the category of propositional functions fails to save logicism from its ontological dilemma, it does help Ramsey's case for accepting impredicativity. Precisely because propositional functions on the liberalized conception are not attributes or conditions, but on the contrary are independent of thought and language, the problem raised earlier about impredicative definitions no longer applies.

The thesis that mathematics is logic

There is surely more to logicism than the claim that classes are extensions of conditions or propositional functions in the Russellian sense. In fact, logicism can dispense with that claim, if we are prepared to accept a liberalized conception of logic, according to which logic includes a theory of Ramseyan propositional functions, or what amounts to the same, a theory of classes that may or may not be extensions of conditions. Classes so conceived are special objects, but the resulting theory has unrestricted application, for there may be classes of anything; so the generality of logic would be preserved. That I think was Ramsey's view, and I propose that it be granted for the sake of exploring further the thesis that mathematics is logic.

Ramsey maintained that thesis, and compared it favourably with what he took to be the alternatives on offer at the time. But he rightly felt that no one had provided an adequate exegesis of it. In *The Principles of Mathematics*, Russell had written as though a logical truth was a truth that can be expressed in terms of variables and logical constants alone, thereby having the topic-neutrality of logic, and no correction of this view had been expressed by the time of the first edition of *Principia Mathematica*. It was not until Russell turned to the matter in his *Introduction to Mathematical Philosophy* that he acknowledged that a true proposition expressible in purely logical terms might fail to be a logical truth.[11] Ramsey gave as an example the claim that any two individuals differ in at least thirty ways. This might be true, and it is expressible in logical terms alone (if identity is a logical constant), but it would not thereby be a logical truth. It might even be a contingent truth.

Once this point is appreciated, it becomes obvious that logicism needs some account of what it is for a truth to be a logical truth. Ramsey adopts a proposal of Wittgenstein. This can be explained simply by introducing some logical terminology. An *atomic* proposition is a simple subject–predicate proposition $F(c)$, where 'c' stands for the subject and 'F' for the predicate, such as those one might express by 'I think' and 'that shines', or a relational proposition $R(c_1, \ldots, c_n)$, such as 'Mike is twice as old as Mary was when she met Tom.' An atomic proposition can be a *constituent* of another proposition in the following ways. A proposition has the atomic proposition $F(c)$ as a constituent if it is formed from $F(c)$ and perhaps other propositions by truth-functional operators or connectives, as for example in a proposition of the form '$\neg Q \rightarrow (F(c) \& R)$'. $F(c)$ is also a constituent of the quantified propositions 'For some x, $F(x)$' and 'For every x, $F(x)$'; and it is a constituent of any proposition that has one of these quantified propositions as a component. These are all the ways in which an atomic proposition can be a constituent of another proposition. Finally, a proposition is a *tautology* if and only if it is true for all assignments of truth-values to its atomic constituents. Here it is assumed that atomic propositions are independent: each may have either truth-value, no matter what the truth-values of the others. A completely general tautology, Ramsey quite reasonably assumed, is a logical truth.[12] The task of logicism, in his view, was to show that mathematical truths are completely general tautologies.

Ramsey thought that this logicist goal was achievable, but he thought that there was one difficulty he had not quite overcome. That problem was based on a highly doubtful view of identity statements that Ramsey had picked up from Wittgenstein, and it evaporates once that view is abandoned. Unsurprisingly, the real difficulties concern the two axioms that look least like logical truths: the Multiplicative Axiom and the Axiom of Infinity.

The Multiplicative Axiom, Ramsey argues convincingly, is not justified if by 'class' we mean 'definable class', as Whitehead and Russell did. But Ramsey asserts without argument that once the definability restriction is dropped the axiom is an obvious tautology. Let us look into this. The axiom, once again, is that, for any (perhaps infinite) class c of pairwise disjoint non-empty classes, there is a choice class for c, that is a class d that shares exactly one member with each member of c. Once one fully digests what this says it does become obvious, as Ramsey says. Obvious though the axiom is, it is not at all clear that it is a tautology. If it were a tautology, we should be able to discern this from our grasp of its structure and of the truth-conditions of its components. To illustrate, let '$\varphi(x)$' be a fixed but arbitrary predicate. We can tell that '[For all x, $\varphi(x)$] $\rightarrow \varphi(c)$' is tautologous by considering the truth-condition of its antecedent: 'For all x, $\varphi(x)$' is true just when every instance of '$\varphi(x)$' is true. As '$\varphi(c)$' is an instance, the antecedent is false when the consequent '$\varphi(c)$' is false, in which case the whole conditional is true; when the consequent '$\varphi(c)$' is true the whole conditional is again true. So the whole proposition is true whatever truth-values are assigned to its atomic constituents. Hence it is a tautology. Nothing so simple is possible for the Multiplicative Axiom, because of its existential part: 'For any class c *there is* a class d such that . . .' However, there are tautologies of universal–existential form, on the Ramsey–Wittgenstein explication of that notion, if it is granted that instances of the class abstraction principle (restricted to type) are tautologous. Omitting indicators of type, the class abstraction principle is this:

For all x, $x \in \{x : \varphi(x)\} \leftrightarrow \varphi(x)$.

Now consider the following proposition, which like the Multiplicative Axiom starts with universal quantifiers followed by an existential quantifier:

For any classes b and c there is a class d such that, for all x, $x \in d \leftrightarrow (x \in b \,\&\, x \in c)$.

This is true just when all instances of the following are true:

There is a class d such that, for all x, $x \in d \leftrightarrow (x \in b \,\&\, x \in c)$.

This in turn is true when some instance of the following is true:

For all x, $x \in d \leftrightarrow (x \in b \,\&\, x \in c)$.

A true instance is the following, which is tautologous by assumption:

For all x, $x \in \{x : x \in b \,\&\, x \in c\} \leftrightarrow (x \in b \,\&\, x \in c)$.[13]

We cannot show the truth of the Multiplicative Axiom this way, by using the class abstraction principle, because we cannot in general find a propositional function by which to define a choice class. Of course, if we could, there would be no need to count the Multiplicative Axiom as an axiom, given the class abstraction principle. With or without that principle, it is not possible to show that the Multiplicative Axiom is true for all assignments of truth-values to its atomic constituents, and we have no other reason to regard its truth as determined by its logical structure. For this reason, we cannot take it to be a tautology in the logical sense.

Ramsey says that 'mathematics is largely independent of the Multiplicative Axiom'. Dropping it would still leave the bulk of analysis, though the comparability of transfinite cardinal numbers could not be proved. But these facts are not germane to our concern. However much or little the axiom contributes to mathematics, Ramsey rightly regarded it as an obvious truth; and, as it is clearly a mathematical truth, we should not accept that all mathematical truths are tautologies.

In type theory the Axiom of Infinity says that there are infinitely many individuals. This is required, because if there are only finitely many individuals, there are only finitely many classes of individuals, and for any type n, if there are only finitely many classes of type n, there are only finitely many classes of type $n + 1$; so there would be no type that contains infinitely many classes. This would make it impossible to represent the natural numbers in a single type, and that in turn would make it impossible to represent any real number in the system. However, there is no self-contradiction in claiming that there are only finitely many individuals, and so the claim that there are infinitely many can hardly be a logical truth. Here Ramsey defers to 'the profound analysis of Wittgenstein', according to which the claim must be either a tautology or a contradiction.[14] The argument for this claim is virtually the same as the argument for the same claim about the proposition that there are at least three individuals. As the latter is easier to state, I present that here. The claim is an existential generalization over a conjunction of distinctness claims:

For some $x, y, z, [x \neq y \, \& \, y \neq z \, \& \, x \neq z]$.

This is tautologous if the bracketed formula has a tautologous instance. It is contradictory if all instances of the bracketed formula are contradictory. Now if a and b are distinct objects they are necessarily distinct, and so the claim that $a \neq b$ will be a tautology; if they are identical they are necessarily not distinct, and the claim that $a \neq b$ will be a contradiction. So any true instance of the bracketed formula will be a conjunction of tautologies and therefore itself a tautology, while any false instance will have a contradictory conjunct and will therefore be a contradiction. Now if the whole claim is true, the bracketed formula has a true, hence tautologous, instance; hence the whole claim is tautologous. If the whole claim is false, all instances of the bracketed formula are false, hence contradictory; so then is the whole claim. As the claim is true or false, it is tautologous or contradictory. To extend this argument to the Axiom of Infinity, it is only required that the axiom can be treated as if it were an existential generalization over an infinite conjunction of distinctness claims.

The fallacy is clear: a distinctness claim '$a \neq b$' may be a necessary truth without being a tautology, or an impossibility without being a contradiction.[15] But setting this aside, what does Ramsey do with the conclusion that the Axiom of Infinity is tautologous or contradictory? He says that we must assume that it is a tautology, unless we prefer the view that real analysis is contradictory. This is defeat. An account on which analysis might be not merely false but contradictory is incompatible with the claim that mathematics is logic, and cannot have satisfied Ramsey.

Simple type theory as a foundation for mathematics

Before concluding I want to consider the adequacy of simple type theory as a foundational system for mathematics, a question largely orthogonal to the assessment of logicism. Classical mathematics, real analysis in particular, can be represented in simple type theory. But the adequacy of simple type theory as a foundational system depends on the epistemic merits and the conceptual naturalness of that representation. As to the epistemic merits, we need only consider the Axiom of Infinity. Any foundational system that accommodates real analysis requires an axiom of infinity in some form or another. In type theory, however, it must entail a claim about the number of individuals, single non-mathematical entities. This dependency on the number of individuals is bizarre. Might mathematics be false in a world with just finitely many individuals? Surely there would be infinitely many prime numbers regardless of the number of individuals. Our confidence in mathematics should not be affected by our view about whether the number of individuals is finite. To the extent that this is a determinate question, our view would have to depend on physics, especially cosmology, and that view would depend on a good deal of mathematics, including parts that entail the existence of infinite sets or sequences.

To assess the naturalness of the representation of mathematics in type theory, let us look at the treatment of cardinal numbers, as so much is built on that. Following Frege, Russell had argued that a cardinal number κ is the class of classes with just κ members.[16] This may seem odd, but when a domain is partitioned according to some spectrum of properties (e.g. shapes, structures) it is now quite common to represent each property in the spectrum by the class of members of the domain that have it. This practice works when the domain is restricted, and in the case at hand it gives a tolerable translation of cardinality attributions. For example, 'The number of prime numbers between 1 and 6 is 3' becomes 'The class of prime numbers between 1 and 6 belongs to the class of 3-membered classes.' But this procedure has problems. One is that it allows circular membership chains. For example, 3 belongs to the class of primes between 1 and 6, and this class (whose members are just 2, 3, and 5) belongs to the class of 3-membered classes, i.e. to 3. The remedy of type theory is to represent each cardinal number κ by an infinity of distinct entities, one for each type above the lowest. For classes of individuals, the number 3 is the class of all three-membered classes of individuals, and in general the cardinal κ of a class of entities of type n is the class of all κ-membered classes of entities of type n. The cardinality of a class of things of type n is a class of type $n + 2$. So, indicating the type of a number by subscript, the cardinality of a three-membered class of individuals is 3_2, that of a three-membered class of classes of individuals is 3_3, and so on. Though 3_n belongs the class of primes$_n$ between 1_n and 6_n, that class is of type $n + 1$ and so belongs not to 3_n but to 3_{n+2}. Thus circularity is avoided, but at a cost. The class whose members are just Mercury, Venus, and Mars has the same number of members as the class whose members are 2_7, 3_7, and 5_7. This is not true in simple type theory: the former class has cardinality 3_2 (being an entity of type 2) while the latter has cardinality 3_9, and these are very different entities. There may not even be a

1-to-1 correlation between 3_2 and 3_9. In general, we cannot capture in simple type theory what it is that κ-membered classes have in common.

This fragmentation of cardinal numbers is a conceptual defect in the account of numbers given in type theory. There are other defects. Which entity is the number κ for a given type becomes a contingent matter, just like the identity of next week's lottery winner. Had Plato's parents never met, the class whose members are Socrates, Plato, and Aristotle would not exist, nor therefore would any class with this class as a member. So the class which on this account is the cardinal number 3_2 would not exist; some other class would have been the number 3_2 instead. The same holds for every κ_n when $\kappa \geq 1$ and $n \geq 2$. This surely is bizarre. The situation for zero is strange in a different way. For each positive type there is a distinct zero, and in each case this will be a class whose sole member is an empty class. These zeros are distinct because for each type there is a distinct empty class.[17] That is counterintuitive, because these classes are indistinguishable with regard to membership, all being empty. These features of the representation of cardinal numbers in type theory are conceptually awkward and should prompt us to ask whether there is a more natural way of representing the cardinal numbers. There is also a mathematical drawback. The ban on mixed types entails that one cannot take the union of finite types to form an initial transfinite type, and this makes it impossible to prove the existence of certain transfinite cardinal numbers.

Conclusion

The alternatives to logicism at the time Ramsey was writing appeared to him to be a formalist view incapable of accommodating simple applications of arithmetic, and a constructivist view incompatible with much of classical analysis. But if logicism was Ramsey's preferred option, he was rightly dissatisfied with the version of logicism presented in the first edition of *Principia Mathematica*, and he was not content to follow the second edition in sacrificing classical analysis to the Vicious Circle Principle. To overcome the main weaknesses, he proposed that the entities of mathematics be regarded as extensional and independent of thought and language. In my judgement this was a large step in the right direction, but the result was still far from satisfactory. The representation of mathematics in type theory is conceptually inadequate, and the constraints of type theory are based on an unjustified doctrine about meaning.[18] Although Ramsey succeeds in extricating logicism from the morass surrounding the Vicious Circle Principle and the Axiom of Reducibility, his defence of it fails. His attempt to overcome the conflict between the logicist conception of a class as the extension of a condition and the need to cater for indefinable classes was not successful, being essentially an abandonment of the logicist conception. Having sharpened logicism by reformulating it as the thesis that mathematical truths are tautologies, the Multiplicative Axiom, in whatever guise, is all the more clearly a counterexample. And the Axiom of Infinity, in the form it must take in type theory, is neither *a priori*[19] nor necessary, let alone tautologous.

Though Ramsey marshalled considerable ingenuity in defending logicism, he cannot have been completely happy, and at one point frankly admits that his attempt is 'vague and unsatisfactory'. But I do not believe anyone could have done better, for the cause was hopeless. His writing shows him not only leaving behind the Russellian outlook but actually straining at the limits of logicism. Though still very young, he was as philosophically acute as anyone working on the foundations of mathematics at the time. Had he lived even half as long as Russell, he may well have abandoned logicism and turned from type theory to axiomatic set theory as a foundational framework for classical mathematics. That is the subject of the next chapter.

Part IV
Axiomatic Set Theory and Hilbert's Programme

Zermelo's Axiomatic Set Theory

As Russell and Whitehead were preparing the first edition of *Principia Mathematica*, Zermelo was formulating axioms for Cantorian set theory without type restrictions. The result was a seminal paper published in 1908. The project was motivated by the paradoxes. Set theory, Zermelo wrote, was an indispensable part of mathematics, but 'the very existence of this discipline seems to be threatened by certain contradictions, or "antinomies", that can be derived from its principles—principles necessarily governing our thinking, it seems—and to which no entirely satisfactory solution has yet been found.'[1]

A satisfactory solution would require the articulation of an alternative to the conception of a set as the extension of a concept, an alternative that would not give rise to the offending principles. At the time, Zermelo frankly admitted, no such alternative conception had been found. How in this circumstance would it help to provide an axiomatization of set theory? Zermelo envisaged a two-stage programme. The first task was to formulate axioms that, taken together, would be generous enough to allow the development of arithmetic and analysis within set theory, thus preserving its foundational role, but which would be too strict to reproduce the paradoxes. The second task was to prove that the axioms would give rise to no new paradox, that is, to prove the axioms consistent. Zermelo's paper of 1908 achieved the first stage.

Zermelo's axioms

The principles that governed most thinking about classes prior to discovery of the paradoxes were the Principle of Extensionality and the Comprehension Principle.[2] The Principle of Extensionality is this:

>If classes A and B have the same members, A is the very same class as B.

Extensionality is what distinguishes being a member of a class from being an instance of a concept. The concept 'odd number' is not the same as the concept 'integer that is not a multiple of an even prime', though they have the same instances. This principle was retained by Zermelo and in all subsequent versions of set theory. But he rejected the Comprehension Principle, which he regarded as the error at the source of the paradoxes.

The Comprehension Principle is this:

>For any condition F there is a class $\{x : F(x)\}$ whose members are exactly the things that satisfy condition F.

As Zermelo's concern was set theory rather than a theory of classes encompassing both sets and Cantor's Absolutely Infinite Multiplicities, what he was really denying is the Comprehension Principle when read as a principle about sets:

>For any condition F, there is a *set* $\{x : F(x)\}$ whose members are exactly the satisfiers of condition F.

In its place, he proposed a restricted version of this principle, the Axiom of Separation:

>For any set m and any condition F that is definite for m, there is a set whose members are exactly the members of m satisfying the condition F.

To say that condition F is *definite* for m is to say that, for each member c of m, either c satisfies F or it does not; there are no intermediate cases. So for any set m, there is a set $\{x : x \in m \ \& \ F(x)\}$ even when there is no set $\{x : F(x)\}$.

This axiom allows one to *separate* from a given set those of its members satisfying a given condition and to regard them as forming a set. It is clearly a restriction of the Comprehension Principle. When it replaces that principle the class paradoxes do not get off the ground. For example, we cannot use the Axiom of Separation to establish the existence of a class of all classes, that is, a class $\{x : x$ is a class$\}$. We could use it to show, for any set m, that there is a class of all classes in m, assuming that 'x is a class' is definite for m. But to show the existence of a class of all classes using the Axiom of Separation, one would have to prove the existence of a set m containing every class among its members. The same obstacle stands in the way of showing that there is a set of all sets. Thus, Cantor's paradox cannot be reproduced using the Axiom of Separation in place of the Comprehension Principle. Parallel considerations apply regarding the other class paradoxes.

The Axiom of Separation provides a way of getting a host of new sets from old. But other ways of getting new sets from old would be needed if the gains of past research with sets were to be saved in the new axiomatic set theory. Zermelo gives three further axioms for getting new sets from old: the Union Set Axiom, the Power Set Axiom, and the Axiom of Choice.

The Union Set Axiom is:

> For any set m, there is a set $\cup m$ (the union set of m) whose members are exactly the objects that are members of a member of m.

Hence for any object x, x is in $\cup m$ if and only if for some member y of m, x is in y.

The Power Set Axiom is:

> For any set m, there is a set $\mathbb{P}m$ (the power set of m) whose members are exactly the subsets of m.

These axioms can be seen as giving instances of comprehension in the following way. For any set m the Union Set Axiom entails the existence of a set whose members are just those objects satisfying the condition 'for some member y of m, x is a member of y'; and the Power Set Axiom entails the existence of a set whose members are just the satisfiers of the condition 'x is a subset of m'.

The Axiom of Choice is:

> For any non-empty set m of non-empty sets with no common member, there is a subset c of $\cup m$ such that, for every set p in m, c has exactly one member in common with p.

Such a set c is said to be a *choice set* for m. It can be thought of as the result of going round all the sets in m choosing just one member from each. Zermelo used it to prove that every set can be well ordered. There were objections to the Axiom of Choice from mathematicians who thought that an existence proof of a mathematical object requires that the object be defined.[3] The Axiom of Choice allows one to assume the existence of a choice set without being able to define one. Thus, it can be regarded as an expression of the view that sets may exist independently of linguistic constructions.

If the axioms so far give us new sets from old sets, what guarantees that there are any sets to begin with? Zermelo proposed two axioms in answer to this. The first, which he called the Axiom of Elementary Sets, has three parts. (i) There exists a set with no members (the empty set). (ii) For any object a there exists a set $\{a\}$ whose sole member is a (the unit set of a). (iii) For any two objects a and b there is a set $\{a, b\}$ having a and b as its only members. Parts (ii) and (iii) can be captured in a single postulate that has come to be known as the Pair Set Axiom:

> For any objects a and b (not necessarily distinct), there is a set $\{a, b\}$ having a and b as its only members.

Then (ii) is the case where $a = b$, and (iii) is the case where $a \neq b$. If we assume that there is an object[4] (call it a), it follows from the Pair Set Axiom that there is a set, namely $\{a\}$. Then we can use the Axiom of Separation to infer the existence of a set whose members are just those members of $\{a\}$ that are not self-identical. As every object is self-identical, this set must be empty. So there is no need to postulate the existence of an empty set. It follows from the innocuous assumption that there is an object, by the Axioms of Separation and Pair Set. The uniqueness of the empty set $\emptyset$ follows from the Axiom of Extensionality.

But another set existence axiom is needed in order to develop arithmetic and analysis within a framework of sets, an axiom guaranteeing the existence of an infinite set. Zermelo would have been aware of attempts to prove the existence of an infinite set by Bolzano and by Dedekind.[5] These attempts were fallacious, and Zermelo rightly thought that the existence of an infinite set is not entailed by his other axioms (unless they are inconsistent). So he would have to postulate the existence of an infinite set. As mathematicians almost universally accepted that the natural numbers formed a set, this was not controversial.

Zermelo's Axiom of Infinity is:

> There exists a set z such that (i) the empty set is a member of z and (ii) for any object x, if x is a member of z, so is $\{x\}$.

For brevity, let us call a set that fulfils both (i) and (ii) a Z-set. A Z-set has an unending sequence of members: $\emptyset, \{\emptyset\}, \{\{\emptyset\}\}, \{\{\{\emptyset\}\}\}, \ldots$ Zermelo used these to represent the natural number sequence. He also proved that there is a unique Z-set that is a subset of every Z-set. Its members are exactly the elements of the sequence just given.

Ordinals and cardinals

An ordinal is the order type of a well ordered set.[6] When we want to reason mathematically about properties of a given kind, such as order types, it is often helpful to represent these properties by mathematical objects. One way of doing this is to represent property P by the set of things in the relevant domain having property P. This usually works when the relevant domain is partitioned by the range of properties under consideration, that is, when everything in the relevant domain has just one of the properties in the range. In this case that condition is met: every well ordered set has just one order type. However, we cannot use the set of all well-ordered sets of a given order type α to represent α within set theory, as there is no such set.[7] In Cantorian language, the well ordered sets of a given order type constitute an Absolutely Infinite Multiplicity (AIM). The alternative way of representing properties is to choose an instance of each property as its representative, using some uniform specification of the representatives. Von Neumann showed how to do this for order types of well ordered sets in a way that is simple to take in and convenient to work with.[8] Let us call the representatives of order types of well ordered sets 'ordinals', as is customary. Von Neumann's proposal was that an ordinal is simply the set of its predecessors.[9] The first ordinal has to be the empty set (as no other well ordered set has the same order type), and this is, trivially, the set of its predecessors. So the sequence of ordinals starts:

$$\varnothing, \{\varnothing\}, \{\varnothing, \{\varnothing\}\}, \{\varnothing, \{\varnothing\}, \{\varnothing, \{\varnothing\}\}\}, \ldots$$

One advantage of von Neumann's proposal is that we can use the membership relation $\in$ to do duty for ordinal precedence; another advantage is that a simple set-theoretic operation does duty for the successor operation on ordinals: the successor of α is defined to be $\alpha \cup \{\alpha\}$, the set whose members are just α's members and α itself.

An ordinal α is *finite* if and only if every ordinal less than or equal to α is $\varnothing$ or a successor ordinal. The finite ordinals can be taken to represent the natural numbers; thus, if $\underline{k}$ is the ordinal representing k, $\underline{n+1} = \{\underline{0}, \underline{1}, \underline{2}, \ldots, \underline{n}\}$. This can be extended comfortably into the transfinite, using an alternative Axiom of Infinity:

There is a set z such that $\varnothing \in z$ and for any set x, if $x \in z$ then $x \cup \{x\} \in z$.

One can show that all the finite ordinals belong to any set z of this kind; hence by the Axiom of Separation there is a set whose members are just the finite ordinals, namely ω. This is the first infinite ordinal, also the first limit ordinal. Cantor's transfinite ordinal arithmetic, so admired by Hilbert,[10] can be easily reproduced using the von Neumann ordinals.

How should cardinal numbers be represented in set theory? A cardinal number is a property of sets and the domain of sets is partitioned by cardinal number, so we might try representing a cardinal κ by the set of all sets having κ members. This again runs into the problem that there is no such set (except when $\kappa = 0$). The alternative is to specify in a uniform way a particular set with cardinality κ as the representative of κ. With the von Neumann ordinals to hand, this is easy: let κ be represented by the first ordinal with exactly κ predecessors. An infinite ordinal has the same cardinal number of predecessors as many other infinite ordinals. So in the realm of the infinite, the ordinals and the cardinals diverge, though the finite cardinals and the finite ordinals coincide.

The set of finite cardinals is the first infinite cardinal, $\aleph_0$. It is commonly believed that an infinite cardinal number cannot be increased by adding 1, and that is true. But one can reach higher infinite cardinals by another operation: the next infinite cardinal after an infinite cardinal κ is the set of ordinals with κ or fewer predecessors. Here I am assuming something that needs to be proved, namely, that for any set x there is a set of all ordinals that can be corelated 1-to-1 with a subset of x; this set is known as aleph(x). Using the aleph operation and the identification of cardinals with initial ordinals, we can define the unbounded sequence of infinite cardinals as follows:

$$\aleph_0 = \omega; \quad \aleph_{\beta+1} = \text{aleph}(\aleph_\beta);$$

and, for any limit ordinal λ,

$$\aleph_\lambda = \text{the union of } \{\aleph_\beta : \beta < \lambda\}.^{11}$$

Assuming that aleph(x) is a set when x is, this is a legitimate definition by transfinite recursion. It can be shown that every infinite cardinal is an $\aleph_\alpha$ for some ordinal α, and that $\aleph_\alpha$ is the least infinite cardinal not in $\{\aleph_\beta : \beta < \alpha\}$.

The Axiom of Replacement

The theory of transfinite numbers informally developed by Cantor and his successors cannot be deduced from the axioms mentioned so far. In particular, we need another axiom to establish that every well-ordered set is isomorphic to a unique ordinal and to establish that aleph(x) is a set when x is. The axiom we use is known as the Axiom of Replacement.

Its source is a principle stated by Cantor: if two multiplicities can be correlated 1-to-1, either both are sets or both are AIMs.[12] Equivalently put, there is no 1-to-1 correlation between a set and an AIM. This is a consequence of Cantor's idea that every set has a cardinal number while AIMs never do. The argument is simply that, if there were a 1-to-1 correlation between a multiplicity (class) B and a set A, B would have whatever cardinality A has; and so B too would be a set. This entails a Cantorian principle of Replacement:

> If there is a 1-to-1 correlation between a set A and a class B, B too is a set.[13]

It turns out to be more convenient to use as an axiom a principle that can easily be proved equivalent to this one, using a couple of the previously stated axioms. This involves the notion of a 'functional relation' in place of correlation. A *functional relation* is a binary relation $F(x, y)$ that assigns to each member x of its domain exactly one object y. Here then is the Axiom of Replacement:

> For any set m and any functional relation F with domain m, there is a set $F[m]$ whose members are exactly the objects assigned by F to members of m.

Here '$F[m]$' abbreviates '$\{y : \exists x[x \in m\ \&\ F(x) = y]\}$'. $F[m]$ is known as 'the image of m under F', and when m is the domain of F, $F[m]$ is the range of F. It is easy to show that the Axiom of Replacement is equivalent to the the Cantorian principle stated earlier.[14]

The problem of 'definiteness'

The main source of discontent with Zermelo's axiomatization of set theory was the notion of a condition that is *definite* for a set, in Zermelo's Axiom of Separation:

> For any set m and any condition $F(x)$ that is definite for m, there is a set whose members are exactly the members of m satisfying the condition $F(x)$.

Zermelo does give an account of definiteness, but it is confusing. It could well be read as saying that condition F is definite for set m when, for every member x of m, it is provable from the axioms that x satisfies F or it is provable from the axioms that x does not satisfy F. That account introduces a vicious circle, as what is provable from the axioms depends on what definiteness amounts to in the Axiom of Separation. An alternative is to stipulate that F is definite for m when, for every x in m, either x satisfies F or x does not satisfy F. This is clear. The problem is that we have no effective test for definiteness in this sense; so we have no effective way of telling what the genuine instances of the axiom are. Attempts to deal with this problem were made by Weyl, Skolem, Fraenkel, and von Neumann.

A related worry is that reference to conditions (or propositional functions) in the Axiom of Separation seems incompatible with the foundational aim of reproducing mathematics in a theory about entities whose natures in no way involve subjective aspects, such as meanings. If meanings or other thought-constructs were allowed into the ontology of the theory, some rules of construction would be needed and then the project would be caught in the web that ensnared *Principia Mathematica*. The same worry afflicts the Axiom of Replacement, as it talks of functional relations. Functional relations are binary conditions of a certain sort, so this axiom requires that the domain of the theory contains conditions as well as sets.

Von Neumann's proposal

Two distinct ways of dealing with these problems were offered in the 1920s, one due to von Neumann and the other due to Skolem. Von Neumann proposed to introduce into the domain of the theory not only sets but also Cantor's Absolutely Infinite Multiplicities, later known as proper classes.[15] The paradoxes are avoided by stipulating that proper classes can never be members. This is no guarantee that contradictions cannot be derived by some other route; like Zermelo, von Neumann pinned his hopes on a consistency proof.

How does the inclusion of proper classes deal with the problems mentioned earlier about the Axioms of Separation and Replacement? The Axiom of Separation can now be stated thus:

For any set m and any class B, $\{x : x \in m \,\&\, x \in B\}$ is a set.

The expression '$\{x : x \in m \,\&\, x \in B\}$' denotes the class of objects in both m and B, that is, the intersection of m and B. Reference to conditions has been eliminated. Bearing in mind that a class may be a class of ordered pairs, we can define a *function* as a class of ordered pairs no two of which have the same first member. What is the intention here? If F is a function in the sense just defined, statements of the form

the ordered pair $\langle x, y \rangle$ is a member of F

can be translated into the more familiar language of functions: 'F$(x) = y$' or, in words, 'the value of F for argument x is y'. (That is nineteenth century terminology. I prefer 'the output of F for input x is y' or, more simply, 'F assigns y to x'.) The class of first members of pairs in a function is its domain and the class of second members is its range. It follows that, for each member x of the domain of a function F, there is a unique member y of its range such that $F(x) = y$. Then in stating the Axiom of Replacement, reference to functional relations can be replaced by reference to functions:

For any set m and any function F, $\{y : \exists x[x \in m \ \& \ F(x) = y]\}$ is a set.

The class $\{y : \exists x[x \in m \ \& \ F(x) = y]\}$ is F[m], the image of m under F.[16] Of course the utility of these axioms depends on what classes one can define in the theory. In some versions of set theory with proper classes, classes are defined by means of a class comprehension axiom. Let 'object' be used for individuals and sets but not proper classes. Then the axiom of comprehension for classes is this:

For any condition $\varphi(x)$ expressible in the language of set theory without proper classes, there is a class $\{x : \varphi(x)\}$ whose members are just the objects that satisfy $\varphi(x)$.

But there is no need for such an axiom. Instead, one can use a finite number of axioms for forming classes from given classes. An example is the Axiom of Complementation:

For any class C there is a class $\sim$C whose members are just the objects not in C.

This is the way von Neumann proceeds.[17] Thus, he avoids mention of propositional functions, conditions, and the like—entities in some way dependent on the nature of thoughts. Such things are excluded from the domain of the theory. Because of this, the problem of finding an adequate characterization of 'definiteness' of a condition vanishes.

However, by authorizing the division of classes into sets and proper classes and bringing proper classes into the domain of the theory, von Neumann's proposal puts the major problem of the Cantorian approach at the heart of his theory: what explains the distinction between sets and proper classes? Without such an explanation, the distinction appears *ad hoc*, and rational confidence in the theory as a foundation for mathematics weakens. Cantor had no satisfactory answer,[18] and von Neumann's answer, while unequivocal, has no merit as an explanation. (Nor was it offered as an explanation.) Von Neumann's account of the difference between sets and proper classes is that proper classes are too big to be members, in the sense that they can be correlated 1-to-1 with the class of all sets.[19] This is clearly no solution of the class paradoxes. Why does size matter? Why should being as large as the class of all sets prevent a class being a member of another class? Why think of classes by analogy with rigid closed containers of bounded volume containing objects of fixed minimum size? It is not at all clear why we should prefer to say that the class of all sets cannot be a member of a class rather than that 'the class of all sets' is non-denoting or ambiguous.

Skolem's proposal

Skolem pointed out that a formal language for set theory could be formulated in a precise and unambiguous way, and that one can specify the sentences of the language in a way that enables us to decide, for any given expression in the language, whether it is a sentence; and we can also give a decidable specification for the open sentences, which are the expressions for conditions. For example, the open sentence

$$\neg \exists y (y \in x)$$

expresses the condition 'x has no member'; and the open sentence

$$\forall z [z \in y \rightarrow z \in x]$$

expresses the binary condition (or relation) 'any member of y is a member of x'. Now, in place of reference to conditions (or relations), we can use a schematic expression whose substitution-instances are open sentences. Here again is Zermelo's Axiom of Separation:

> For any set m and any condition F that is definite for m, there is a set whose members are exactly the members of m satisfying the condition F.

Here is the corresponding axiom schema:

> For any set m, there is a set whose members are exactly the members x of m such that $\psi(x)$.

Here it is understood that '$\psi(x)$' is schematic for open sentences of the formal language of set theory with exactly one free variable, which are just those that express unary conditions. Any instance of this schema is an axiom. This entails that there are infinitely many axioms, the instances of the schema. But that is not a problem, as the schema enables us to tell, for any given sentence in the language of set theory, whether it is an axiom—the matter is effectively decidable.[20] That is Skolem's proposal, and it can be as easily applied to the Axioms of Separation and Replacement.[21] In this way Skolem overcame the weaknesses of Zermelo's initial axiomatization of set theory.

Conclusion

Zermelo's axioms plus the Axiom of Replacement preserve everything of value in set theory that was known by the early 1920s. This included not only Cantor's theory of the transfinite but also the foundational gains of set theory: the representation of natural-number arithmetic within set theory, and set-theoretic accounts of the real numbers and, building on that, the development of analysis within set theory. The resulting theory, though clearly not a system of logic, is more powerful, more flexible, and more consonant with intuition than the simple theory of types. But by the time the Axiom of Replacement was on the books, in the early 1920s, there was still no clear conception that the axioms, taken collectively, could be seen as articulating. Rather, the axiomatization was the result of an attempt to preserve as much as possible of naïve set theory short of reproducing the paradoxes. Thus, there was at the time no strong ground for confidence that the axiomatic theory was consistent. Hence the need for a consistency proof was pressing. That aside, there were other sources of discontent with axiomatic set theory as a foundation for mathematics. This is the subject of the next chapter.

Blitz on Paradise   2

Despite the discovery of the paradoxes around the end of the nineteenth century, Cantor's set theory continued to be developed in the following years and used fruitfully both in clarifying the infinitesimal calculus and in the study of sets of spatial points and its generalization to the study of topological spaces.[1] There is no doubt that set theory, including the theory of the transfinite, has an intuitive content that reveals an apparent realm of considerable beauty, 'Cantor's paradise', in Hilbert's memorable phrase.[2] Zermelo's axiomatization of the theory dispelled immediate concern about the paradoxes, as those routes to contradiction were not passable in Zermelo's system. But confidence in the theory would remain shaky as long as positive reason for believing the theory consistent was lacking. And new attacks were on the way.

Skolem's critique

In the early 1920s Skolem refined Zermelo's axiomatization, ironing out its major flaw. At the same time, however, Skolem battered the idea that by axiomatizing set theory its role as a foundation for mathematics could be preserved. But why in the first place might one think that axiomatizing set theory would help? We have some grasp of sets and membership from examples of sets whose members we can name, such as the set of letters of the English alphabet. But our liability to fall into paradox revealed that our initial understanding did not extend to a grasp of the general nature of set-hood and membership. So in place of direct understanding one might hope that an axiomatization of set theory would give us an implicit definition of set-hood and membership. That view, though not promoted by Zermelo, was current in the early 1920s. Von Neumann, for example, gave expression to it in the following way.

To replace [the naïve notion of set] the axiomatic method is employed; that is, one formulates a number of postulates in which, to be sure, the word 'set' occurs but without any meaning. Here (in the spirit of the axiomatic method) one understands by 'set' nothing but an object of which one knows no more and wants to know no more than what follows about it from the postulates.[3]

It was hoped, perhaps expected, that, for a given set of individuals (objects that are not sets or classes), the axioms would determine the universe of sets and the central properties and relations of set theory, such as those concerned with cardinality.

Skolem pointed to a couple of mathematical facts which, he argued, show that axiomatization did not have this benefit. He focused his attack on the system of axioms consisting of the Skolem-style version of Zermelo's axioms, counting the instances of the schema of Separation as axioms. But Skolem's arguments still apply when we adopt his earlier proposal to add the instances of the axiom schema of Replacement. The resulting system is known as ZFC.[4] First, Skolem pointed out that if the axiom system is consistent it does not determine a unique domain, even when the axioms are interpreted as intended (that is, with '$x \in y$' for membership and 'S(x)' for set-hood) and the set of individuals is held fixed. Moreover, there would be domains that have distinct membership structure. For the axioms do not rule out the existence of infinitely descending membership chains:

$$\ldots \ldots x_{n+1} \in x_n \in x_{n-1} \in \ldots \in x_2 \in x_1 \in x_0.$$

But if a domain for which ZFC is true has such chains, it has a subdomain without such chains, and ZFC is also true for this subdomain.[5] This is not a serious threat to the foundational goals of axiomatization, as an axiom could be added to exclude infinitely descending membership chains.[6] But Skolem had another shaft, one that could not be evaded.

The downward Löwenheim-Skolem theorem

Skolem drew attention to a theorem that seems to show that properties central to our understanding of the infinite cannot be pinned down by means of a precise formal theory of sets. To state the theorem simply, some abbreviations are needed. A precise formal language is *enumerable* if and only if the set of its expressions can be enumerated by the natural numbers (or by an initial segment thereof); and it is *first-order* if and only if its variables range over members of the domain only (hence none of its variables range over subclasses of the domain). Let L be any first-order language whose simple non-logical symbols are categorized as relation symbols, function symbols, predicate symbols, or names. L need not have symbols of all these categories. For example, if L is a formal language for set theory with individuals, it need only have a two-place relation symbol for membership and a predicate symbol for set-hood. Then an *interpretation* of L consists of a domain D, plus an interpretation function that assigns to each simple non-logical symbol σ of L a value appropriate to the category of σ:

Symbol category	Value type
n-place relation symbol	class of ordered n-tuples of members of D
predicate symbol	subclass of D
n-ary function symbol	extension of an n-ary function on D[7]
name	member of D

To illustrate, if D is the domain of an interpretation of set theory, its interpretation function must assign a class of ordered pairs of members of D to the two-place relation symbol '$x \in y$' and a subclass of D to the predicate symbol '$S(x)$'. A *model* of a system of axioms is an interpretation of the language of the axioms under which all the axioms are true. Here then is the theorem, known as the downward Löwenheim–Skolem theorem for enumerable languages, which I will shorten to 'LS':

> Any system of axioms in an enumerable first-order language has a model with an infinite domain only if it also has a model whose domain is enumerable.

A version of this was first presented by Löwenheim; Skolem improved Löwenheim's argument and proved a generalization now known as the Löwenheim–Skolem theorem.[8]

To see why LS might be significant, it will be helpful to consider a more specific theorem, an application of LS to set theory. Again, it will be convenient to have some abbreviations. A *language for set theory* is a formal language whose only non-logical symbols are a two-place relation symbol for membership and, if we want to allow for individuals as well as sets, a predicate symbol for set-hood. (In practice, we introduce new symbols as abbreviations for expressions defined in terms of the original symbols, but the new symbols are eliminable.) An *intended interpretation* of a language for set theory is an interpretation that (i) has a domain containing nothing but sets and perhaps individuals, and (ii) assigns to the predicate symbol the class of sets in the domain, and (iii) assigns to the relation symbol the class of ordered pairs $\langle x, y \rangle$ of elements of the domain such that the first, x, is a member of the second, y. Finally an *intended model* of a system of axioms in a language for set theory is an intended interpretation under which all the axioms of the system are true. Applying LS to set theory yields the following theorem:

> Any system of axioms in an enumerable first-order language for set theory has an intended model with an infinite domain only if it has an intended model whose domain is enumerable.

Skolem's paradox

Why is this a problem for the view that ZFC could serve as a foundation for mathematics by implicitly defining the notions of set and membership? The main argument starts as follows. If ZFC does not have an intended model with an infinite domain, it does not characterize a universe of sets in which the rest of the mathematical realm can be represented. So let us assume that it does have such a model. Then, by the theorem just mentioned, it has an intended model M with an enumerable domain. This gives rise to a puzzle known as Skolem's paradox, though, as Skolem noted, it is not an antinomy. From the axioms of ZFC, we can prove the existence of sets that are much too large to be enumerated, for example $\mathbb{P}\omega$, the power set of the set of finite ordinals. So in M it must be true that there is a non-enumerable set. 'How can it be', asked Skolem, 'that the entire domain [of M] can already be enumerated by means of the finite positive integers?'[9] Skolem knew the answer and used it to argue that central concepts of set theory have an inescapable relativity if we rely solely on axiomatic set theory for our understanding of set-hood and membership. Let us go into the matter.

The puzzle can be sharpened by assuming that M has the additional property that it is *transitive*: every set that is a member of M's domain is also a subset of the domain.[10] This will be used in the argument to follow. One theorem of ZFC, informally put, is that there is a non-enumerable set. What this means is that there is a set c such that no set d enumerates c.[11] I will put square brackets round an informal expression of the theorem to denote its formal expression. Since any logical consequence of a set of axioms is true in any model of the axioms, [there is a non-enumerable set] is true in M. Now let c be any set in the domain of M. As M is transitive, c is a subclass of the domain of M. But any subclass of an enumerable set is enumerable, and the domain of M is enumerable. Hence any set c in the domain of M is enumerable. But this seems to contradict the fact that [there is a non-enumerable set] is true in M.

To solve this puzzle, one needs to unpack a little what it means to say that

[there is a non-enumerable set] is true in M.

The locution 'φ is true in M' is just a stylistic variant of 'φ under interpretation M is true'. A formal sentence expresses no proposition as long as it is uninterpreted and so cannot be true or false. But a formal sentence φ under an interpretation M (denoted φ^M) does express a proposition, hence can be true or false. So we need to unpack 'It is true that [there is a non-enumerable set]^M', or simply

[there is a non-enumerable set]^M.

Then we can see whether this proposition really contradicts the fact that every set in the domain of M is enumerable. Here is a first step in unpacking the statement:

[there is a set x such that no y enumerates x]^M .

Writing 'dom(M)' for the domain of M, this can be further unpacked by extracting the quantifiers:

there is a set x in dom(M) such that no y in dom(M) [enumerates]^M x.

Rather than continue unpacking, the puzzle can now be solved quite simply by considering in turn two jointly exhaustive possibilities. Let c be any set in dom(M) such that no y in dom(M) [enumerates]^M c. The first possibility is that 'no y in dom(M) [enumerates]^M c' does *not* entail 'no y in dom(M) enumerates c'. In that case the paradox evaporates immediately because the non-existence of an [enumeration]^M of c is compatible with the existence of an enumeration of c. The second possibility is that 'no y in dom(M) [enumerates]^M c' *does* entail 'no y in dom(M) enumerates c'. Then it would be true that there is no enumeration of c in the domain of M, and that might seem to conflict with the fact that c, being a subclass of an enumerable domain, is enumerable. But there is no conflict at all here, as the absence from the domain of M of any enumeration of c is compatible with the existence of an enumeration of c *outside* the domain of M. If c is a set in the domain of M that is [non-enumerable]^M, the situation is that there is an enumeration of c, but not in the domain of M. That is the solution to the puzzle.

Relativity

The real significance of LS is not that it generates a paradox. The paradox is benign, but, by reflecting on the situation described in solving it, the significance of LS begins to emerge. Let c and M be as above: there is no enumeration of c in the domain of M, but outside that domain there is an enumeration of c. In that case there is a more encompassing intended model of ZFC—call it M^+— in which c is enumerable. That is, c is in the domain of M^+ and satisfies [x is enumerable]$^{M^+}$. As c is also in the domain of M but does not satisfy [x is enumerable]^M, what 'enumerability' comes to is relative to a model of the axioms: 'enumerability' in the sense of M^+ is not co-extensive with 'enumerability' in the sense of M, as only the former applies to c.

This applies also to 'non-enumerability', of course, and to other concepts connected with cardinality, such as 'finite' and 'infinite', 'x has the same cardinality as y', and even 'x is the power set of y'. This relativity extends to certain defined terms of the theory. This can be illustrated with reference to a stronger version of LS: for any model C of a first-order theory T, there is a model B of T that is an enumerable submodel of C. For models of set theory B and C, B is a *submodel* of C when (i) B's domain is a subclass of C's domain, (ii) anything in B's domain that satisfies [x is a set]^B also satisfies [x is a set]^C, and (iii) any ordered pair $\langle b_1, b_2 \rangle$ of members of B's domain that satisfies [$x \in y$]^B also satisfies [$x \in y$]^C. Now let B and C be intended models of ZFC, with B a submodel of C. The term '$\mathbb{P}\omega$' is relative in the sense that the object in C's domain that satisfies [$x = \mathbb{P}\omega$]^C need not be the same as the object in the domain of B that satisfies [$x = \mathbb{P}\omega$]^B. The reference of this term of set theory may vary from model to submodel.

Thus, ZFC not only fails to determine a universe of sets (given a set of individuals) but also fails to determine properties and relations for central concepts of the theory. The axioms cannot, therefore, be taken as an implicit definition of set-hood and membership; otherwise they would also define notions built up from the notions of set and membership, such as the notion of enumerability. Since the argument does not depend on the details of the axiomatization but applies to all the other axiomatizations in an enumerable first-order formal language, no first-order axiom system for set theory can by itself fix the references of some of the central concepts of set theory.

I will canvass three possible responses and say briefly why they are insufficient. First, one could object that the argument presupposes an informal *absolute* property of enumerability in saying that there is a model of ZFC with an enumerable domain; thus, the acceptability of the argument is destroyed by its conclusion that there is no absolute property of enumerability. This objection rests on a mistake about the conclusion of the argument. The conclusion is not that there is no absolute property of enumerability (although Skolem in later writing clearly drew that conclusion too); the conclusion is that there is no absolute property of enumerability *if* set-hood and member-ship are determined solely by a first-order axiom system in an enumerable language. What is under attack is the idea that the references (or extensions) of the concepts of set-hood and membership, hence of concepts defined in terms of them, are implicitly determined by the axioms.

Secondly, one could object that the restriction to *enumerable* languages is unreasonable; we could use infinitary languages, languages with a non-enumerable number of expressions. Although we can exclude some models this way, it is not a way of saving the idea that the axioms of set theory can serve as an implicit definition of set-hood and membership. From a set of primitive symbols that we can know and a set of rules that we can comprehend, only an enumerable number of expressions can be generated; so if there were a language with a non-enumerable number of expressions only an enumerable part of it would be accessible to us; so our understanding of sets, and our concepts of their properties and relations, would be no superior to their counterparts framed in an enumerable language.

Finally, one could object that the restriction to *first-order* languages is unreasonable. It should be conceded that we would better capture our idea of a universe of sets in a second-order language, a language that has variables that range over all the subsets of the domain. But as a way of defeating Skolem's considerations against the purely axiomatic approach to foundations, this response has two weaknesses. First, in order to understand such a language one must have a grasp of second-order quantification; this means that in order to grasp the second-order version of ZFC one already needs a grasp of 'all subsets' of an infinite domain; so our understanding would not rest on the axioms alone. Secondly, there is an analogue of LS for sets of axioms in a second-order language.[12] So, although some of the relativity is cut out by moving to a second-order language, much remains. There is more to be said in connection with these objections. But it should be clear that Skolem's considerations are substantial enough to cast into doubt the idea of definition by axiomatization: if our intuitions about sets are too weak or unreliable to provide a foundation for mathematics, an axiomatization of set theory is not going to make up the shortfall.[13]

Brouwer's intuitionist challenge

Set theory was the focus of interest because the whole of established mathematics, especially the mathematical analysis of continua, could be recast in the language of set theory and derived from its principles. The groundwork for recasting analysis in set theory had already been done by Dedekind, Cantor, and others, and the decades following Dedekind's seminal work on real numbers[14] saw the advance of this programme in the development of point-set theory. This work was generally regarded as valuable; only the basis, set theory, was felt to need straightening out and securing against paradox, as Zermelo proposed. But some voices were raised against the early work too, and not just on matters of detail.

The arch critic was Brouwer. Brouwer himself had made a substantial contribution to point-set theory, specifically topology and dimension theory, and the depth, rigour, and originality of his work had won him international acclaim by 1913. But his philosophical view led him to reject the framework within which his discoveries had been made. Brouwer's 'intuitionism', as he called his view, is the analogue in mathematics of phenomenalism about the physical world, in that the entities and facts of mathematics, on this view, are creations of the mind and in that sense are *in* the mind. One focus of dispute was the proper treatment of continuous magnitudes. We acquire an idea of a continuous interval from our experience, such as our experience of the duration of an uninterrupted event. It is not part of this pre-theoretical idea that a continuous interval is made up of points, and many paradoxes arise from that view, unless it is beaten into form by mathematical artifice. But there is a natural idea of 'homing in on a point' by an unending succession of ever shorter steps. This idea can be given a mathematical explication, as the activity of constructing a Cauchy sequence.[15] So mathematical analysis would be more securely tied to experience, it seems, if in place of the ready-made point we put the ongoing construction. Brouwer's intuitionism can be thought of as a generalization and development of this outlook: mathematical entities and facts are mental constructions that are directly accessible to the mind of the constructor; this direct access is known as intuition. At no time, on this view, is there a mathematical object or fact that is currently beyond intuition.

That doctrine bars the classical way of defining real numbers in terms of infinite sets or sequences of rational numbers. On the classical approach, infinite sets or sequences of rationals are taken to exist in entirety from the start, without any constructive activity. On Brouwer's approach, an infinite or 'indefinitely proceeding' sequence is a *choice* sequence. A choice sequence is a sequence of elements chosen freely or with some specified constraints; what exists of the sequence at any time are (i) the finite sequence of elements so far chosen and (ii) any choice-constraining rule. Some choice sequences are determined at every step by a given rule; those are known as *lawlike* sequences. There are no facts about a sequence beyond facts about the part of it that has so far been constructed plus the rules governing or constraining construction and what has been constructively deduced therefrom. This has important consequences for logic. For it means that a true-or-false question about a sequence beyond its currently constructed part has no current answer, unless an answer has been constructively proved from the rules governing or constraining construction of that sequence. To use a well-worn example, it is at present neither true nor false that somewhere in the decimal expansion of π there occurs a sequence of nine consecutive 9s. Thus, the classical Law of Excluded Middle, according to which every proposition of the form 'P or not-P' is true, is unacceptable on this view. The consequences of this for mathematics can hardly be overestimated. For example, even such a straightforward item as a step function is ruled out. In classical analysis, we can define a function on an interval [0, 2] thus:

$$\text{For all } x \in [0, 2], f(x) = \begin{cases} 1, \text{ if } 0 \le x < 1. \\ 2, \text{ if } 1 \le x \le 2. \end{cases}$$

But from the intuitionist viewpoint this is illegitimate, as it assumes that, for every real number x between 0 and 2, $x = 1$ or $x \neq 1$.[16]

Also unacceptable is the classical Law of Double Negation, according to which every proposition of the form 'If not-not-P, then P' is true. This would be acceptable only if, in every case, a proposition follows from its double negation. On Brouwer's view this is not so. For a mathematical truth, on his view, is nothing but a constructively established fact; and a mathematical falsehood is a state of affairs that has been constructively shown to be impossible to construct. Now let s be an unconstrained choice sequence whose currently constructed initial segment does not contain nine consecutive 9s. Given this information, we can be sure now that at no time can it be ruled out that nine consecutive 9s will occur somewhere in s, as s is an unconstrained choice sequence. Thus, we have constructively shown that it is not possible to establish constructively that s does not contain nine consecutive 9s. Hence it is *not* the case that s does *not* contain nine consecutive 9s. If the Law of Double Negation were acceptable, we should be able to conclude that s *does* contain nine consecutive 9s. But this is not a fact, as it has not been constructively established: the segment of s so far constructed does not contain nine consecutive 9s, and there is no constraining rule from which one might have deduced that nine consecutive 9s will occur in s at a later stage.

138

What Brouwer objected to, then, was not confined to one or two principles of set theory. Basic modes of reasoning used throughout mathematics were rejected as invalid, with devastating effect wherever the infinite is involved, notably in analysis and set theory. Intuitionism was not merely an attack on axiomatic set theory; it was a total repudiation of the heart of nineteenth-century mathematics and much of mathematics from ancient times on. Whereas others sought to bring clarity, system, and rigour to classical mathematics, the major task in Brouwer's eyes was to construct mathematics anew according to intuitionist lights.[17]

Weyl's predicativism

A less radical view accepts classical logic but bans impredicative definitions in mathematics, thus heeding the Vicious Circle Principle:

> No entity is definable only in terms of a class to which it belongs.

This was Weyl's view at the time he wrote *Das Kontinuum*.[18] All of the classical ways of developing mathematical analysis in set theory violate this principle at a fairly basic stage, namely, when it comes to defining the least upper bound of a set of real numbers. The problem was explained in Part III Chapter 2 on *Principia Mathematica*. To see how Weyl intended to deal with it, we first need to see how the problem is manifested when real numbers are represented as left Dedekind cuts (which I will call simply 'cuts' from here on).[19]

The special structural characteristic of the continuum, according to Dedekind, is that every non-empty set of real numbers that has an upper bound has a least upper bound.[20] This is a principle used in the proofs of many theorems of analysis. Recasting this development of classical analysis within set theory requires a set-theoretic definition of the least upper bound of a non-empty set of reals bounded above. Using cuts, this is easy: if S is a non-empty set of reals bounded above, the least upper bound of a set S is just ∪S, the union set of S:

> The least upper bound of S = $\{q : \text{for some } r, q \in r \,\&\, r \in S\}$.

The variables 'q' and 'r' range over the rationals and reals, respectively. It is not difficult to show that ∪S is itself a real, i.e. a cut, and that it is the least upper bound of S (with respect to inclusion). Precisely because ∪S is a real and the variable 'r' in its definition ranges over the reals, ∪S is here defined in terms of a totality to which it belongs. So this definition is unacceptable if one wants to ensure that the Vicious Circle Principle is respected by avoiding impredicative definitions.

Weyl proposed to get round this by replacing Dedekind's axiom (that every non-empty set of reals that has an upper bound has a least upper bound) by the principle that every non-empty *sequence* of reals that has an upper bound has a least upper bound. Let r be a sequence of reals $r_1 \, r_2 \, r_3 \ldots$ that has an upper bound. Then Weyl defined its least upper bound as the union of the reals in the sequence. That is,

The least upper bound of $r = \cup r[\mathbb{N}]$.

To see that this does not violate the Vicious Circle Principle, it will help to spell this out without the union symbol:

The least upper bound of $r = \{q : \text{for some } n, q \in r_n\}$

where 'n' ranges over natural numbers and 'q' over rationals. Thus defined, the least upper bound of r is a real (a cut); it is neither a rational nor a natural number; hence it does not fall into the range of either of the variables used in its definition.

This left Weyl with the task of developing analysis in terms of sequences of reals rather than sets of reals. The ban on impredicative definitions entails that mathematics should observe distinctions of order, where the order of an entity depends on the ingredients that went into its definition.[21] But a reconstruction of analysis with real numbers of different orders becomes impractical and loses intuitive simplicity. So Weyl proposed to reconstruct analysis with real numbers of the lowest order only. Weyl had not advanced very far when he was swept off his feet by the extent of Brouwer's development of his radical intuitionist programme. He then revised his conception of the continuum along intuitionist lines, and he publicly aligned himself with Brouwer, though there were real differences between Brouwer's views and his own.[22] The alignment was temporary. Weyl soon became aware how much is lost by taking the intuitionist position: 'With Brouwer,' he later wrote, 'mathematics gains the highest intuitive clarity; his doctrine is idealism thought through to the end. But, full of pain, the mathematician sees the greatest part of his towering theories dissolve in fog.'[23] At the same time, he was coming to see the merits of an alternative programme initiated by Hilbert.

Hilbert, possibly alarmed by seeing his brightest former doctoral student, Weyl, join his brightest former protégé, Brouwer, in rejecting set theory and classical analysis, attacked them both: 'if we follow such reformers,' Hilbert wrote, 'we run the risk of losing a large number of our most valuable treasures';[24] and he concentrated his efforts on the development of a programme to defend classical mathematics.

In order to explain Hilbert's Programme, we first need an account of its basis, Hilbert's finitist philosophy. That is the subject of the next chapter.

Hilbert's Finitism 3

It must be admitted, Hilbert said in 1925, that the present situation in which we run up against the paradoxes is intolerable. 'Where are we to find certainty, if even mathematical thinking fails us?' This lament is followed by the cheerful declaration that 'there is a completely satisfactory way of escaping the paradoxes without betraying our science.'[1] In fact, neither Hilbert nor his co-workers believed that the paradoxes showed that mathematics, in particular set theory and analysis, was in any way defective. Hilbert stoutly asserted that there is nothing wrong with Zermelo's axioms, but if we use them 'as starting points and foundations for the proofs, mathematics thereby loses the character of absolute certainty'.[2] To settle what Hilbert called the foundational question, it is not enough to find axioms for set theory which do not generate contradictions, as it was believed Zermelo had done; it was also necessary to prove that the axioms do not generate contradictions or patent falsehoods.

Finitism and logic

Of course, a collection of axioms does not generate anything on its own. Only in conjunction with some logic, that is, some rules of inference and perhaps some logical laws, can axioms lead to contradictions. This is important because we may find that uncertainty about a theory, characterized by a set of axioms and its logic, is due to the logic rather than the axioms. In Hilbert's view, the familiar logic can be assumed to be valid only in contexts meeting certain conditions. This is where finitism enters. One of these conditions is that the domain of discourse is finite. When, as in the arithmetic of positive integers, the domain is infinite, Hilbert held that certain laws of classical logic are not valid; hence their use introduces uncertainty except when the domain is known to be finite. A central example is the Quantifier Law of Excluded Middle[3] (QLEM):

Every x satisfies $\varphi(x)$, or some x satisfies the negation of $\varphi(x)$

where $\varphi(x)$ is any one-place condition. For the sake of illustration, let *Goldbach's property* be: if x is an even number greater than 2, x is the sum of a pair of numbers each of which is prime. Goldbach, an eighteenth-century Prussian diplomat and amateur mathematician, conjectured that all positive integers have this property.[4] The negation of Goldbach's property is: x is an even number greater than 2 that is not the sum of a pair of integers each of which is prime. When the domain is the class of positive integers, to satisfy the negation of Goldbach's property is just to lack Goldbach's property. QLEM entails that every positive integer has Goldbach's property or some positive integer lacks it. This may sound perfectly obvious. And it can be derived from simpler logical laws. These are (1) the Law of Excluded Middle (LEM): θ or not-θ, where 'θ' stands for any statement; (2) one of the laws governing transfer of negation across quantifiers, namely that statements of the form (i) and (ii) are logically equivalent:

(i)   Not every x satisfies $\varphi(x)$;   (ii)   some x satisfies not-$\varphi(x)$.

QLEM follows from these laws by the rule permitting replacement of one part of a statement by something logically equivalent to it (in transparent contexts[5]).

None the less, from Hilbert's finitist point of view, QLEM is not to be trusted unless the domain of discourse is known to be finite. To see why, we must take account of the finitist understanding of universal and existential statements. A universal statement such as Golbach's conjecture can be construed as the simultaneous attribution of a property to infinitely many objects, the positive integers, as if it were an infinite conjunction

G(1) & G(2) & G(3) & G(4) & . . .

This construal is not acceptable to finitism, as it makes the content of the statement a kind of infinite object. An alternative is that Goldbach's conjecture is a kind of schema,

G(c),

acceptance of which involves a general disposition to answer positively, whenever the question arises for a given positive integer whether it has Goldbach's property. Acceptance of the schema is correct if and only if we have a finitary procedure by which, given any numeral for a positive integer, we can prove the instance of 'G(c)' for that numeral. We can say that 'G(c)' indicates the truth of each of its instances. Now prefixing an expression for

143

negation to a general schema does not result in the negation of a universal statement, but just in another general schema. 'Not-G(c)' indicates that every instance of 'c lacks Goldbach's property' is true. It does not say or indicate that not every instance of 'G(c)' is true. On the finitist view, the sentence

Not every positive integer has Goldbach's property

fails to say anything at all. It does not even have a schematic construal. So the following is not a logical truth:

Every positive integer has Goldbach's property or not every positive integer has Goldbach's property.

This shows that LEM is not universally valid, given the finitist understanding of universal statements.[6] Hence the route to QLEM given above is not passable from the finitist standpoint.

To show that QLEM is not valid given finitism, we must also take account of the finitist construal of existential statements. One way of understanding an existential statement is as an infinite disjunction, each disjunct attributing the property expressed by the predicate '$\varphi(x)$' to one of the positive integers. So 'There is an x such that x lacks G' would be understood thus:

Not-G(1) or not-G(2) or not-G(3) or not-G(4) or . . .

On this reading of the existential statement, there is an implicit allusion to the infinite totality of natural numbers, which is unacceptable to the finitist. On a finitist construal, an existential statement is either a finitely bounded existential statement or it is incomplete, just part of a proposition, which we can justifiably state only when we can complete it. An example of a finitely bounded existential statement is: 'There is a fourth power less than one million that is the sum of four fourth powers.' This can be verified or refuted by running through the finitely many natural numbers less than one million and checking. But the following is an unbounded existential statement and therefore incomplete: 'There is a fourth power that is the sum of four fourth powers.' Another unbounded existential statement is that there is a positive integer that does not have Goldbach's property. We can utter this without impropriety only when we can specify some bound within which we know it is true, but even then the statement is incomplete, hence not a genuine proposition, according to finitism.

Let us return to QLEM. Consider the following instance of it:

@   Every positive integer has Goldbach's property or there is one that lacks it.

In the absence of LEM, which was seen to be unacceptable to the finitist, a disjunction can be correctly asserted only when one of its disjuncts can be correctly asserted. So we can only correctly assert @ when either we can correctly assert that every number has the Goldbach property, or we can correctly assert that there is one that lacks it. So it follows from the finitist account of universal and existential statements that we can correctly assert @ only when either we have a finitary procedure by which, given any positive integer n, we can prove that n has Goldbach's property, or we can specify a bound b for which we can prove that some positive integer less than b lacks Goldbach's property. Since we have neither procedure nor bound, we cannot correctly assert @. Hence QLEM cannot be assumed to be true in every instance, from the finitist point of view.

Finitism and content: real and ideal propositions

Two tenets of finitism have been illustrated by the foregoing. One is that in contexts in which the domain of discourse is infinite the laws of classical logic cannot be assumed to hold. The other is that in contexts in which the domain of discourse is infinite not all sentences of the discourse express real propositions. Some theorems of arithmetic[7] do not express what the finitists count as real propositions, others do. For the same reasons, the finitist division between real and non-real propositions also runs through the theorems of analysis and set theory. For a reason to be given in the next section, Hilbert called the non-real propositions 'ideal propositions'. The real–ideal distinction is important to the finitist view of higher mathematics, and so it is worth trying to set it out.

Real propositions are statements with 'finitary content'. They fall into two classes, those that are strictly finitary and those that are finitary but general. Strictly finitary statements must satisfy the following conditions:

(a) The denotation of each singular term (noun phrase) must be perceptible and completely surveyable, or it must have an isomorphic representative which is perceptible and completely surveyable, just as for instance each positive integer n can be represented by a succession of n short vertical strokes (the Hilbert numerals), or by a succession of n occurrences of 's' followed by one '0'. Thus, terms for natural numbers are admissible, but terms for irrational numbers and infinite numbers and sets are not.

(b) The denotation of each complex term must be computable from its components in a finite number of steps. Thus, '$3 \times (7 + 6)$' is admissible but 'the limit, as n increases, of $[1 + (1/n)]^n$' is not. (Here any numeral counts as a simple term; a multidigit numeral is a simple *term* but a compound *symbol*.)

(c) Predicates must be decidable for terms fulfilling conditions (a) and (b). This means that for an admissible n-place predicate there must be a way of deciding in a finite number of determinate steps whether, for any sequence of n terms fulfilling (a) and (b), the predicate truly applies to that sequence of terms. For example, the arithmetical predicates '$x < y!$', '$\neg(x = 0)$', and '$w \times z^2 + y \times z^1 = 0$' are decidable.

(d) Sentential connectives and operators must be truth-functional. This means that the truth value of a sentence composed of sentences conjoined by connectives must be computable from the truth values of those component sentences in a finite number of steps; the truth value of a sentence whose immediate subcomponents are a sentence and a sentential operator must be finitarily computable from the truth value of the subsentence.

(e) Quantifiers must be finitely bounded.

The part of a mathematical subject consisting entirely of sentences that satisfy (a)–(e) has a special perspicuity: the truth value of every sentence in this part is decidable by means of precise determinate procedures in a finite number of steps. But no kind of generality is expressible within these bounds, and that seems to exclude some statements that are acceptable as certain even from a finitist point of view. We can illustrate this using the Hilbert numerals for the positive integers: I, II, III, IIII, . . . The number 1 is represented by 'I', 2 by 'II', and so on. Addition of two positive numbers is represented by concatenating their Hilbert numerals, thus forming the Hilbert numeral of their sum. There is a simple finitary method for telling when two Hilbert numerals are equal: write down each numeral; simultaneously erase one stroke from each numeral inscription; repeat this until one of the inscriptions is completely erased; then stop. If both are completely erased, the numerals are equal; otherwise the numeral whose inscription is completely erased is the lesser. Using this, we have an obviously finitary way of demonstrating any given instance of the equation that results from substituting a numeral for 'c' in '$c + 1 = 1 + c$'.

For this reason, Hilbert counted that equation and others like it as real rather than ideal propositions, but he acknowedged that they have a problematic character.[8] They are distinguished from the strictly finitary statements by their generality. I will call them *finitary general* statements.[9] Let a finitary general term (of arithmetic) be a variable or a complex term with one or more free variables such that its value is computable when numerals are substituted for all of its variables. The finitary general statements include not only equations between finitary general terms but any formula with some finitary general term(s) that is finitarily decidable when numerals are substituted for the free variables. They are problematic for finitism because it is difficult to explain why they should be counted as real rather than ideal when their content appears to involve a tacit reference to an infinite totality.

Neither Hilbert nor Bernays really addressed this problem. To examine it, let us return to the equation 'c + 1 = 1 + c'. The crux of the matter is how we are to understand 'c' in this context. To make sense of the finitist position, I tentatively suggest that one has the appropriate understanding of 'c' just when, for any arithmetical condition $\varphi(x)$ that one recognizes as finitely decidable, one is disposed (i) to accept any inference from $\varphi(c)$ to any numeral instance $\varphi(1)$, $\varphi(2)$, etc. when the question of that instance arises, and (ii) to reject $\varphi(c)$ given the negation of any numeral instance.[10] Clearly, this *account* of the disposition involves a reference to an infinite totality (all numeral instances). But equally clearly, the disposition itself can be possessed and activated without the possessor thinking of an infinite totality. The disposition to accept the proposition expressed by any substitution instance of the equation 'c + 1 = 1 + c' does not require one to think of the totality of positive integers, for one could have this disposition without having acquired a general concept of positive integer, though one must have concepts expressed by the numerals. So the thought expressed by the equation 'c + 1 = 1 + c' does not involve a general concept of positive integer, and is therefore distinct from the thought

For every positive integer n, $n + 1 = 1 + n$.

Similarly, the thought does not employ a general concept of numeral, so it differs from the metalinguistic thought

For every numeral α, the result of substituting α for 'c' in 'c + 1 = 1 + c' is true.

The thought then is finitary, as it does not involve reference to any infinite object or totality; and it can be counted as real, rather than ideal, because we have a finitary procedure for verifying its instances.[11] Hence the charge that generality in arithmetic depends essentially on infinitary thinking is not warranted.

To sum up, the real statements fall into two kinds, the strictly finitary and the finitary general. All other statements in mathematics are ideal statements.

These will involve quantification over an infinite domain or reference to an infinite object, such as an irrational number, a function defined on all integers, the set of all rational numbers between two integers, the first infinite cardinal number, and so on. Arithmetic, analysis, and set theory all have both real and ideal statements.

Instrumentalism

Given the finitist view that the theorems of the non-finitary parts of mathematics are not real propositions, and therefore that they are not truths, one might advocate a wholesale rejection of classical mathematics beyond its finitary parts, especially analysis, which, Hilbert pointed out, is replete with apparent reference to the infinite, as well as the major part of set theory. But Hilbert was a staunch defender of analysis and set theory. He described analysis as 'a symphony of the infinite' and Cantor's theory of the transfinite as 'the most admirable flower of the mathematical intellect, . . . one of the highest achievements of purely rational human activity'. His goal was to save analysis and set theory from the advocates of rejection. Famously, Hilbert wrote: 'No one shall be able to drive us out of the paradise that Cantor has created for us.'[12]

How could Hilbert consistently defend Cantor's theory of transfinite sets and at the same time hold that it is all talk without truth? The answer is that Hilbert could regard Cantor's theory as a system which, though not a body of knowledge, is useful as an instrument for reaching finitary truths. The instrument is aesthetically admirable and very useful, giving us formal proofs of finitary truths, proofs that are simpler and easier to find than finitary proofs of the same truths. In particular, it allows us to use the formal laws of classical logic that do not hold universally within the finitary part of a theory ostensibly about an infinite realm. We have already seen that the Quantifier Law of Excluded Middle fails; so do the Laws of Quantifier Interdefinability and the Laws of Negation Transfer.[13] Thus, a serious loss of convenience and simplicity results from confining oneself to finitary mathematics.

There is, then, a practical motive for seeking a justification of non-finitary mathematics. Hilbert used a mathematical analogy to make the point. In geometry the introduction of points at infinity and a line at infinity as ideal elements permits the simplifying law of duality,[14] and in analysis the introduction of imaginary numbers (terms of the form ir, where r is a real number and $i = \sqrt{-1}$) permits us to treat equations with and without real roots in a uniform manner. In the same way, we can regard the non-finitary theorems of a

theory as ideal elements, added to the real elements which are its finitary theorems, so as to preserve the laws of classical logic. Of course, adding ideal elements and laws has to be legitimate. Legitimacy requires that any conclusion
about real elements that one can reach via laws made available by the introduction of ideal elements be true. In the case of a non-finitary theory, this is
the requirement that finitary conclusions reached with the aid of non-finitary
statements and classical logic be true. When this is the case, the non-finitary
theory can be a useful instrument.

At the time that Hilbert was putting forward the instrumentalist view of set
theory and analysis, parallel views about physics were in the air. In particular,
theories that did not consist of generalizations of observable states of affairs,
such as general relativity theory and quantum theory, were sometimes looked
upon not as bodies of propositions, but as instruments for deriving predictions verifiable by observation.[15] Hilbert draws the parallel, in responding to
the reproach that on his view non-finitary mathematics would be just a game:

> To make it a universal requirement that each individual formula then be interpretable by
> itself is by no means reasonable; on the contrary, a theory by its very nature is such that
> we do not need to fall back upon intuition or meaning in the midst of some argument.
> What the physicist demands precisely of a theory is that particular propositions be
> derived from laws of nature or hypotheses solely by inferences, hence on the basis of a
> pure formula game, without extraneous considerations being adduced. Only certain
> combinations of and consequences of the physical laws can be checked by experiment—
> just as in my proof theory only the real propositions are directly capable of verification.[16]

A caveat: real propositions are here contrasted with ideal propositions, not
with fictitious or pseudo propositions. So it would wrong to infer that Hilbert
was endorsing a verificationist view of meaning. The point is rather that we
do not need to interpret the untestable sentences in our theory: they can be
treated in a purely formal way. What matters is that the testable ones are true.

Of course, any proponent of instrumentalism about analysis and set theory faces the question: How do we know that the instrument is reliable? How
do we know that all its finitary theorems are true? How do we know that the
ideal part does not lead to inconsistency in the real part? In view of the class
paradoxes, these were pertinent questions.

Finitary reasoning: subject matter

To prove that analysis and set theory are reliable, we need a mode of reasoning whose reliability does not have to be proved. This bedrock in Hilbert's

view is finitary reasoning; its methods, its rules of definition and inference, and the restrictions on their application are designed to give us the maximum degree of security compatible with the possibility of proving general truths. The subject matter of finitary reasoning must be transparent to human awareness; in so far as the methods can be applied to abstruse subject matter, such as things posited on the basis of 'arbitrary abstract definitions', the applications will fall outside finitary reasoning. Hilbert gave the following characterization of finitary subject matter:

as a condition for the use of logical inferences and the performance of logical operations, something must already be given to us in our faculty of representation, certain extralogical concrete objects that are intuitively present as immediate experience prior to all thought. If logical inference is to be reliable, it must be possible to survey these objects completely in all their parts, and the fact that they occur, that they differ from one another, and that they follow each other, or are concatenated, is immediately given intuitively, together with the objects, as something that can neither be reduced to anything else nor needs reduction.[17]

This is not entirely clear, partly because of the troublesome word 'intuitively', or 'anschaulich' in the original. I am inclined to interpret 'objects that are intuitively present as immediate experience prior to all thinking' to mean objects whose presence is directly perceived rather than inferred or abstracted from what is perceived; and in general, facts 'immediately given intuitively' are directly perceived rather than inferred from what is perceived. But this interpretation may be a bit too narrow. Intuitive presence may include objects or situations that are represented by clear and stable imagery in visual imagination.

Hilbert and his co-workers showed that set theory, analysis, and number theory (including its non-finitary part) could be set out as purely formal systems. So any study of those systems would be a study of purely formal objects—specifically, finitely many primitive symbols, finite strings of symbols, and finite sequences of such strings. Moreover, the properties under investigation would also be purely formal: being a primitive symbol of the system, being a term, being a formula are purely formal properties of symbols or strings of symbols; being a derivation is a formal property of finite sequences of formulas. At first sight this makes formal systems promising subjects for the valid application of finitary methods, given Hilbert's preconditions. First, symbols, finite strings of symbols, finite sequences of such strings and their constituent parts are perceptible, surveyable objects; we can distinguish one from another, and the spatial relations between them in any finite array are completely perspicuous. Secondly, whether a given mark is a symbol of the system, whether a given string is a term, whether a given string is a formula, whether a given formula is an axiom of the theory—these are always decidable by perceptual check.[18] It is also perceptually decidable whether a formal rule has been followed in a transition to a formula from earlier formulas in a sequence; consequently it is perceptually decidable, for any given finite sequence of strings, whether it is a formal derivation.

Two problems about finitary subject matter

However, there are a couple of problems about Hilbert's characterization of finitary subject matter. One of these problems becomes apparent when we distinguish between actual physical inscriptions of a single formal entity, known as *tokens*, and the common form of these inscriptions, known as the *type*. Here are two tokens of the same type, the capital first letter of the English alphabet: A A. Each of these tokens is a concrete perceptible object. But the type is abstract. Although the tokens of that type have location, the type does not. Although the tokens are directly perceptible objects, the type is recognizable only by abstraction from perception of some token(s). True, we can see that the two marks are tokens of the same type; but no object that we can see *is* the type.

Now when Hilbert talks about a symbol, for example when he places '→' in his list of logical signs, he is talking about a type. He is not talking about one particular ink mark on his manuscript, nor about the corresponding printed ink marks in copies of the publication. So the symbols that are the objects of study are not the concrete, perceptible objects that Hilbert seems to demand in the quoted passage. Similar remarks apply to formulas and derivations. When Hilbert says that he will try to prove that the formula '1 ≠ 1' is not derivable in a formalization of real-number theory, he clearly refers to the formula type, not to any particular inscription of it. So the subject matter of Hilbert's undertaking does not satisfy his stated criterion for the legitimate application of the prescribed methods. This is the type–token problem.

It is not a deep problem. Hilbert's stated requirement on the subject matter to which finitary methods may be validly applied is too strict for his intentions. Finitist certainty would not be impugned if one counted as finitary subject matter any abstract object whose tokens are concrete and perceptible, provided that (i) we can tell directly by perception whether a given perceptible mark in a relevant context is a token of the abstract object, and (ii) we attribute a property to the abstract object only when we can tell by finite

151

inspection of one of its tokens whether the attribution is correct. If one says of a given string of symbols, meaning the type, that it is a formula, the truth of the statement can be checked by inspecting a token of that string. If one says of a given sequence of formulas that it is a derivation ending with '1 ≠ 1', meaning the type, that too can be checked by inspecting a token of the derivation, that is, an actual inscription of it. No epistemological loss, no loss of certainty, is incurred by applying finitary inferences to abstract objects, provided that the kinds of thing we want to say about them can be checked by perceptual inspection of their tokens.

The second problem, the problem of practical limits, is that some formulas, and some sequences of formulas, are just too long for perceptual checking. A token of a formula with ten times as many symbols as there are subatomic particles in the whole of space–time is not physically realizable; and even if it were, no one could inspect it. This is a problem that one is tempted to brush off by saying that such monsters are in principle possible to check. For any given formula, beings like us but mentally better endowed in a more copious space–time would be able to do the inspecting. But this is not satisfactory. Suppose, for example, that a long sequence of formulas is described, and suppose that we cannot in practice prove or disprove from its description that it is a derivation. Then in order to tell whether it is a derivation we must inspect a complete token of the sequence. If we cannot make such an inspection, we cannot know whether the sequence is a derivation. It is entirely irrelevant that in some physically richer possible world some super-human beings could make the inspection. They might be able to find out whether the sequence is a derivation, but that has no bearing on what *we* can find out. So a further relaxation of Hilbert's stated preconditions is necessary.

If we actually look at the work of Hilbert and his co-worker Paul Bernays, we see very few tokens of actual formulas. Practically the entire work is carried out by means of schemas using a metalanguage, that is, a language in which we speak about the formal language of a mathematical theory. Formulas in the metalanguage serve as schemas for formulas of the system to be studied. They use schemas to specify axioms and inference rules of a formal system, and to state general claims about its theorems. For example, in formalizing the logical part of number theory, Hilbert and Bernays stipulate that any formula that instantiates the following schema is an axiom:

$$A \to (B \to A).$$

They add that instances of the following schema count as inferences by Modus Ponens:

$$\frac{A, A \to B}{B}.$$

Of course, it must be made clear when a formula is an instance of the axiom schema, and when a sequence of formulas is an instance of the inference schema: the same formula must be substituted for the same schematic letter. They then make the general claim that, in a formal system with those axioms and Modus Ponens,

If A is an axiom, $F \to A$ is a theorem.

A simple derivation schema enables us to establish this:

$$A$$
$$A \to (F \to A)$$
$$F \to A.$$

Now to see that this establishes the claim, we have to see that this is a token of a schema which results in a derivation when any axiom is substituted for the occurrences of 'A' and any formula is substituted for the occurrences of 'F'. For this it is not necessary that we be able to inspect tokens of all formulas including the monsters. It is enough that we can see that this schema represents any sequence of formulas such that the step from the first two to the last is an instance of the specified inference rule, and that any instance of the formula schema on the second line is an instance of the specified axiom-schema; for then we can see that any sequence of formulas conforming to the schema is a derivation (i.e. that each formula in the sequence is an axiom or follows from earlier formulas by an inference rule). This we can in practice check by inspecting a token of the sequence schema, and tokens of the axiom schemas and the inference schema. The general situation is presented in Figure 3.1.

In this way the epistemological problem for monstrously long formulas can be overcome. If the metalanguage has schematic variables for sequences of formulas, as well as formulas, there is no reason why we cannot prove statements about derivations, including monstrously long ones, in like manner. The consequence of this is that Hilbert's statement of preconditions for valid use of logical reasoning must be relaxed to include reasoning about objects by means of schemas that those objects instantiate, provided that the schemas used in any piece of reasoning have tokens that can be inspected in practice by us.

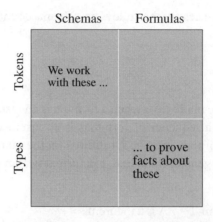

	Schemas	Formulas
Tokens	We work with these ...	
Types		... to prove facts about these

Figure 3.1

Finitary reasoning: methods

The methods of finitary reasoning were identified by Hilbert and Bernays with the methods of Skolem's free-variable arithmetic, which is equivalent to what is now known as primitive recursive arithmetic (PRA).[19, 20] We can think of this as the theory of explicit computation. Its axioms include some principles for defining complex terms from simple terms. The value, for any given input, of a function term defined by these methods can be computed. Thus, the value of any term built up from the basic referring terms, e.g. Hilbert numerals, and basic function symbols by the prescribed methods can be worked out in a finitary way.[21] Let us call these terms primitive recursive terms. The truth value of any equation or inequation between primitive recursive terms can be determined by computing the values of the terms and comparing them. Since the truth value of any combination of statements using truth functional connectives (e.g. conjunction, disjunction, and nega-tion) can be computed given the truth values of those statements, the truth values of any truth functional combination of equations and inequations whose terms are primitive recursive can be computed. Computing is what you expect it to be: determining an output value from some input values in a finite sequence of steps in accord with precise rules (equivalently, by follow-ing a program, that is, a finite sequence of precise instructions[22]). An illus-tration is given in part A of the appendix to this chapter. Computations can be represented as proofs in PRA.

The axioms include propositional axioms, e.g. the instances of A → (B → A), and equality axioms, the instances of $\tau = \tau$ and of Leibniz's Law that one term can be substituted for another to which it has been proven equal.[23] The rules include rules of substitution and Modus Ponens, and one contentious axiom or rule, free-variable induction. Here it is, in the form of a rule:

$$\frac{\varphi(1),\ \varphi(y) \to \varphi(sy)}{\varphi(y)}$$

where 'y' stands for a numerical variable and 'sy' is read 'the successor of y'.[24]

When is a purported proof of a finitary general proposition acceptable from the finitist standpoint? The answer is: when we have a finitary procedure for obtaining from the purported proof a finitary proof of any given instance of the general proposition. For instance, if from a purported proof of $\varphi(y)$ we can obtain a proof of $\varphi(n)$, for any number n, just by replacing 'y' throughout by the numeral for n, the purported proof is indeed a proof by finitary standards. For an example, see part B of the appendix to this chapter.

But a proof by induction cannot be turned into a proof of a given instance just by substituting the relevant numeral for the inductive variable. Suppose we have finitary proofs of

[a] $\varphi(1)$ and
[b] $\varphi(y) \to \varphi(sy)$

from which we inferred

[c] $\varphi(y)$.

This is an application of induction. But, taking the numerals to be '1' and any finite string of 's's followed by a '1', we do not get a finitary proof of $\varphi(ss1)$ by substituting 'ss1' for 'y' in [a], [b], and [c]. What we need to do is to write down after [a] and [b] the first two instances of [b]:

[b1] $\varphi(1) \to \varphi(s1)$
[b2] $\varphi(s1) \to \varphi(ss1)$

and then to apply Modus Ponens twice, starting with [a] and [b1], to get

[c1] $\varphi(s1)$,

and then to [c1] and [b2] to get

[c2] $\varphi(ss1)$.

The result is a clearly finitary proof of the desired instance of [c]. Obviously, the prescription can be generalized to obtain a finitary proof of any instance $\varphi(n)$.[25] This completes our sketch of finitary reasoning.

155

Conclusion

There are three quite distinct doctrines to which the title 'finitism' might be given, and all three get some airing in Hilbert's writings. Ontological finitism says that there are no infinite entities. Semantic finitism says that no statement alluding to an infinite entity expresses a genuine proposition. Epistemological finitism says that finitary reasoning is as secure as one could reasonably require, whereas non-finitary reasoning using classical logic introduces uncertainty, though it might be possible to show by finitary reasoning that formal counterparts of some non-finitary mathematics do not lead to absurdities.

As far as I am aware, there is no good reason to accept ontological or semantic finitism. Epistemological finitism is different. Finitary reasoning, in particular its embodiment in primitive recursive arithmetic, has a special kind of security, owing to the fact that it need involve nothing beyond the application of simple, precise rules of symbol manipulation, rules whose validity for finitary subject matter is obvious, given basic visual cognitive capacities. It is true that this will not ward off Cartesian global scepticism—probably nothing does that, and so it is unreasonable to require it. The claim for finitary reasoning is that it gives as much certainty as one could reasonably demand. Against this, it can be said that we are prone to make slips when manipulating symbol arrays of great length or complexity, and this can be a source of uncertainty. But presented with a particular sequence of moves, thorough checking of what is present at each stage of the sequence always makes clear whether it accords with the given rules of symbol manipulation. There is no possibility of error arising from vagueness or equivocation, since those kinds of error involve interpreting the symbol sequences and operating on the interpretations, rather than on the symbol sequences themselves. Moreover, the paradoxes were not produced by the kind of slip involved in erroneous symbol manipulation. In fact, they were not produced by a slip at all, that is by our failure to abide by rules or laws we have endorsed. The fault lay instead with the rules or laws. The class paradoxes, for example, depend on the law that for any precise condition there is a class of all entities that satisfy the condition, which is very far from being a finitary principle. So finitary reasoning is not prey to paradoxes of the kind that threaten non-finitary mathematics.

For Hilbert's foundational goal, it is only epistemological finitism that matters. One can coherently reject (or be agnostic about) ontological and semantic finitism and yet accept that, if Hilbert and his co-workers were to present a sound finitary argument for the consistency of set theory, that conclusion would thereby have been established beyond reasonable doubt. In fact, the merit of finitary reasoning as a tool in foundational studies lies partly in this very fact, that its reliability can be accepted by people of almost any philosophical persuasion.[26] So Hilbert was not at all irrational in hoping that finitary reasoning was the light by which the ghosts of paradox would be finally laid to rest. How Hilbert and his co-workers thought this could be accomplished is the subject of the next chapter.

APPENDIX

A: Sample definitions and a computation

Here are two definitions by recursion. First is the cut-off predecessor function:

$$p(1) = 1; \qquad p(sx) = x.$$

Second is the cut-off subtraction function $y - x$:

$$y - 1 = p(y); \qquad y - sx = p(y - x).$$

Here is a computation of the value of $sss1 - s1$ using the above:

$sss1 - s1$	
$p(sss1 - 1)$	(by definition of $-$)
$p(p(sss1))$	(by definition of $-$ and substitution)
$p(ss1)$	(by definition of p and substitution)
$s1$	(by definition of p and substitution).

B: A finitary proof of a finitary general proposition, without induction

We use a derived rule not mentioned in the chapter. 'Transitivity of $=$' is the rule: from $\rho = \sigma$ and $\sigma = \tau$ one can infer $\rho = \tau$.
The statement is [a]: $sx - s1 = x - 1$. Here is the proof:

(1)	$sx - s1 = p(sx - 1)$	(by definition of $-$)
(2)	$p(sx - 1) = p(p(sx))$	(by definition of $-$ and substitution)
(3)	$sx - s1 = p(p(sx))$	(from (1) and (2) by transitivity of $=$)
(4)	$p(p(sx)) = p(x)$	(by definition of p and substitution)
(5)	$sx - s1 = p(x)$	(from (3) and (4) by transitivity of $=$)
(6)	$p(x) = x - 1$	(by definition of $-$)
(7)	$sx - s1 = x - 1$	(from (5) and (6) by transitivity of $=$).

To obtain from this derivation a finitary proof that $sn - s1 = n - 1$, where 'n' stands in for a numeral, simply replace 'x' by the numeral n throughout.

Hilbert's Programme 4

Hilbert aimed to justify acceptance and use of arithmetic,[1] analysis, and set theory. A natural way of approaching this task is to look for indubitable truths to serve as axioms for a comprehensive theory, along with inference rules that are indubitably truth-preserving. This may have been Frege's approach, but following discovery of the contradiction, Russell concluded that some element of doubt about the truth of the axioms is unavoidable. The best one could hope for, on Russell's view, was that the axioms were inductively[2] well supported by their known consequences. Accordingly, Russell distinguished between epistemological foundations and deductive foundations.[3] In making this move, Russell had performed a half-revolution. The epistemological basis was now regarded as comprising the simplest and most immediately evident truths of mathematics, together with quasi-empirical induction. The goal, however, was still to establish the truth of the axioms, beyond reasonable doubt if not beyond all doubt. For this goal the permitted means were inadequate. Russell never found a sufficiently powerful set of axioms that he felt met the required standard. Had he abandoned the goal of a comprehensive theory and decided to treat the subjects of real analysis and transfinite sets separately, he would have fared no better: recall the troubles over Dedekind's Continuity Axiom, the Axiom of Infinity, and the Axiom of Choice.[4]

Justification for analysis and set theory must come in a different way. A successful foundational programme would need either a more modest goal than Russell's or a more secure means of achieving it. Hilbert's programme had both. The goal was no longer to establish the *truth* of theories of arithmetic, analysis, and transfinite sets, but to establish their finitary reliability. The permitted means for achieving this goal was not quasi-empirical induction but the methods of finitary reasoning. A theory has finitary reliability when it has no false finitary consequences. So the goal of Hilbert's programme, put in terms of his distinction between real and ideal statements, was to show that no conclusion one can reach using the ideal statements of arithmetic and the simplifying laws of classical logic is false, and the same for analysis and set theory in place of arithmetic. In short, to justify non-finitary means, finitary statements reached by those means must be true, and this must itself be shown by finitary means.[5] The finitary means to be used are captured by primitive recursive arithmetic, a proper part of arithmetic far removed from the axioms of higher mathematics.

Thus, Hilbert's programme completed the revolution began by Russell, inverting the foundationalism of Frege. Frege assumed the reliability of the axioms and rules of his system, whereas for Hilbert the reliability of the axioms and rules was what had to be shown: as Marx did to Hegel, so Hilbert did to Frege. This was an eminently sensible revolution: finitary arithmetic is much more evident to us than the axioms of analysis and set theory, not to mention the axioms of Frege's system. If Hilbert had no more than conceived of this approach to the foundations of mathematics, he would have deserved great credit. As it was, he and his co-worker Bernays developed an ingenious strategy.

The strategy, part (1): formalization

The strategy has two parts. The first is to set out arithmetic, analysis, and set theory as completely precise formal systems. The second is to show by finitary means that no finitary falsehood is derivable in any of these systems. The main concern was with analysis and set theory, as few doubted the reliability of arithmetic, that is, first-order Dedekind–Peano arithmetic. But the latter goes well beyond finitary arithmetic, that is, primitive recursive arithmetic; and so success in executing the strategy for arithmetic would have been a substantial rehearsal for dealing with analysis and set theory.

The first part of the strategy was relatively easy, though not trivial. The relevant theories had been axiomatized, to be sure, but formalization is a further step. A *formal system* is not just a set of axioms and inference rules, but a completely specified formal language together with a completely specified formal theorem-generator. These terms of art need explaining. Let us describe as *effective* any way of deciding some question that consists in a precise, determinate, and totally reliable procedure that terminates after a finite number of steps. Then we can define the terms as follows:

(I)   A *formal language* consists of a finite list of primitive symbols and a finite list of formation rules specified in a manner that provides an effective way of deciding, for any given string of primitive symbols, whether or not it is a formula.

(II)   A *formal theorem-generator* consists of, first, a collection of formulas, *axioms*, specified in a manner that provides an effective way of deciding, for any formula, whether or not it is an axiom; secondly, a finite collection of *inference rules* such that, for each rule, there is an effective way of deciding whether or not the last formula in any explicitly given finite sequence of formulas is obtainable by applying the rule to earlier formulas.

Two more definitions complete our account of a formal system. For a formal system T, a *derivation* in T is any finite sequence of formulas in the language of T each one of which is either an axiom of T or is obtainable from earlier formulas in the sequence by one of the inference rules of T. A *theorem* of T is the last formula of some derivation in T. It follows from these definitions that there is an effective way of deciding, for any given finite sequence of formulas in the language of T, whether or not it is a derivation in T.[6]

The strategy, part (2): reliability and consistency

Hilbert and his followers acknowledged that the task of formalizing arithmetic, analysis, and set theory was greatly facilitated by the efforts of Russell and Whitehead. It remained to construct formal systems for these theories in such a way that conditions (I) and (II) are clearly fulfilled. The second part of the strategy then comes into play. This is the hard part. The task is to show that the formal systems of arithmetic, analysis and set theory have no false finitary consequence. The immediate problem with this is that falsehood is a semantic concept rather than a formal concept. So the task must be reformulated if it is to be tractable by finitary means.

Each of the formal systems to be investigated contains finitary arithmetic, in the sense that we can specify a translation of the language of finitary arithmetic into the language of the formal system, such that the translation of each strictly finitary truth of arithmetic is a theorem of the system. We can be more specific. If T is a formalization of some mathematical theory, the *finitary theorems* of T are those theorems of T that are formalizations of finitary statements. Then the translation of finitary arithmetic into the formal language of T satisfies the following condition. If S is the set of T's finitary theorems, S will contain translations of the strictly finitary truths of arithmetic.

Because of this, it turns out that to establish T's reliability, i.e. that T has no false finitary consequence, it suffices to show of some particular finitary false-hood, e.g. that $1 \neq 1$, that its translation in the language of T is not derivable in T. So the notions of truth and falsehood would not have to be imported into the reasoning. The whole quest would then be reduced to establishing the purely formal claim that no derivation in T has as its last formula the T-trans-lation of '$1 \neq 1$' (or whatever strictly finitary falsehood is chosen).

How can it suffice to show this? In the case of arithmetic and analysis, the answer is fairly straightforward. For ease of exposition I will let the sentences '$1 \neq 1$' and '$1 = 1$' stand for their translations in T. Let T be a formal system of arithmetic or analysis, whichever is under investigation, and let S be T's fini-tary part. The sentences of S will all be arithmetical sentences, and they will include the translations of the strictly finitary truths of arithmetic. The argu-ment uses three facts about the formal logic of these systems. The first is that, if φ is derivable in T and χ is derivable in T, so is their conjunction $\varphi \,\&\, \chi$. This is known as &-*introduction*. The second is that, if the conjunction of a formu-la and its negation $\varphi \,\&\, \neg\varphi$ is derivable in T, so is any other formula of the lan-guage. This is known as the *inconsistency effect*.[7] The third is that, if a general formula $\varphi(x)$ with a free variable x is derivable in T, so is any numerical instance $\varphi(n)$. This is a subkind of the rule of *universal instantiation*.[8] For brevi-ty, I will call a formula in the language of T a finitary truth or falsehood if it is the formalization of finitary truth or falsehood. The argument runs as fol-lows. Let φ be any false finitary theorem of T. Then there are two possibilities: (i) φ is strictly finitary, or (ii) it is a finitary general statement. We consider each case in turn.

In case (i), $\neg\varphi$ is a strictly finitary truth of arithmetic, hence it is in S; as sen-tences in S are all theorems of T, $\neg\varphi$ is derivable in T. Since φ is derivable in T by hypothesis, the contradiction $\varphi \,\&\, \neg\varphi$ is derivable in T (by &-introduction); then '$1 \neq 1$' is derivable in T (by the inconsistency effect).

In case (ii) φ has some false instance χ whose negation $\neg\chi$ is a finitary truth of arithmetic; hence $\neg\chi$ is in S. As members of S are theorems of T, $\neg\chi$ is derivable in T. By hypothesis, φ is derivable in T, so χ is derivable in T (by universal instantiation). Hence $\chi \,\&\, \neg\chi$ is derivable in T; so '$1 \neq 1$' is derivable in T.

Therefore if some false finitary formula is derivable in T, so is '$1 \neq 1$'. (The converse is trivial.) It follows that we only need show that this single formula is not derivable in T, in order to establish that no false finitary formula is deriv-able in T. The argument for set theory is essentially the same but more com-plicated, so we leave it aside.

What has all this to do with consistency? The answer is that for the systems of concern to us the consistency of the system is equivalent to the underivability of a given false finitary formula in the system: show the latter and you have shown the former. A formal system is *consistent* if and only if there is no formula in the language of the system such that both it and its negation are derivable in the system. The equivalence is shown as follows. Suppose that '$1 \neq 1$' is derivable in T. As S contains all finitary arithmetical truths, it contains '$1 = 1$'; as the members of S are theorems of T, '$1 = 1$' is derivable in T. So both '$1 = 1$' and its negation '$1 \neq 1$' are derivable in T, and so T is inconsistent. Conversely, suppose T is inconsistent. Then some formula φ and its negation $\neg\varphi$ will both be derivable in T. So, by &-introduction and the inconsistency effect, '$1 \neq 1$' will be derivable in T. So T is inconsistent if and only if '$1 \neq 1$' is derivable in T.

So there are two characterizations of the aim of Hilbert's Programme: to show, of formal systems of arithmetic, analysis, and set theory, (a) that in none of the systems is a false finitary sentence derivable, and (b) that each system is consistent. For the standard formal systems of arithmetic, analysis, and set theory (a) and (b) are equivalent. As we have seen, to establish these claims it suffices to show that no derivation in the formalization has (the translation of) '$1 \neq 1$' as its last formula. Hilbert and his co-workers intended to do this by showing that every derivation in T of a finitary formula could be transformed by a finitary procedure into a derivation in a formal version of finitary arithmetic of the same formula. They had a specific kind of transformation in mind, and Ackermann and von Neumann had made enough progress by 1927 to inspire confidence that completion of the proof for arithmetic was just around the corner.

Objections and responses

Echoing Poincaré, Brouwer objected that the use of induction in a proof of the consistency of number theory would be circular.[9] The argument is that induction on the natural numbers would be needed in any proof of the consistency of a theory and yet induction is something that is not evident from the finitist point of view. This point can be met by distinguishing between unrestricted induction and induction on an effectively decidable quantifier-free predicate. Unrestricted induction does indeed lie beyond what is finitistically evident, since its instances may involve predicates with unbounded existential quantifiers. But induction on an effectively decidable predicate without quantifiers is finitistically acceptable, as was explained in the previous chapter, and it is this restricted form of induction that was to be used to establish consistency.

A more serious objection was voiced by Brouwer thus:

the (contentual) justification of formalistic mathematics by means of the proof of its consistency contains a vicious circle, since this justification rests upon the (contentual) correctness of the proposition that from the consistency of a proposition the correctness of the proposition follows . . .[10]

A consistent theory may be false. What Brouwer is adding here is that, for all we know, a consistent extension of finitary arithmetic into the non-finitary may be false; so a finitary proof of consistency of the extension cannot establish its correctness. This objection can be met. First, from Hilbert's point of view, non-finitary statements cannot be either true or false, being ideal rather than real propositions. But even if this response is set aside, the objection can be met. There is no need to establish the correctness of non-finitary theorems, since only instrumental reliability is required of a non-finitary formal system, and this requires the correctness of only its finitary consequences: a non-finitary extension of finitary arithmetic is reliable if and only if it has no false finitary consequences. But the consistency of any of the formal systems in question is equivalent to the underivability in the system of '$1 \neq 1$', and the latter entails that no false finitary sentence is derivable in the system, as was shown in the previous section for formal systems of arithmetic and analysis. So this was Hilbert's trump card: an extension of finitary arithmetic, if consistent, has no false finitary consequences. The converse follows by the inconsistency effect. The equivalence of consistency and finitary reliability for the systems of interest can be shown in a finitary way, so there is no circularity in taking finitary reliability to follow from consistency for those systems. In fairness to Brouwer, it must be noted that the equivalence of consistency and reliability was not mentioned by Hilbert until 1927, a few months before Brouwer made the criticism.[11] For years Hilbert had been stressing consistency, and he may himself have been unaware that consistency entails reliability in the relevant cases before 1927. None the less, Hilbert did find a perfectly cogent reply to this objection.

If the objection fails to dent Hilbert, it may yet worry those who do not accept that non-finitary statements lack truth value, and are not satisfied with instrumentalism about analysis and set theory. For we have no reason to think that the consistency of an extension of finitary arithmetic ensures that none of its *non*-finitary consequences is false. The response to this is

163

that it would still be valuable to establish consistency, since this would rule out the kind of incoherence exposed in Frege's theory by Russell's paradox; and it would establish finitary reliability, which guarantees instrumental utility. If consistency and finitary reliability of analysis and set theory were established, the continued investigation and use of these theories would be justified.

There was a rival programme that promised truth: Brouwer's intuitionism. Should Hilbert's Programme have been abandoned for intuitionism? No. Hilbert's Programme was both epistemologically safer than Brouwer's intuitionistic programme and mathematically less damaging: intuitionism was based on an abstract phenomenology of mental constructions that had not been made precise, whereas Hilbert's Programme was based on well defined mechanical reasoning about finite arrays of symbols; intuitionism banned the convenient and natural methods of classical analysis even after its rigorous reformulation, while Hilbert sought to justify them. If successful, Hilbert's Programme would have provided surer justification for classical mathematics than the intuitionists could provide for the restricted mathematics acceptable to them. It is not surprising then that Weyl, who had been sympathetic to Brouwer's outlook, accepted Hilbert's Programme once he realized that its success would establish the finitary reliability of classical mathematics.[12] Unfortunately, success was not to be had.

Part V
Gödel's Underivability Theorems

Incompleteness, and Undefinability of Truth

Hilbert's Programme placed formal systems at the centre of foundational research. This work was proceeding apace in the late 1920s in the direction that Hilbert envisaged. Then in 1931 a paper was published by Gödel, then only 25, that was to change the landscape of foundational studies permanently. This paper contained a couple of theorems about formal systems of great significance, and presented a new and powerful technique for metamathematics (the study of formal systems). This chapter presents the first of these two theorems, plus a related theorem of Tarski, and then assesses their wider significance. The following chapter then presents the second theorem and assesses its significance.

The significance of these theorems is a controversial and delicate matter. In order to make any real headway, some background is needed. In particular, one needs to have some grasp of what came to be known as the arithmetization of syntax, a central technique of metamathematics invented by Gödel. I will call it *coding*, for short. This will also provide the basis for a proper understanding of the theorems and of the lines of thought leading to them.

Coding

Hilbert intended to show that formal systems of arithmetic, analysis, and set theory were consistent by applying the resources of finitary arithmetic to the syntactic objects of the systems and to formal properties of those objects. A formal system, recall, has a list of primitive symbols; the syntactic objects of the system comprise those symbols and finite strings of them, and finite sequences of those strings. Formal properties of syntactic objects include those of being a term, being a formula, and being a derivation in the system, a derivation being the formal counterpart of a proof. Gödel realized that one could conduct finitary reasoning about the syntactic objects of a formal system and their formal properties without any explicit mention of those objects and properties, by using numbers as codes for the objects and by using arithmetical conditions to represent formal properties. This can be done in such a way that arguments about the formal system can be expressed entirely within finitary arithmetic. As the formal systems of concern have the resources of finitary arithmetic needed for expressing those arguments, one can use each of these systems to reason about that very system within itself.

First, Gödel showed how to specify an enumeration of the syntactic objects of any given formal system T. (From now, 'T' will be used for any formal system of the kind under discussion.) The place of a syntactic object in the specified enumeration is known as its Gödel-number or code. If α is a syntactic object I will use '$\lceil \alpha \rceil$' for the *numeral* in the language of T that denotes the code number of α. No harm is done if we say that α's code numeral (as well as its code number) *codes* α. We can ensure that the coding fulfils the following condition: each syntactic object is assigned a unique code number in such a way that (i) given any syntactic object, we can compute its code numeral, and (ii) given any numeral, we can decide whether it codes a syntactic object and, if so, we can tell which syntactic object it codes. Encoding and decoding are finitary processes of computation. There are many different codes fulfilling these conditions. Any textbook in mathematical logic will provide an example.

The second part of Gödel's idea is that one can represent formal properties, such as that of being a derivation in T, by means of arithmetical predicates. For each relevant formal property F Gödel showed how to find an arithmetical predicate that is true of exactly those numbers that code syntactic objects having F. Let us look into this. Let S be a theory of arithmetic including PRA. A formal property F (of the system T) is *represented* in S by a predicate $\varphi(x)$ in the language of S if and only if the following two conditions hold: for any numeral **n** in the language of S,

(1)   if **n** codes an object that has F, $\varphi(\mathbf{n})$ is derivable in S, and

(2)   if **n** does not code an object that has F, $\neg\varphi(\mathbf{n})$ is derivable in S,

where '$\neg\theta$' stands for the negation of θ. This definition can be extended in a fairly obvious way to cover formal relations, such as 'x is a derivation in T of y'.[1] Assuming that S is true (under its intended arithmetical interpretation), it follows that, for any predicate φ representing property F in S,

α has F if and only if $\varphi(\lceil \alpha \rceil)$ is true,

where α is a syntactic object of the system T and $\varphi(\ulcorner \alpha \urcorner)$ has its standard arithmetical interpretation. In this case, the predicate φ is true of just those num-
bers that code objects having F. In some cases of interest, S is *contained in* T, in
the sense that S is (or is translatable into) a subtheory of T. In that case syntactic features of T can be internally represented.

In some expositions of these matters, once it is established that a predicate
φ represents in S a formal property F, it is said that the sentence $\varphi(\ulcorner \alpha \urcorner)$ 'says
that' or 'expresses that' α has F. This is misleading, even when S is a true the-
ory of arithmetic. In that case, φ's representing F guarantees that '. . . has F'
and '$\varphi(\ulcorner . . . \urcorner)$' are co-extensional. But it does not guarantee that the latter,
when decoded, means the same as the former.[2] Crucially, for some predicates
representing a formal property F it will not be possible to tell just by decoding
them that they represent F.[3] There is no general procedure for determining
which formal property, if any, is represented by a given predicate. For these
reasons we should not think that, because arithmetical predicate φ represents
F in a true formal system of arithmetic, the arithmetical sentence $\varphi(\ulcorner \alpha \urcorner)$ *says*
or *expresses* in code that α has F. Expressing, unlike representing, requires that
we should be able to tell which formal property is represented just by decoding the numerical terms while keeping the definition of the formal property
in mind. That can be done when the representing predicate φ is constructed
in parallel with the definition of F. The idea of parallel construction can best
be conveyed by means of an illustration. Suppose the primitive symbols of
the language of T include the following:

- an individual constant **0** (for zero)
- infinitely many individual variables $\mathbf{v}_i$ for $i = 1, 2, 3, . . .$[4]
- a unary operation symbol **s** (for the successor operation)
- a binary operation symbol + (for addition)
- another binary operation symbol × (for multiplication).

Suppose also that the formal property of being a *term* of the language of T is
defined recursively as follows:

α is a *term* if and only if α is **0** or, for some i, α is $\mathbf{v}_i$ or, for some terms **r**
and **t**, α is **sr** or + **rt** or × **rt**.

Suppose now that the codes of the symbols listed above are defined as follows:

$\ulcorner \mathbf{0} \urcorner = 1$,
$\ulcorner \mathbf{v}_i \urcorner = 3^i$,

and, where **r** and **t** are terms,

$$\lceil sr \rceil = 2 \times 3^{\lceil r \rceil},$$
$$\lceil +rt \rceil = 4 \times 3^{\lceil r \rceil} \times 5^{\lceil t \rceil},$$
$$\lceil \times rt \rceil = 8 \times 3^{\lceil r \rceil} \times 5^{\lceil t \rceil}.$$

We can now construct an arithmetical predicate $\tau(x)$ true of just the code numbers of terms of T by proceeding in parallel with the definition of 'term' given above:

$\tau(x)$ if and only if $x = 1$, or, for some $u < x$, $x = 3^u$, or, for some $u < x$ and some $v < x$, $\tau(u)$ and $\tau(v)$ and [$x = 2 \times 3^u$, or $x = 4 \times 3^u \times 5^v$, or $x = 8 \times 3^u \times 5^v$].

This can be transcribed in formal languages containing (directly or by translation) the language of arithmetic. From the definition of 'term' and the specified coding of terms, we can tell from this definition of τ that it is true of just those numbers that code terms, simply by decoding the numerical expressions.[5] In this case, then, it is reasonable to regard the arithmetical sentence $\tau(\lceil \alpha \rceil)$ as saying or expressing that α is a term.

In general, if $\varphi(x)$ is a predicate that represents in S a formal property F, $\varphi(\lceil \alpha \rceil)$ *expresses* the proposition that α has F if and only if the construction of $\varphi(x)$ parallels the definition of F. This can be extended to cover formal relations, such as 'α is a derivation in T of β'. In what follows I will use '$\mathrm{Pr}_T(x, y)$' for a two-place predicate that both represents in S the relation 'α is a derivation in T of β' and is constructed in parallel with the recursive definition of that relation. So for syntactic objects α, β of the language of T, the sentence $\mathrm{Pr}_T(\lceil \alpha \rceil, \lceil \beta \rceil)$ expresses in code the proposition that α is a derivation in T of β.

Coding the syntactic objects of the language of a formal system T, constructing arithmetical predicates in parallel with the recursive definitions of formal properties of the syntactic objects, and showing that those predicates represent in S those properties and relations—all this is much of the work involved in the proofs of Gödel's Underivability Theorems. Gödel showed that this could be done provided that S contains the resources of a certain finitary portion of arithmetic, known as primitive recursive arithmetic (PRA), which can be thought of as explicitly computable arithmetic.[6]

Self-reference and Tarski's theorem on the undefinability of truth

By means of the arithmetization of syntax just described, Gödel devised a way of formulating self-referring expressions. Let T be a formal system containing a formal theory S of arithmetic encompassing PRA, and let $\varphi(x)$ be a formula in the language of T with just one free variable (i.e. a one-place pred-icate). We can then consider sentences of the form $\varphi(\ulcorner \alpha \urcorner)$, where α is a syntactic object in the language of T. It is possible to show within S that, for any one-place predicate φ of T, there is a sentence β in the language of T that is equivalent in S to the sentence $\varphi(\ulcorner \beta \urcorner)$:

$$\beta \leftrightarrow \varphi(\ulcorner \beta \urcorner).$$

This is known as the *Diagonalization Lemma*. See the appendix to this chapter for a proof-sketch of it and an explanation of its name. Its significance is that, if φ represents a formal property F of sentences, and if the construction of φ parallels the definition of F, then some sentence β expresses the claim that β itself has F.

This kind of self-reference is involved in the Liar paradox, which was set out in Part III Chapter 3. The Liar says 'I am now lying' or 'This statement is not true.' Should we not fear that the diagonalization lemma leads to the Liar's self-contradiction? No. That would be to assume that there is an arithmetization of the property of *being untrue*. Noticing this, Tarski argued that the property of being a true arithmetical sentence is not defin-able in arithmetic. The argument is so simple that I will present it here. Let $\mathscr{L}$ be a formal language of arithmetic. A property F of sentences of $\mathscr{L}$ is *definable in arithmetic* when there is a one-place arithmetical predicate φ such that, for every number n, $\varphi(\mathbf{n})$ is a truth of arithmetic if and only if n is the code of a sentence in $\mathscr{L}$ that has the property F.[7] The argument is a *reductio ad absurdum*. Suppose that the property of being an arithmetical truth is arithmetically definable. Then there is an arithmetical predicate $Tr(x)$ true of exactly those numbers that code sentences in $\mathscr{L}$ that are true given their standard arithmetical interpretation. So, for any sentence χ in $\mathscr{L}$, χ is true if and only if $Tr(\ulcorner \chi \urcorner)$ is true. In short,

(i) $\chi \leftrightarrow Tr(\ulcorner \chi \urcorner)$.

Now consider the negation of $Tr(x)$. This is a predicate of $\mathscr{L}$ which, given our initial supposition, arithmetically defines failure to be an arithmetical truth. So, by the Diagonalization Lemma, there is a sentence β of $\mathscr{L}$ that says 'β is not an arithmetical truth.' More precisely, there is a sentence β such that

(ii) $\beta \leftrightarrow \neg Tr(\ulcorner \beta \urcorner)$.

Since (i) holds for any sentence of $\mathscr{L}$, it holds for β:

(iii) $\beta \leftrightarrow Tr(\ulcorner \beta \urcorner)$.

Two claims equivalent to a third are equivalent to each other; hence

$$\text{Tr}(\lceil \beta \rceil) \leftrightarrow \neg \text{Tr}(\lceil \beta \rceil).$$

This is absurd; so the property of being an arithmetical truth is not arithmetically definable.

That is Tarski's *Undefinability-of-Truth* Theorem. It is one of several discoveries indicating that it is impossible to pin down mathematical truth, even arithmetical truth. This was important at the time (the early 1930s) when the idea of a realm of mathematical entities that are abstract and independent of human intellectual constructions was widely felt to be vacuous metaphysics. A concept of mathematical truth is admissible, it was believed, only if it can be explicated without a commitment to any such realm. For a more precise grasp of the significance of Tarski's theorem, we need to see it in the context of Gödel's earlier First Underivability Theorem.[8]

Incompleteness

Gödel's proof of his underivability theorems also involves self-reference. Let T be any formal system containing PRA. Having constructed a formula $\text{Pr}_T(x, y)$ in the language of T that expresses the relation 'is a derivation in T of', Gödel constructed a sentence γ in the language of T that says of itself that it is not derivable in T. Let us look into this. $\text{Pr}_T(x, y)$ expresses in PRA, hence in T, the relation 'is a derivation in T of'. So $\neg \text{Pr}_T(x, y)$ expresses 'is not a derivation in T of'. Then binding the x with a universal quantifier prefix gives a predicate $\forall x \neg \text{Pr}_T(x, y)$, which says that, for every x, x is not the code of a derivation in T of the formula coded by y. Using '$\langle n \rangle$' for the syntactic object coded by n, the predicate means that for no x is $\langle x \rangle$ a derivation in T of $\langle y \rangle$. In short, the predicate $\forall x \neg \text{Pr}_T(x, y)$ expresses the property of being underivable in T. By the Diagonalization Lemma, there is a sentence γ in the language of the arithmetical part of T which is equivalent in T to a sentence that expresses that γ is underivable in T:

$$\gamma \leftrightarrow \forall x \neg \text{Pr}_T(x, \lceil \gamma \rceil).$$

A formula fulfilling this condition is a *Gödel sentence* for T. From this equivalence, we know that γ is true if and only if it is underivable in T. We also know that, if γ were derivable in T, T would be inconsistent: for some numeral $\mathbf{n}$, $\text{Pr}_T(\mathbf{n}, \lceil \gamma \rceil)$ would be true and, as T contains PRA, derivable in T; and as both γ and the above equivalence would be derivable in T, the sentence

$\forall x \neg \text{Pr}_T(x, \ulcorner \gamma \urcorner)$ would also be derivable in T; hence $\neg \text{Pr}_T(\mathbf{n}, \ulcorner \gamma \urcorner)$ would also be derivable in T.[9] Hence both $\text{Pr}_T(\mathbf{n}, \ulcorner \gamma \urcorner)$ and its negation would be derivable in T, and T would be inconsistent. This yields the first part of Gödel's First Underivability Theorem:

> Let T be a formal system containing PRA.
> (i) If T is consistent, γ is underivable in T.

The proof of the second part of the theorem is more complicated and so I will just state it. It requires T to have a stronger condition than consistency, called ω-consistency.[10] The second part of the theorem is:

> (ii) if T is ω-consistent, $\neg\gamma$ is underivable in T.

A formal system T is defined to be *incomplete* if and only if there is a sentence α in the language of T such that neither α nor its negation is derivable in T.[11] So the theorem's import can be stated thus:

> Any ω-consistent formal system containing PRA is incomplete.

A few years after Gödel proved this, it was shown by Rosser that if, in place of the Gödel sentence γ expressing its own unprovability, one used a sentence δ expressing a certain more complicated claim, the condition of ω-consistency could be replaced by simple consistency: neither δ nor its negation is derivable in T, if T is consistent.[12] So the theorem, sometimes called the Gödel–Rosser Theorem, can be summed up thus:

> Any consistent formal system containing PRA is incomplete.

This is the First Underivability Theorem.

Incompleteness via the undefinability of truth

There is a close link between the undefinability of truth and incompleteness, which Gödel himself made clear in lectures he gave in 1934.[13] Let T be a formal system of number theory containing PRA, and let '$\mathcal{L}(T)$' be the formal language of T. Suppose now that T is arithmetically *sound*, in the sense that every T-derivable sentence is true when standardly interpreted as a sentence of arithmetic. The Liar's self-contradiction would be reproducible in arithmetic if 'being a true sentence of $\mathcal{L}(T)$' were representable in T; so it is not. But 'being a T-derivable sentence of $\mathcal{L}(T)$' is representable in T, as T contains PRA. So the class of codes of true sentences of $\mathcal{L}(T)$ does not coincide with the class of codes of T-derivable sentences of $\mathscr{L}$(T). So there must either be a sentence of $\mathscr{L}$(T) that is true but underivable in T, or a sentence of $\mathscr{L}$(T) that is derivable in T but untrue. The latter, however, is ruled out by the soundness of T: all T-derivable sentences are true. Hence there must be a sentence α that is a truth of arithmetic but underivable in T. As α is true, its negation ¬α is untrue; and so, by the soundness of T, ¬α is underivable in T. Hence both α and its negation ¬α are underivable in T; that is, T is incomplete. Thus, consideration of the Liar paradox reveals that any sound formal system of arithmetic containing PRA is incomplete. This theorem is weaker than the First Underivability Theorem for systems of arithmetic, as the latter attributes incompleteness to all *consistent* systems of arithmetic containing PRA rather than to all *sound* systems of arithmetic containing PRA, and consistency is a less demanding condition than soundness.[14]

Gödel first discovered the incompleteness of number theory in this way, reaching the weaker incompleteness theorem from considering the Liar's self-contradiction.[15] The point of then attempting to prove incompleteness for consistent (rather than sound) systems was not just because consistency is a lighter condition than soundness, but also because consistency is a syntactic concept that was accepted by all, whereas the concept of soundness, which involves a notion of truth applicable to non-finitary sentences, would have been regarded with suspicion by finitists and by influential philosophers of the time.

The significance of Gödel's First Underivability Theorem

What is the significance of the First Underivability Theorem? Large claims have been made for the significance of this theorem regarding the nature of human minds, a subject beyond the concerns of this book.[16] What is the theorem's significance for the philosophy of mathematics? In my judgement, the theorem bears on the nature of mathematical truth and mathematical existence, concerns central to the philosophy of mathematics. In the rest of this chapter I will substantiate this claim, and will then turn to the question of the theorem's bearing on Hilbert's Programme.

Truth and derivability

One consequence of the theorem is that a formal system of mathematics, however comprehensive, cannot be totally comprehensive. Thus, the goal of a formal all-encompassing set of principles of mathematics is unachievable. But this, Gödel pointed out, was known prior to his discovery of incompleteness. For if T is or contains a formal system of analysis, the real numbers definable in the language of T can be enumerated; then, by diagonalizing,[17] we can define a real number not among those definable in T. This definition will not be in the language of T, and so true statements involving the term introduced by this definition will not be derivable in T. What Gödel's First Underivability Theorem adds is that, even if we confine ourselves to truths expressible in the language of T, not all of them are derivable in T, unless T is inconsistent; and this holds for any formal system containing PRA. It follows that for any such system truth in the language of the system cannot be equated with derivability in the system. Prior to Gödel's discovery, derivability in an adequate formalization of arithmetic was thought to be a possible way of pinning down the notion of truth in the language of arithmetic; similarly for analysis and set theory. Gödel showed that this was not so.

Tarski's theorem extends this message. Derivability in T, where T contains PRA, can be represented by an arithmetical predicate of a fairly low level of quantificational complexity. Tarski showed that no arithmetical predicate, however complex, represents the property of being a true sentence of arithmetic. If, as seems plausible, all purely formal properties are representable in arithmetic at some level, truth in the language of arithmetic cannot be reduced to a formal property. The hope of accommodating a concept of arithmetical truth (let alone mathematical truth) within a philosophy that abhors the abstract was dealt a severe blow by these theorems of Gödel and Tarski.

Existence and consistency

A quarter of a century before Hilbert's major statement of his finitist philosophy, Hilbert had espoused a view apparently in conflict with it: namely, that the consistency of an axiom system guarantees the existence of a domain of entities about which the axioms and their consequences are true. One expression of this view can be found in his famous address to the International Congress of Mathematicians held in Paris in 1900. Talking about an axiom system for real-number arithmetic, Hilbert said:

the proof of the consistency of the axioms is at the same time the proof of the mathematical existence of the totality of real numbers or of the continuum. Once the proof of the consistency of the axioms has been fully accomplished, the doubts occasionally expressed as to the existence of the totality of real number will become completely groundless.[18]

To see the relevance of Gödel's First Underivability Theorem to the view that consistency entails existence, we need some preliminary reminders about formal languages and their logic.

The language of a formal system has syntax, that is, a specification of its primitive symbols and of various categories of primitive and complex symbols such as variables, terms, and formulas. It also has semantics. This includes a specification of the ingredients for an interpretation: a domain, relations and operations on the domain, and distinguished elements. An example might be the set of natural numbers, the operations of successor, plus, and times, and the distinguished element zero. Also included in the semantics is an assignment of these ingredients to some of the symbols. For example, one could assign to each symbol of the form 'v_n' the set of natural numbers as its range of variation, to the symbols 's', '+', '×' the operations for successor, plus, and times, and to the symbol '0' the number zero. Then the semantics gives a recursive definition of the denotations of terms, and finally a recursive definition of the truth of sentences under the given interpretation.[19]

There is an important semantic distinction between first-order languages and second-order languages. A first-order language has variables that range over elements of the domain, which we may call first-order variables, but no other variables. A second-order language has first-order variables and in addition variables that range over *subsets* of the domain, second-order variables. Hilbert and Ackermann devised a derivation system for first-order languages and showed that it was sound, in the sense that, if sentence α is derivable from a set of sentences Γ, α is a semantic consequence of Γ.[20] As before, a set of sentences Γ is consistent if and only if there is no contradictory pair of sentences α and ¬α both of which are derivable from Γ. So consistency is relative to a derivation system. Using a definite first-order language and derivation system, Gödel showed that for any consistent set of sentences Γ, there is an interpretation under which all the sentences of Γ are true; or, as we now say, if Γ is consistent Γ has a model. Gödel's proof of this can be adapted to reproduce the result for the other usual first-order languages and derivations systems. Summarizing, we can say that any consistent first-order theory has a model.[21] So this is a partial vindication of the view that the consistency of an axiom system ensures the existence of a model of it.[22] It is only partial, because the result covers only first-order axiom systems.[23]

Can the result be extended to second-order axiom systems? Given that the formalized second-order version of Dedekind–Peano arithmetic is consistent, the answer is: No. This is established by the First Underivability

Theorem, in the light of a theorem of Dedekind. I will say why this is so after explaining the difference between the first-order and second-order versions of Dedekind–Peano arithmetic (DPA).[24] The difference lies in the way that the principle of induction is presented. In the first-order version the principle is fragmented into infinitely many axioms, the instances of the single axiom schema:

$$[\varphi(\mathbf{0}) \ \& \ \forall \mathbf{v}_0(\varphi(\mathbf{v}_0) \to \varphi(\mathbf{sv}_0))] \to \forall \mathbf{v}_0 \varphi(\mathbf{v}_0).$$

The symbol 'φ' here is purely schematic; its role is to mark the place of a predicate in the first-order language of arithmetic. In second-order DPA the principle is captured by a single second-order axiom:

$$\forall R \, ([\, R(\mathbf{0}) \ \& \ \forall \mathbf{v}_0(R(\mathbf{v}_0) \to R(\mathbf{sv}_0))] \to \forall \mathbf{v}_0 R(\mathbf{v}_0)).$$

The symbol 'R' is a second-order variable. In the intended interpretation it ranges over sets of natural numbers.[25] The sentence says that, for any set of natural numbers, if zero is in it and the successor of each of its members is also in it, then all natural numbers are in it. This applies both to sets of natural numbers that are definable by some first-order condition and to those that are not so definable. Second-order DPA also includes a restricted comprehension axiom schema:

There is an S such that, for all n, S(n) if and only if $\varphi(n)$,

where '$\varphi(n)$' is a predicate in the language of second-order arithmetic and 'S' is a variable intended to range over sets of natural numbers. As first-order formulas are included in the language of second-order arithmetic, every sentence derivable using the first-order induction schema is derivable using the second-order induction axiom plus the second-order comprehension schema. The converse is clearly not true.

Let us return to the question whether the consistency of a system entails the existence of a model of it. Dedekind proved that any two models of *second*-order DPA are isomorphic.[26] The relevant background fact is that any sentence true in a model M is true in any model isomorphic to M; so if α is true in M, α is true in all models isomorphic to M and, therefore, $\neg\alpha$ is false in all models isomorphic to M (including of course M itself). Writing '$\mathfrak{N}$' for the standard model of second-order DPA, it follows that:

If α is true in $\mathfrak{N}$, $\neg\alpha$ is false in any model of second-order DPA.

Call this the Dedekind fact. Let T be second-order DPA, which certainly incorporates PRA. Then the first part of Gödel's original version of the First

Underivability Theorem applies to T: if T is consistent, the Gödel sentence γ for T is underivable in T. As we are assuming that T has a model, hence that T is consistent,[27] this has the following relevant consequences. (i) The theory $T+\neg\gamma$ that results from adding $\neg\gamma$ to T's axioms is consistent.[28] And, as γ is true in the standard model $\mathfrak{N}$ of T if and only if γ is underivable in T, (ii) γ is true in $\mathfrak{N}$. Applying the Dedekind fact to (ii), it follows that $\neg\gamma$ is *false* in all models of T. So (iii) $T+\neg\gamma$ has no model. Putting (i) and (iii) together, we see that $T+\neg\gamma$ is a counterexample to the claim that every consistent theory has a model.[29]

Consistency then does not guarantee existence. Still, consistency does entail existence for first-order theories, and so one might think that the exceptions are of marginal significance. That would not be right. The theories that best capture our beliefs about natural numbers, real numbers, and sets are second-order,[30] and so some second-order theories are highly significant. Mathematical discourse is thoroughly committed to realms of abstract entities, and that commitment cannot be justified by reference to the consistency of formalizations of the relevant theories. Still less can one reconstrue apparent commitment to a realm of some kind of mathematical entity, such as the natural numbers, as commitment to nothing more than the consistency of a formal theory of entities of that kind: one cannot shed the metaphysical burden of talk about the existence of models by shifting down to talk about formal consistency.

Finitary truth and derivability

From the finitist point of view, the questions of the truth of a theory such as first or second-order DPA, and of the existence of a model of the theory, have no finitary content. So the fact that truth (as non-finitistically conceived) does not coincide with derivability, and the fact that consistency does not guarantee existence, would not worry a finitist of the Hilbert mould. But finitists may be disturbed by the First Underivability Theorem for other reasons. For they may believe that finitary truths are just those that can be proved by finitary means, and that finitary proof in arithmetic can be precisely captured by derivability in a formal system of finitary arithmetic. If that were right, there would be a way of pinning down finitary arithmetical truth to something fairly concrete, namely, derivability in a formal system of finitary arithmetic. However, Gödel's proof of his First Underivability Theorem shows that truth in finitary arithmetic does not amount to derivability in a formal system of finitary arithmetic. Let S be a formal system of finitary arithmetic. Then S will be consistent and will contain PRA.[31] So, given a coding for the language of S, the Gödel sentence for S—call it γ—is not derivable in S. But γ is inter-derivable in S with the finitary general sentence $\neg Pr_S(x, \lceil \gamma \rceil)$, a true sentence that expresses the underivability in S of γ. So there will be a finitary truth not derivable in an adequate formalization of finitary arithmetic. Finitists may well have been surprised by this. Either truth in finitary arithmetic does not coincide with finitary provability (for arithmetic), or finitary provability cannot be precisely captured by derivability in a formal system. Either way, finitary arithmetical truth does not have the unproblematic character of the syntactic property of derivability.[32]

Is Hilbert's Programme blocked by the First Underivability Theorem?

It has been contended that the goal of Hilbert's Programme is shown to be unattainable by the First Underivability Theorem.[33] Recall that the goal was to show the finitary reliability of number theory, analysis, and set theory. This was to be done by showing that formal number theory is conservative over its finitary part; and the same was then to be shown for formal theories of analysis and set theory. A formal theory T is *conservative over* a subtheory S just when every formula in the language of S that is derivable in T is also derivable in S. So it was to be shown that any finitary formula derivable in formal first-order DPA is already derivable in its finitary part. The alleged problem for Hilbert's Programme is that Gödel's result gives reason to doubt that formal number theory is conservative over its finitary part. Let S be a formalization of finitary arithmetic and T its extension to number theory, and for a given coding let γ be the Gödel sentence for S. Then γ is a finitary general formula which, by part (i) of the First Underivability Theorem, is not derivable in S, as S is consistent and contains PRA. But γ may be derivable in T, and if it is, T is not conservative over S.[34] If T is a formal system of analysis or set theory, γ will be derivable in T. So Hilbert's Programme, at least for analysis and set theory, appears doomed by the First Underivability Theorem.

This argument has been cogently rebutted by Detlefsen.[35] To spell this out we need a definition: a finitary sentence α is *refutable* in S if and only if $\neg \alpha$ is derivable in S or, if α is a finitary general sentence $\varphi(x_1, \ldots, x_k)$, a counterinstance $\neg \varphi(\mathbf{n}_1, \ldots, \mathbf{n}_k)$ is derivable in S. The goal of Hilbert's Programme is to show that there are proper formalizations of arithmetic, analysis, and set theory in which no false finitary sentence is derivable. Suppose that finitary sentence α is false. If α is not a general sentence, its falsehood can be shown by a finitary calculation which can be transformed into a derivation in S of $\neg\alpha$; if α is a general sentence $\varphi(x_1, \ldots, x_k)$, it has a false instance $\varphi(\mathbf{n}_1, \ldots, \mathbf{n}_k)$, and as this is a non-general finitary sentence its negation $\neg\varphi(\mathbf{n}_1, \ldots, \mathbf{n}_k)$ is derivable in S. So any finitary sentence of arithmetic that is false is refutable in S; and, as S is by stipulation a correct formalization of finitary arithmetic, any finitary sentence of arithmetic that is refutable in S is false. In sum, for finitary arithmetic, falsehood coincides with refutability in S. Hence, taking T to be an adequate formalization of arithmetic (or analysis, or set theory) that contains S, the desired conclusion of Hilbert's Programme can be restated thus: for any finitary sentence[36] of arithmetic α,

> if α is derivable in T, α is not refutable in S.

That is the finitary reliability of T. Detlefsen points out that this is not the same as the conservativeness of T over S: for any finitary sentence of arithmetic α,

> if α is derivable in T, α is derivable in S.

The impossibility of showing the finitary reliability of T could be validly inferred from the impossibility of showing that T is conservative over S only if we knew that any finitary sentence of arithmetic that is not refutable in S is derivable in S. But the First Underivability Theorem shows that this is not so: the Gödel sentence for S (shorn of its initial universal quantifier) is a finitary general arithmetical sentence in the language of S that is neither derivable in S nor refutable in S, as S is ω-consistent.[37] So the impossibility of showing that T is conservative over S does not, on its own, entail the impossibility of showing that T is reliable with respect to finitary claims.

It is true that the *strategy* used by Hilbert and his colleagues for their goal was to find a way of showing that every derivation in T of a finitary sentence could be transformed into a derivation of the same sentence in S, and that would be a way of proving conservativeness of T over S. We may conclude then that this strategy cannot succeed; but this leaves open the possibility of achieving the goal of Hilbert's Programme by some other strategy. This possibility is discussed in the next chapter, on Gödel's Second Underivability Theorem and its significance.

Appendix: The Diagonalization Lemma

Let T be a formal system containing a true arithmetical theory S encompassing PRA. The one-place predicates of T can be effectively enumerated φ_0, φ_1,

$\varphi_2, \ldots$ according to the size of their code numbers. Then we can think of the codes of all formulas of the form $\varphi_k(\lceil \varphi_j \rceil)$ as if set out in a rectangular array, with the code of $\varphi_k(\lceil \varphi_j \rceil)$ in the kth row and jth column. Of interest to us is the diagonal of this array, which consists of codes of sentences of the form $\varphi_k(\lceil \varphi_k \rceil)$. We can define a primitive recursive function $\mathbf{d}$ such that $\mathbf{d}(\lceil \varphi_k \rceil) = \lceil \varphi_k(\lceil \varphi_k \rceil) \rceil$. This is known as the diagonal function. To spell this out, let $\langle n \rangle =$ the expression coded by n. Then $\langle n \rangle$ is φ if and only if n is $\lceil \varphi \rceil$. The *diagonal function* $\mathbf{d}$ is defined so that:

$$\mathbf{d}(n) = \lceil \langle n \rangle(n) \rceil \quad \text{if } n \text{ codes a one-place predicate;}$$
$$= n \quad \text{if not.}$$

With this diagonal function, a certain kind of self-reference can be achieved in a wide range of cases. The argument is this. Let $\mathbf{d}$ be transcribed in the language of S, hence of T. This is possible because $\mathbf{d}$ is a primitive recursive function. Let $\varphi(y)$ be any one-place predicate in the language of T. Put '$\varphi(\mathbf{d}(x))$' for the result of replacing all occurrences of the free variable 'y' in $\varphi(y)$ by occurrences of '$\mathbf{d}(x)$'. For ease of comprehension, we let $\mathbf{m} = \lceil \varphi(\mathbf{d}(x)) \rceil$ and we let α be the sentence '$\varphi(\mathbf{d}(\mathbf{m}))$'. Then

$$\mathbf{d}(\mathbf{m}) = \lceil \langle \mathbf{m} \rangle(\mathbf{m}) \rceil \quad \text{[by definition of } \mathbf{d}]$$
$$= \lceil \varphi((\mathbf{d}(x))(\mathbf{m}) \rceil \quad \text{[by definition of } \mathbf{m}]$$
$$= \lceil \varphi(\mathbf{d}(\mathbf{m})) \rceil = \lceil \alpha \rceil \quad \text{[by definition of } \alpha].$$

Hence $\varphi(\mathbf{d}(\mathbf{m}))$ is equivalent in S to $\varphi(\lceil \alpha \rceil)$. Hence, by the definition of α,

α is equivalent to $\varphi(\lceil \alpha \rceil)$.

This is the Diagonalization Lemma. Its significance is that, given any one-place predicate $\varphi(y)$ of T, we can construct a sentence α of T that is true (under its arithmetical interpretation) if and only if α has the property represented by $\varphi(y)$.

Underivability of 'Consistency'

Gödel's Second Underivability Theorem is widely thought to pose a direct threat to Hilbert's Programme. It is sometimes referred to as the 'unprovability of consistency' and glossed as showing that a proof of the consistency of a theory that contains a bit of arithmetic must depend on assumptions that lie beyond the theory itself. It is impossible to assess such claims about the implications of Gödel's Second Underivability Theorem without going some way into the fine print. This requires that we keep in mind the facts about coding and arithmetization of syntax mentioned in the last chapter. This chapter outlines the proof and then turns to the controversial matter of the theorem's significance for Hilbert's Programme.

The path to the theorem

Let T be a formal system containing primitive recursive arithmetic (PRA). To describe the path to the theorem, a fixed coding of the language of T is assumed. Let $Pr_T(x, y)$ be a two-place predicate in the language of T that both represents in T the syntactic relation 'x is a derivation in T of y' *and* is constructed in parallel with the recursive definition of that relation. As $Pr_T(x, y)$ is constructed that way, one can tell by decoding the predicate that it represents that relation. For this reason we say that the predicate *expresses* in code[1] 'x is a derivation in T of y'. For any syntactic object α, let $\lceil \alpha \rceil$ be the code numeral of α in the language of T. So for syntactic objects α, β of the language of T, the sentence $Pr_T(\lceil \alpha \rceil, \lceil \beta \rceil)$ expresses that α is a T-derivation of β.

As before, γ is the Gödel sentence for T constructed from $Pr_T(x, y)$. So γ is equivalent to a sentence that expresses its own underivability in T. To say that

T is consistent is to say that no sentence and its negation are both T-derivable or, equivalently, that for any ζ, η, θ it is not the case that η is a T-derivation of ζ and θ is a T-derivation of $\neg\zeta$. So the proposition that T is consistent can be expressed in the language of T thus:

$$\forall x \forall y \forall z \neg(\, \mathrm{Pr}_T(y, x) \, \& \, \mathrm{Pr}_T(z, \mathrm{neg}(x))\,),$$

where $\mathrm{neg}(\lceil \varphi \rceil) = \lceil \neg\varphi \rceil.$[2] For all the systems of interest, consistency of the system is trivially equivalent to underivability in the system of a false equation with numerals (such as '$0 = s0$') or the negation of a true equation with numerals (such as '$\neg\, 0 = 0$').[3] So consistency of the system can be identified with the underivability in it of a chosen falsehood of this category. Given this, consistency of a system T can also be expressed in the language of T thus:

$$\forall y \neg[\, \mathrm{Pr}_T(y, \lceil \neg\, 0 = 0 \rceil)\,].$$

So any of several easily interderivable sentences in the language of T can be used to express the consistency of T. Let 'Con_T' stand for whichever of these is chosen for the job. Now we can outline the proof of the Second Underivability Theorem.

Recall that, by part (i) of the First Underivability Theorem,

(a)   if T is consistent, γ is underivable in T.

This conditional (a) can be expressed in the language of T by the sentence

(b) $\mathrm{Con}_T \rightarrow \forall x \neg \, \mathrm{Pr}_T(x, \lceil \gamma \rceil).$

As the first part of the First Underivability Theorem, hence (a), is provable by finitary reasoning, one would expect (b), the arithmetical expression of (a), to be provable in finitary arithmetic. So by formalizing the proof of part (i) of the First Underivability Theorem, one might hope to get a derivation of (b) in PRA, hence in T, as T contains PRA. This can be done but the matter is not straightforward. It must be shown that the formula $\mathrm{Pr}_T(x, y)$ satisfies certain conditions, known as the derivability conditions.[4] To show this, one relies on the fact that the relation 'x is a T-derivation of y' has certain standard characteristics, and that the formula $\mathrm{Pr}_T(x, y)$ not only represents that relation but is also constructed in parallel with its recursive definition.[5] As the formula $\mathrm{Pr}_T(x, y)$ satisfies the derivability conditions, (b) can be shown to be derivable in T. As the equivalence

$$\gamma \leftrightarrow \forall x \neg \, \mathrm{Pr}_T(x, \lceil \gamma \rceil)$$

is derivable in T, and as (b) is derivable in T, so is

(c) $\text{Con}_T \to \gamma$.

From this fact a short and simple argument establishes Gödel's Second Underivability Theorem. Suppose that Con_T is derivable in T. Appending a T-derivation of (c) to a T-derivation of Con_T is again a T-derivation. Then the result of appending γ to that derivation is again a T-derivation, as Modus Ponens[6] is a rule of T. That is, we can infer:

Con_T	(assumed previously derived)
$\text{Con}_T \to \gamma$	(previously derived)
γ	(from the above by Modus Ponens).

Hence if Con_T were derivable in T, γ would be derivable in T. However, we know from part (i) of the First Underivability Theorem that γ is underivable in T. So Con_T is not derivable in T.

This is the idea underlying the Gödel–Bernays proof of the Second Underivability Theorem.[7] The theorem is usually proved for some particular formal system, and then something more general is left to be gathered from the proof. Feferman has given a precise general account of standard formal systems and has shown that the argument works for all standard formalizations of arithmetic, analysis, and set theory.[8] For some non-standard formalizations it does not work. So we can state the theorem as follows:

> If T is a consistent standard formal system containing PRA, a sentence in the language of T expressing the claim that T is consistent is not derivable in T.

A feature of this theorem, rare in mathematics, is that it involves the meaning or intension of some mathematical symbolism, as opposed to just its reference or extension. This is signalled by the condition that Con_T *expresses* the T-underivability of T's consistency. This is not an optional extra, added for the philosophical market. If a candidate consistency sentence does not express consistency of T, if it is constructed from a predicate that represents but not does express 'x is a T-derivation of y', the argument for the Second Underivability Theorem cannot be guaranteed to go through for that sentence, as the predicate is liable to fail the derivability conditions.[9] Even if one could show that that sentence is underivable in T, it is hard to see what significance that underivability fact would have, given that the sentence does not express that T is consistent. By contrast, the underivability in T of a sentence that *does* express that T is consistent is significant, as it poses a *prima facie* threat to Hilbert's Programme.

The significance of the Second Theorem for Hilbert's Programme

The threat to Hilbert's Programme is encapsulated in the following argument. Let T be a standard formalization of arithmetic, analysis, or set theory containing PRA. Let us assume for the sake of *reductio* that there is a finitary proof of T's consistency. So T is consistent. Then the Second Underivability Theorem tells us that Con_T, a sentence in the language of T expressing that T is consistent, is underivable in T. The proof of the theorem in fact shows us how to construct Con_T. Now let **C** be the canonical statement of T's consistency, in finitary general form:

> It is not the case that η is a T-derivation of ζ and θ is a T-derivation of ζ's negation,

where 'ζ', 'η', and 'θ' are variables for syntactical objects of the language of T. Let **C'** be a statement that results from decoding Con_T, for example that nothing is a T-derivation of '$\neg(0 = 0)$', or, in finitary general form,

> It is not the case that η is a T-derivation of '$\neg(0 = 0)$',

where 'η' is again a variable for syntactical objects. Then **C'** is deducible from **C** by finitary reasoning about the syntax of T. So if T's consistency were provable by finitary means, say by a proof of **C**, we could extend that proof to a finitary proof **C'**, which is the sentence whose expression in code is Con_T. Then, via the coding, this could be transformed into a proof within finitary arithmetic of Con_T. As T contains PRA and possibly much more, this proof could be formalized as a derivation in T of Con_T. That, however, is just what the Second Underivability Theorem shows cannot be done. Hence the assumption that there is a finitary proof of T's consistency is false.

To complete the argument, one must link that conclusion to Hilbert's Programme. The goal of the programme is to show by finitary means that no false finitary sentence is derivable in T, where T is a proper formalization of arithmetic; and the same for analysis and set theory. But if T is a proper formalization of any of these theories it will satisfy the Inconsistency Effect: if a sentence and its negation are both derivable in T, any sentence in the language of T is derivable in T. So if T is inconsistent, the sentence '$\neg(0 = 0)$' is derivable in T, as is any other sentence in the language of T which, under its standard arithmetical interpretation, expresses a finitary falsehood. Hence the underivability in T of any false finitary sentence entails that T is consistent. Let us say that a system is *reliable* when no false finitary sentence is derivable in it. The argument just given, from T's reliability to T's consistency, lies within the scope of finitary reasoning, and so any finitary proof of the former could be extended to a finitary proof of the latter. But we have already concluded that there is no finitary proof of T's consistency. So there is no finitary proof of T's reliability—and this applies to any formal system of concern for Hilbert's Programme. Hence the goal of the programme cannot be achieved. This argument, allowing for variations of detail, is what sustains the orthodox view of the import of the Second Underivability Theorem for Hilbert's Programme.

The argument is not watertight. Ignoring quibbles, there are just two weaknesses. One lies in the tacit assumption that the Second Underivability Theorem applies to any formal system that properly formalizes one of the relevant bodies of mathematics. My informal statement of the Second Underivability Theorem restricts its scope to standard formal systems. Perhaps some *non*-standard formal system properly formalizes Dedekind–Peano arithmetic (DPA). For such a system the theorem does not rule out that a coded expression of its consistency is derivable within it, even within a part of the system that formalizes some finitary arithmetic. Then Hilbert's Programme may be achievable for arithmetic, and similar possibilities might arise for analysis and set theory. I will call this the problem of non-standard formal systems.

The second problem concerns the assumption that a formal system can capture in code any finitary argument about that system, provided that the system contains PRA. There might be finitary methods beyond those that are formalized in a system T that contains PRA. If so, a finitary proof of T's consistency using those methods would not be transformable via coding into a derivation in T. So the underivability in T of any sentence expressing T's consistency would fail to block Hilbert's Programme. That is the problem of finitary reasoning. I treat these two problems in turn.

The problem of non-standard formal systems

Perhaps Hilbert's Programme can evade the Second Underivability Theorem by means of a non-standard formalization of arithmetic. This is the contention of Detlefsen in his defence of Hilbert's Programme against orthodoxy.[10] In fact, there are non-standard formal systems of arithmetic whose consistency is guaranteed by the way they are presented.[11] Moreover, for any standard formal system of arithmetic, there is a consistency-guaranteed system with the very same theorems, assuming that the standard system is consistent. How does a consistency-guaranteed system evade the Second Underivability Theorem?

The answer lies in the non-standard nature of the derivability relation of a consistency-guaranteed system. The proof of the Second Underivability Theorem requires that the derivability relation of the system fulfils certain conditions, the derivability conditions mentioned earlier,[12] but in consistency-guaranteed systems one of these conditions is not fulfilled.[13] Hence the proof does not go through for those non-standard systems.

Consistency-guaranteed systems seem to offer a means of side-stepping the obstacle to Hilbert's Programme constituted by the Second Underivability Theorem. There are three grounds for thinking that the hope offered here is illusory. The first questions the claim that consistency-guaranteed systems can be proper formalizations of arithmetic. The second is that we cannot know that a given consistency-guaranteed system formalizes the intended set of theorems without knowing that some standard system is consistent. The third is that there is a version of the Second Underivability Theorem that applies even to the non-standard systems. I will now substantiate these points in order.

There are two species of consistency-guaranteed systems, Feferman systems and Rosser systems, with many variants. Systems of both sorts are parasitic on some standard formalization T of DPA. Feferman systems employ an effective enumeration e of the axioms of T, e.g. by code number. The language and inference rules of T^F are those of T. But an axiom of T^F is defined to be an axiom of T that is consistent with the set of e-prior axioms of T.[14] A derivation of T^F is defined to be a T-derivation whose e-maximal T-axiom is a T^F-axiom.[15] If T is consistent, the axioms and derivations of T^F are just those of T. But T^F, unlike T, is obviously consistent. Before describing Rosser systems let me explain why Feferman systems do not count as proper formalizations of arithmetic, at least for the purposes of Hilbert's Programme. Even if one had a finitary proof that no derivation in the system yields a false finitary sentence, efforts to establish certainty about the body of mathematics the system is intended to formalize will be futile if we cannot effectively determine whether a candidate derivation is in fact a derivation. That is why the definition of formal systems given in Chapter 4 of Part IV requires that the property of being a derivation in the system be effectively decidable. Feferman systems fail this requirement. There is no effective method for telling whether a given set of sentences is consistent,[16] hence no effective method for telling whether a sentence is an axiom of T^F, hence no effective method for telling whether a sequence of sentences is a T^F-derivation.[17]

Let T be a standard formalization of DPA as before. Rosser-style systems employ an effective enumeration e of the derivations in T, rather than the axioms of T. (It is assumed that one can effectively determine, given any n, what is the nth derivation in e, and given any derivation, what its place is in e.) The language, axioms, and inference rules of T^R are as for T. But a derivation in T^R is a derivation in T whose conclusion is not the contradictory of the conclusion of any e-prior derivation of T, two formulas being contradictories when one is the negation of the other.[18] If T is consistent, T and T^R are identical with respect to axioms, rules, derivations and therefore theorems; yet only the latter is obviously consistent. Unlike Feferman systems, one can effectively decide whether a candidate derivation, i.e. a derivation η in T, is a derivation in T^R: find the place of η in the enumeration e of T-derivations and inspect all e-prior T-derivations to see if any have a conclusion that is a contradictory of η's conclusion—η is a T^R-derivation if and only if the answer is 'no'. There is no reason to deny that T^R is a genuine formal system. But there is genuine doubt about its adequacy as a formalization of arithmetic. For the logic of T^R may be so far removed from the logic of non-formal arithmetic that T^R is not really a formalization of arithmetic considered as a body of procedures as well as theorems. The major defect of Rosser systems is that the Cut Rule fails for them. This is the principle that allows us to accept a sentence as a theorem on the basis that it has been derived from premises that are not axioms but have been previously derived.[19] This is a universal feature of mathematical reasoning which we could not forgo without a severe reduction in what could actually be proved. Thus, a system for which the Cut Rule fails cannot be an adequate formalization of ordinary arithmetic, analysis, or set theory.[20]

Consistency-guaranteed systems of the Feferman or Rosser varieties are parasitic on standard systems. A second problem for the use of such systems as a means of evading Gödel's Second Underivability Theorem is that we cannot find out by finitary means whether the theorems of a parasitic consistency-guaranteed system comprise a relevantly comprehensive body of arithmetic. The belief that they do is based on the assumption that the host system T, designed as an obviously proper formalization of DPA, is consistent. If T is consistent, the theorems of the parasitic system T* are exactly those of T, and so T* formalizes the intended body of arithmetical propositions. But this is not something that can be established by finitary reasoning, given that that reasoning can be codified in T. For if there were a finitary proof that T and T* have the same theorems, that could be added to a finitary proof of T*'s consistency, thus yielding a finitary proof that T is consistent. That proof could then be translated into a derivation in T of the sentence Con_T expressing T's consistency. But that is ruled out by the Second Underivability Theorem. So we could not establish by finitary means that T* has the same theorems as T, given that T contains enough finitary arithmetic. What we can establish by finitary means is that the set of T*'s theorems is a consistent subset of T's theorems. But, for all we can tell by finitary means, that subset might be quite narrow. So, given a plausible assumption about the host system, we cannot establish by means acceptable within Hilbert's Programme that the theorems of a parasitic system comprise a body of mathematics of relevantly wide scope. If DPA is the theory that T* is supposed to formalize, finitary means will not suffice to show that T*'s theorems formalize more than a narrow portion of the theorems of DPA. So finitary knowledge of the consistency of the parasitic system T* cannot give us finitary knowledge of the consistency of the body of mathematics that T* is supposed to formalize.

These arguments are not decisive. One might deny the assumption just made that all finitary methods can be codified in a proper formalization of DPA, even though DPA encompasses PRA. That question will be discussed in the next section. Also, there may be non-standard formalizations that no one has yet thought of which evade these objections. But if we grant, for the moment, that DPA does encompass finitary reasoning, the considerations given reveal that non-standard systems of the kinds on offer to date are useless for the purpose of rescuing Hilbert's Programme.[21]

The third objection to the project of rescuing Hilbert's Programme by means of non-standard systems strikes at the heart of the programme. A consistency proof was not the only goal, nor the ultimate goal of Hilbert's Programme. The reliability of arithmetic, analysis, and set theory is what has to be shown in order to justify the use of those non-finitary bodies of mathematics. Reliability of a theory here means the impossibility of deducing from the theory any finitary falsehood. The programme requires that the reliability of these bodies of mathematics be shown by obviously reliable means: it must be shown by finitary reasoning alone. For the systems studied by Hilbert and his co-workers, reliability and consistency are equivalent; but they are not equivalent for some non-standard systems. So a crucial question for the viability of Hilbert's Programme is whether the Second Underivability Theorem reformulated with reliability in place of consistency can be proved for all systems containing PRA. To put the question more precisely, can we prove that, in any reliable formal system containing PRA, there is no derivation of a sentence expressing that the system is reliable? If the answer is positive, the main goal of Hilbert's Programme is unachievable, given that PRA contains all finitary arithmetic.

The answer is indeed positive. Gödel summed up the situation in 1966 in a note he later headed 'The best and most general version of the unprovability of consistency in the same system'. He acknowledges that some consistent systems T containing PRA *may* have an internal consistency proof, if consistency is taken in the sense of the underivability in T of a contradictory pair of sentences. He then formulates a version of reliability which he calls 'outer consistency', and states that, if T is outer consistent, its outer consistency is not provable within T. Finally, he points out that a proof of T's outer consistency is what is needed to justify the non-finitary axioms of T, if justification is taken in the sense of Hilbert's Programme.[22]

Outer consistency is a precise version of reliability: for any finitary statement α, if α is false, α is not T-derivable.[23] Let $\text{Prov}_T(y)$ be $\exists x \, \text{Pr}_T(x, y)$, thus expressing that y is T-derivable. Then T is reliable if and only if, for any finitary sentence α in the language of T, $\text{Prov}_T(\lceil \alpha \rceil) \to \alpha$.[24] By a technical modification of the Gödel–Bernays proof of the Second Underivability Theorem, it can be shown that, if T contains PRA and is reliable, there is a finitary sentence α in the language of T such that $\text{Prov}_T(\lceil \alpha \rceil) \to \alpha$ is not derivable in T.[25] The proof does not require that T be a standard formal system, unlike the proof of the normal version of the Second Underivability Theorem. So its conclusion is a strengthened version of the theorem:

> If T contains PRA and is reliable, there is a formal instance of the claim that T is reliable which is not derivable in T.

This pertains directly to the goal of Hilbert's Programme, given that DPA encompasses finitary arithmetic. Let T be a formalization of DPA. Then T contains PRA and finitary arithmetic (which may be the same as PRA). So, if there were a finitary proof of the reliability of DPA, that proof could be formalized in T to yield a derivation of $\text{Prov}_T(\lceil \alpha \rceil) \to \alpha$, for any given finitary sentence α. But that is precisely what is ruled out by the version of the Second Underivability Theorem just given. Thus, the major goal of Hilbert's Programme is shown to be unachievable by a version of Gödel's Second Underivability Theorem, on the sole assumption that finitary reasoning about numbers can be captured in a formal system of arithmetic (hence also of analysis and set theory).

The question of finitary reasoning

Perhaps that assumption does not hold. Gödel mentions this as a possible way out for Hilbert's Programme, in the first presentation of his underivability theorems:

I wish to note expressly that Theorem XI (and the corresponding results for M and A) do not contradict Hilbert's formalistic viewpoint. For this viewpoint presupposes only the existence of a consistency proof in which nothing but finitary means of proof is used, and it is conceivable that there exist finitary proofs that *cannot* be expressed in the formalisms of P (or of M or A).[26]

Theorem XI is the Second Underivability Theorem for a version of *Principia Mathematica* (with Reducibility), and M and A are formal systems of set theory and analysis respectively. Despite this initial caution, Gödel soon came to believe that in fact all finitary proofs are expressible within these systems and that a finitary consistency proof of arithmetic was not possible, a view shared by Bernays, Hilbert's closest co-worker.[27] Here is a quotation from a fairly late article by Gödel:

Due to the lack of a precise definition of either concrete or abstract evidence there exists, today, no rigorous proof for the insufficiency (even of the consistency proof of number theory) of finitary mathematics. However, this surprising fact has been made abundantly clear through the examination of induction by ε_0 used in Gentzen's consistency proof of number theory.[28]

Let us look into this a little. The ordinal ω is the first infinite ordinal. The ordinal ε_0 lies well beyond ω; it is the limit of the infinite denumerable sequence that starts with ω and proceeds to the next element of the sequence by taking the ωth power of the last:

$$\omega, \omega^\omega, \omega^{\omega^\omega}, \ldots$$

The principle of induction mentioned in previous chapters is a version of induction up to ω, as the natural numbers can be identified with the ordinals less than ω. Induction up to ε_0 is an extension of induction up to ω. It can be expressed as an inference rule thus: one can infer that

all ordinals less than ε_0 have given property P

from the information that

for every ordinal α less than ε_0, if all ordinals less than α have P, α itself has P.

If we restrict P to decidable properties formalized by a quantifier-free predicate, we have an induction principle of the kind investigated by Gentzen. Gentzen proved the consistency of a standard formal system of arithmetic, using induction up to ε_0 together with purely finitary methods.[29] Following Gentzen's consistency proof, it was shown that, for any ordinal α less than ε_0, induction up to α can be proved in number theory.[30] From this and the Second Underivability Theorem, Gentzen inferred that induction up to ε_0 is the weakest induction principle that, together with principles of finitary arithmetic, suffices for proving the consistency of arithmetic.

Yet it is reasonable to assume that by and large this correlation [of ordinal numbers with derivations] is already fairly *optimal*, i.e. that we could not make do with *essentially lower* ordinal numbers. In particular the totality of all our derivations cannot be handled by means of ordinal numbers all of which lie below a number which is smaller than ε_0. For transfinite induction up to such a number is itself provable in our formalism; a consistency proof carried out by means of this induction would therefore contradict Gödel's theorem (given, of course, that the other techniques of proof used . . . have not assumed forms that are non-representable in our number-theoretical formalism).[31]

This of course applies only to standard formal systems. Since arithmetic is included in analysis and (by translation) in set theory, corresponding consistency proofs of analysis and set theory require induction up to an ordinal at least as far into the transfinite and in fact beyond.

Thus, our attention is directed to the question whether the principle of induction up to ε_0 has the degree of evidential certainty that Hilbert required of finitary principles. Clearly, the principle is not literally finitary, as it has non-redundant variables ranging over infinite ordinals. But Gödel suggests that this need not be decisive, as induction up to ω^2, which for the same reason is not literally finitary, has an experiential basis:

On the other hand, the validity of [induction up to ε_0] can certainly not be made *immediately* evident, as is possible for example in the case of ω^2. That is to say, one cannot grasp at one glance the various structural possibilities which exist for decreasing sequences, and there exists, therefore, no *immediate* concrete knowledge of the termination of every such sequence. But furthermore such *concrete* knowledge (in Hilbert's sense) cannot be realized either, by a stepwise transition from smaller to larger ordinal numbers, because the concretely evident steps, such as $\alpha \rightarrow \alpha^2$, are so small that they would have to be repeated ε_0 times to in order to reach ε_0.[32]

Gödel's contrast between ω^2 and ε_0 can be illustrated in the following way. One can think of the ordinals up to ω^2 as if arranged in a two-dimensional rectangular array consisting of infinitely many rows enumerated by the positive integers, row $n + 1$ beneath row n, each row consisting of infinitely many places enumerated from the left by the positive integers. In the natural ordering of ordinals, those in higher rows precede those in rows further down; and, within each row, an ordinal precedes all those further to the right. Given this way of imagining the ordinals less than ω^2, it is easy to appreciate that for any decreasing sequence of these ordinals there must be a first (highest) row in which the sequence has a member, and among the members of the sequence in this row there must a leftmost, which will be the least, member of the sequence. So every decreasing sequence of ordinals less than ω^2 has a least element. Induction up to ω^2 is an easy consequence of this fact, and so it does have some basis in visual or visualizing experience. But it is doubtful that this kind of experience, involving visually imagined spatial representation, can be produced for ω^ω, and it is out of the question for ε_0. So induction up to ε_0 does not have the evidential status of a finitary principle.[33]

Could there be some completely different kind of consistency proof of arithmetic, one that *is* finitary? This cannot be decisively ruled out, because there is no agreed definition of finitary methods. But I am not aware of any candidates. Gödel's Second Underivability Theorem shows that, if this is to be a live possibility, some finitary methods would have to be unprovable within natural number arithmetic; for a finitary consistency proof of analysis, some finitary methods would have to lie beyond analysis; the same holds regarding set theory. Gentzen revealed how much *is* provable within arithmetic. These findings, together with Tait's analysis of finitary reasoning,[34] sharply reduce the plausibility of the idea of finitary methods beyond arithmetic. It is still less credible that there are finitary methods beyond analysis, not to mention set theory. Thus, the evidence weighs heavily against the existence of finitary consistency proofs of these bodies of mathematics, so much so that it is hardly reasonable to continue regarding it as a serious possibility.

Gentzen's theorems hold for standard formalizations of arithmetic. Some non-standard systems are trivially consistent, but for those systems consistency does not entail reliability, and reliability is what matters for Hilbert's Programme.[35] So the question arises whether there are results corresponding to Gentzen's concerning proofs of reliability for the non-standard formal systems. I do not know the answer. But we should keep in mind that the non-standard systems are parasitic on standard systems and can be considered relevant only on the basis that they have the same theorems as their standard host systems. That is something we cannot establish by finitary means without also obtaining a finitary proof of the consistency of the standard formalization. But for reasons given above, that is not a serious possibility. The outcome is that, for any formal system of arithmetic, standard or non-standard, we cannot show by finitary means both its relevance and its reliability.

Two positive results

Before concluding, I would like to mention two positive results, to say why they do not count as fulfilling Hilbert's Programme for arithmetic. The first is another discovery by Gödel. This is about the relation of classical arithmetic to intuitionistic arithmetic. By 'classical arithmetic' I mean first-order DPA, or some similar first-order axiomatization of arithmetic, using standard first-order logic. Intuitionistic arithmetic results from attempts to recast mathematics as a theory about mental constructions immediately accessible to the thinker. Heyting, a student and follower of Brouwer, presented a formalization of intuitionistic arithmetic and explained how it was to be interpreted.[36] Gödel showed that there is a translation of the theorems of a standard formal system of classical arithmetic into theorems of Heyting's formal system of intuitionistic arithmetic such that a contradictory pair among the former would be translated into a contradictory pair among of the latter. Hence, if classical arithmetic is inconsistent, so is intuitionistic arithmetic.[37] If intuitionist arithmetic could be regarded as falling within the realm of finitary truth, this would be a finitary proof that classical arithmetic is consistent. But intuitionist arithmetic cannot be regarded as finitary. A central reason is the abstract nature of the subject matter of intuitionistic arithmetic. The intuitionist interpretation of a sentence of the form $A \rightarrow B$ is that we have a procedure which, applied to any proof of A, yields a proof of B. (Here, of course, procedures and proofs are restricted to those that are intuitionistically acceptable.) The intuitionist interpretation of $\neg A$ is that $A \rightarrow \perp$, where $\perp$ is some obvious absurdity not involving negation, such as '$0 = 1$'. Thus, all intuitionistic theorems of these forms are about proofs. Proofs here are not purely syntactic objects but are essentially meaning-laden entities, whereas the subject matter of finitistic reasoning is confined to spatial configurations of types of definite perceptible objects.[38] If sentences of the form $A \rightarrow B$ are interpreted not in terms of intuitionistic proofs but in terms of derivations in a formal system of intuitionist arithmetic, the subject matter becomes finitary, but some of the axioms of intuitionistic arithmetic are no longer true under that reinterpretation of '$\rightarrow$'. So we have no reason to hold that the theorems of intuitionistic arithmetic are all finitary truths. There are also reasons for thinking that intuitionistic arithmetic transgresses constructive requirements of finitary reasoning.[39] This is because the notion of intuitionistic proof is not constructively defined and may even harbour circularity, for what counts as an intuitionistic proof of a conditional depends on the intuitionistic interpretation of conditionals, and that, we have seen, involves the totality of intuitionistic proofs. That particular problem may have been overcome by the later development of intuitionistic type theory.[40] But there remains the fact that proofs, as opposed to formal derivations, are not finitary objects. So the proof of the consistency of arithmetic relative to intuitionistic arithmetic does not count as a finitary consistency proof of arithmetic.

Having shown that classical arithmetic is consistent if intuitionist arithmetic is, Gödel later used the same method to show that intuitionist arithmetic is consistent if a certain constructive theory is. Putting the two results together gives a proof that classical arithmetic is consistent relative to this constructive theory, which I will refer to as D.[41] This is the second positive result I wanted to mention. Broadly speaking, D preserves the constructive methods of finitary arithmetic, but its subject matter is clearly non-finitary. The domain of finitary arithmetic consists of the numbers, which can be iso-morphically represented by numerals in some system. The numerals are fini-tary because they are types of directly perceptible configurations of basic objects whose identity is fixed by size and shape. The subject matter of D con-sists not only of the numbers but also of computable functions of higher and higher levels. At the lowest level there are functions that deliver a number as output, given a finite sequence of numbers as input; then there are functions that can have lowest-level functions as well as numbers among their inputs; then functions that can have *those* functions, as well as lowest-level functions and numbers, among their inputs; and so on. All these functions are required to be computable and their computability is required to be constructively evi-dent. But functions of even the lowest level fail Hilbert's criteria for finitary subject matter. For a function on the natural numbers has an infinite domain, and its identity depends on its output for each member of the domain. Even if we identify a function with a programme for computing its values, a func-tion would not be a spatial configuration of perceptible objects, as a pro-gramme is not a configuration of marks that express it, but the interpretation of that configuration in some language. So the lowest-level computable func-tions are too abstract to count as finitary objects; and higher-level functions, which are those with functions as well as numbers among their inputs, have a yet higher degree of abstraction. Clearly, then, Gödel's constructive theory D is not a finitary theory, nor was it presented as such. Though the proof of the consistency of classical arithmetic relative to D is an epistemic advance,[42] it is not a finitary consistency proof of number theory; still less are the relative consistency proofs of analysis obtained by extending Gödel's method.

Conclusion

Hilbert and his co-workers did not have a precise definition of the scope of finitary mathematics, and so there can be no mathematical proof of the impossibility of achieving the goal of Hilbert's Programme for arithmetic: a finitary proof of reliability. The argument stemming from Gödel's Second Underivability Theorem is convincing for standard formalizations of arithmetic on the assumption that they encompass finitary reasoning. That leaves open just two possible avenues for Hilbert's Programme for arithmetic: non-standard formalizations, and finitary methods beyond DPA. Those avenues are effectively blocked by further considerations, as argued above. So I conclude that there is no serious possibility of achieving the goal of Hilbert's Programme for arithmetic.[43] *A fortiori*, there is no hope of achieving the goal of the programme for analysis and set theory. Few, if anyone, doubted the reliability of arithmetic. Analysis and set theory, plagued with paradoxes almost from their inception, are the real objects of concern. With regard to them, it becomes clear after reflection on Gödel's theorems and subsequent discoveries that the search for certainty through Hilbert's Programme cannot succeed.

APPENDIX: INTENSIONALITY OF THE SECOND UNDERIVABILITY THEOREM

The sentences γ and $\mathrm{Con_T}$ are built up using the predicate $\mathrm{Pr_T}(x, y)$ representing the T-derivation relation, and that in turn is built up using a predicate $\mathrm{A_T}(x)$ representing the property of being an axiom of T. For the proof of the First Underivability Theorem, it suffices that these predicates *represent* the intended property or relation. This ensures a kind of extensional correctness of the predicates: writing '**n**' for the numeral in T for n, and ‹*n*› for the syntactic object it codes,

$\mathrm{A_T}(\mathbf{n})$ is derivable in T if and only if ‹*n*› is an axiom of T;

$\mathrm{Pr_T}(\mathbf{n}, \mathbf{m})$ is derivable in T if and only if ‹*n*› is a T-derivation of ‹*m*›.

If T is a true formal system of arithmetic, this entails that $\mathrm{A_T}(x)$ when arithmetically interpreted has the same as extension as 'x codes an axiom of T'; so $\mathrm{A_T}(x)$ is extensionally correct. Similarly for $\mathrm{Pr_T}(x, y)$. For the proof of the Second Underivability Theorem these predicates must also be intensionally correct. That is, they must *express* the corresponding syntactic predicates, in the sense that it must be possible to tell by decoding which syntactic predicates they represent.

Suppose that T is a consistent formalization of Dedekind–Peano arithmetic and that $A_T(x)$ is a predicate that is constructed in parallel with the definition of the property of axiomhood in T, so that the predicate is both extensionally and intensionally correct. Similarly, let $Pr_T(x, y)$ be both extensionally and intensionally correct and let Con_T be constructed just as before. Then we can construct a predicate $A^*_T(x)$ that is co-extensional with $A_T(x)$ but intensionally distinct from it. While $A_T(x)$ expresses that x codes an axiom of T, $A^*_T(x)$ expresses (roughly) that x codes an axiom of T and, for any sentence code y no greater than x, the axioms of T with codes no greater than y form a consistent set. Yet $A^*_T(x)$ and $A_T(x)$ have the same extension, as T is consistent. The example is Feferman's, and he used it to show the relevance of intensional correctness for the Second Underivability Theorem. Using $A^*_T(x)$ in place of $A_T(x)$ to construct a predicate $Pr^*_T(x, y)$ to represent the T-derivability relation, and using $Pr^*_T(x, y)$ to construct a 'consistency sentence' Con^*_T for T, Feferman proved that Con^*_T is derivable in T (Feferman 1960: 68, 69, th. 5.9). This does not reduce the significance of the Second Underivability Theorem, as the sentence Con^*_T does not express that T is consistent. But it does show that the proof of the Second Underivability Theorem depends on the intensional correctness of the coding of syntactical predicates and relations.

Mostowski gives another example.[44] Let T be a true system of arithmetic containing PRA, and let $Pr_T(x, y)$ express T's derivability relation, as before. Now define

$$Pr^\square_T(x, y) \leftrightarrow Pr_T(x, y)\ \&\ \neg Pr_T(x, \ulcorner 0 = s0 \urcorner).$$

'$0 = s0$' is the sentence of T whose arithmetical interpretation is that 0 equals 1. As T is arithmetically correct, that sentence is underivable in T. So the formula $\neg Pr_T(x, \ulcorner 0 = s0 \urcorner)$ is true for all numbers x. Hence the predicate $Pr_T(x, y)$ $\&\ \neg Pr_T(x, \ulcorner 0 (s0 \urcorner)$ is true of exactly the same ordered pairs of numbers as the predicate $Pr_T(x, y)$. That is, the predicates $Pr_T(x, y)$ and $Pr^\square_T(x, y)$ have the same extension. But they have different intensions, as the latter expresses the relation: ⟨x⟩ is a T-derivation of ⟨y⟩ but not of '$0 = s0$'. Suppose we use $Pr^\square_T(x, y)$ in place of $Pr_T(x, y)$ to construct a 'consistency sentence' $Con^\square_T$ for T, by defining

$$\mathrm{Con}^{\square}{}_T \leftrightarrow \forall x \,\neg\, \mathrm{Pr}^{\square}{}_T(x, \lceil \mathbf{0} = \mathbf{s0} \rceil).$$

Then $\mathrm{Con}^{\square}{}_T$ is a theorem of predicate logic that is easily derivable in T:

$$\mathrm{Con}^{\square}{}_T \leftrightarrow \forall x \,\neg\, [\, \mathrm{Pr}_T(x, \lceil \mathbf{0} = \mathbf{s0} \rceil) \,\&\, \neg \mathrm{Pr}_T(x, \lceil \mathbf{0} = \mathbf{s0} \rceil) \,].$$

Again, this does not detract from the significance of the Second Underivability Theorem, as $\mathrm{Con}^{\square}{}_T$ clearly expresses something much weaker than that T is consistent, namely that nothing both is and is not a T-derivation of '$\mathbf{0} = \mathbf{s0}$'. But, again, it does show that the proof of the theorem depends on the intensional correctness of the coding of syntax.

Part VI
Aftermath

Paradise Restored? 1

How worrying is the fact that a finitary proof of the consistency of set theory is not a serious possibility? Zermelo's axiomatization of set theory made explicit positive principles of set existence while avoiding the essential ingredient of all the class paradoxes, the Comprehension Principle. But at the time that Zermelo first published his axioms (1908), no one could present a unifying picture of a universe of sets for which the axioms could be seen to be true, and so the axiom system was viewed as an *ad hoc* weakening of the inconsistent theory. Hence consistency of the axioms was a pressing concern, as Zermelo himself noted. But in 1930, the year when Gödel made his underivability discoveries, Zermelo published a paper that did present a unifying picture,[1] and when eventually it was recognized that his axioms were a partial articulation of this picture, confidence in the axioms rose sharply.[2] The next section presents the core of Zermelo's picture.

A universe as a cumulative hierarchy of stages

The structure of a universe of sets, in Zermelo's view, is a cumulative hierarchy of stages. Each universe has a unique lowest stage, which may be empty; alternatively, it may have one or more members, but these must be memberless entities, called *Urelemente* by Zermelo but also called atoms or individuals. As any set of individuals can serve as the lowest stage of a universe, there is a plurality of universes each with a different initial stage.

The hierarchy of stages after the first is built up from lower stages in two ways. First, given any stage of the hierarchy, there is a unique next stage above. This contains all members of the given stage plus, for each possible selection from the given stage, a set whose members are just those of the selection. Any plurality of members of the given stage whatsoever constitutes a possible selection, as does the empty selection and selections of just one item. We can summarize by saying that the next stage above a given stage is just the set of all members and all subsets of the given stage. A selection can contain everything in the given stage; hence each stage is itself a set in the next stage up and so is in the domain of the universe. It is not assumed that for each selection there is an expressible condition satisfied by just the objects selected; on the contrary, there can be arbitrary selections. But, given any expressible condition, the members of a stage that satisfy it constitute a selection, provided that for no member of the stage is it indeterminate whether it satisfies the condition.

The second way in which stages are built out of lower stages is this: given any endless sequence of consecutive[3] stages, the union of these stages is the first stage above all the stages in the sequence. Such stages are known as limit stages. So an object (individual or set) is in the limit stage of a given sequence if and only if it is in at least one of the stages in that sequence. Every stage after the lowest is either a successor stage or a limit stage, and every stage is *cumulative* in the sense that it contains everything in every lower stage. As any universe has a unique lowest stage and each stage has a unique successor, the cumulative hierarchy of stages of a universe starts with an endless sequence that can be numbered: V_0 for the lowest stage and V_{n+1} for the next stage above V_n. Then the second kind of operation guarantees the existence of an infinite stage V_ω, which is the union of all the lower stages V_n (for n in ω).

By the first kind of operation, there is again an endless succession of stages starting with V_ω: $V_{\omega+1}$ is the result of adding to V_ω all the subsets of V_ω; $V_{\omega+2}$ results from adding to $V_{\omega+1}$ all subsets of $V_{\omega+1}$; in the same way, $V_{\omega+n+1}$ is obtained from $V_{\omega+n}$. The second kind of construction gives the next limit stage $V_{\omega+\omega}$. In fact, the process continues in a way that parallels the ordinals.

This conception of a universe of sets as a cumulative hierarchy of stages is the core of Zermelo's picture.[4] What now of the conception of a set? As before, sets are classes and therefore obey extensionality: sets are the same if they have the same members. But what is it for a class to be a set? Let us call the objects in the domain of a universe the elements of that universe. A class of elements of a universe is a set if and only if it is a subclass of some stage. A class of elements of a universe that is not a subclass of any stage is a *proper class* relative to that universe, and is therefore not an element in that universe—only the atoms and the sets in a universe are elements of it. Examples of proper classes of a universe are the class of all its stages and the class of its elements. This relativity is important: the proper classes of a universe will be sets in a more encompassing universe.

Comparisons

There is a major difference between the conception of sets as members of a cumulative hierarchy and the older conception of classes as predicate extensions, championed by Frege. For some predicates in the language of set theory there is no set in a cumulative hierarchy to serve as its extension, for example the predicate 'x is an ordinal'; and some sets in a cumulative hierarchy are not extensions of any predicate in the language, since the language has an enumerable infinity of predicates whereas the sets in a cumulative hierarchy are beyond enumeration. The older conception assumed that there is a totality of all things whatsoever and that a predicate in a mathematical language divides that totality into mutually exclusive and exhaustive classes, the class of things that satisfy the predicate and the class of all other things. This conception led to the antinomies. Gödel contrasts this conception with Zermelo's, which (following Gödel's usage) came to be known as the *iterative conception*:

This concept of set, however, according to which a set is something obtained from the integers (or some other well-defined objects) by iterated application[5] of the operation 'set of', and not something obtained by dividing the totality of all existing things into two categories, has never led to any antinomy whatsoever.[6]

The conception of class that Russell settled on by the time he and Whitehead published the first edition of *Principia Mathematica* maintained the idea that a class is the extension of a predicate, but added two conditions: (1) a class can have members of just one type; (2) the predicate must satisfy syntactic restrictions designed to guarantee respect for the Vicious Circle Principle. This second condition issues from the view that classes are intellectual constructions, a view that places Russell's conception at too great a distance from Zermelo's conception for useful comparison. But we may usefully consider simple type theory with arbitrary sets (or classes: there is no set–class distinction in type theory). The lowest type is reserved for individuals; the sets of each type above the lowest are the possible selections of objects of the type immediately below and nothing else.

How does that compare with the universe of a cumulative hierarchy? In a cumulative hierarchy the sets of each stage above the lowest are the possible selections of objects from *any* stage below it, not just from the stage *immediately* below it. But an important feature of the universe of types is preserved. Just as every set in the latter has a type, so every set in a cumulative hierarchy has a level, which is the unique lowest stage of which it is a member. The stages of a cumulative hierarchy are well-ordered, so for each set there must be a lowest stage of which it is a subset, and then its level is the next stage up. Clearly, the level of a set must be higher than the level of any of its members. This is enough to prevent circular membership chains; it is not necessary to demand that a set have members only of the level immediately below its own. Avoiding this extra demand increases flexibility. A cumulative hierarchy is to a universe of types as a community that allows social mixing is to a rigid caste system. A set in a cumulative hierarchy can have members with a mixture of levels lower than its own. This allows the formation of a stage that is the union of all finite stages, and greatly facilitates the development of the theory of transfinite sets. Furthermore, there are no restrictions in the language of set theory corresponding to the type restrictions. Predicates in the language of set theory are true or false for sets of any level; and nothing is wrong with the predicate 'x is not a member of itself', though no set in a cumulative hierarchy is its extension, as every object in the hierarchy satisfies it.

From principles about stages to axioms of set theory

Implicit in the foregoing conception are a number of principles about stages and sets. Some of these were explicitly formulated by Dana Scott, who showed how axioms of set theory could be derived from them.[7] As sets are just those classes that are subclasses of some stage, one principle is *Restriction*:

> Every set is a subset of a stage.

A converse of this is that any selection of members of a stage is a set. This yields *Separation for Stages*:

> For any stage V, there is a set whose members are precisely the objects x in V such that $\theta(x)$.

Here '$\theta(x)$' is schematic for one-place predicates expressing a precise condition. It is not difficult to see that these two principles yield Zermelo's Axiom of Separation:

> For any set m, there is a set whose members are precisely the objects x in m such that $\theta(x)$.

From the principle of Separation for Stages, it follows that every stage is a set, hence a subset of itself. Every stage is therefore a member of the next stage up, and in fact is a member of all higher stages, as the stages are cumulative. So if V is lower than W, V ∈ W. The converse is also true.[8]

A stage W that has a set among its members cannot be an initial stage. Every non-initial stage is just the set of all members and all subsets of all lower stages. This is Scott's principle of *Accumulation*:

> For any set m, m is a member of a stage W if and only if there is a stage V in W such that m is in V or is a subset of V.

Assuming only the Axioms of Extensionality, Separation, Restriction, and Accumulation, Scott proved that the stages are well ordered by the membership relation. He did this by way of proving the Axiom of Foundation (or Regularity):[9]

> Every non-empty set m has a member none of whose members are also in m.

This is the axiom that ensures that there is no set whose members form an infinite descending membership chain: $\ldots x_{n+1} \in x_n \in x_{n-1} \in \ldots \in x_2 \in x_1 \in x_0$.[10] This in turn rules out membership circles: $y \in x \ldots \in y$.

As mentioned before, it follows from the fact that the stages are well ordered that for each set there is a unique lowest stage of which it is a member, the *level* of the set.[11] The level of any individual is V_0. Let b and c be any objects (individuals or sets); if they are both of the same level V, both b and c will be in V; if they are of different levels W and V and if V is the higher of the two, W is a subset of V, and so again both b and c will be in V. So the selection $\{b, c\}$ is a set in the stage after V. That yields the Pair Set Axiom.

By Separation, the empty set $\emptyset$ is in V_1, hence in V_ω, which is just the union of all V_n, where n is a natural number. For any object x in V_ω, there is some natural number n such that x is in V_n; hence the unit set $\{x\}$ is in V_{n+1}, hence in V_ω. Therefore there is a set, namely V_ω, that contains $\emptyset$ and that contains $\{x\}$ if it contains x. This is Zermelo's Axiom of Infinity.

The lowest stage W that contains a given set m, the level of m, is the first stage above the lowest stage containing all the members of m. As the stages are cumulative, it follows that W, and each higher stage, contains every member of m. This entails that

(#)   For any set m and any stage W, if m is in W, m is a subset of W.

Using this fact, it is not difficult to show that the rest of Zermelo's original axioms apart from the Axiom of Choice are implicit in his conception of a universe of sets.

First, the Power Set Axiom:

> For any set m, there is a set $\mathbb{P}m$ whose members are exactly the subsets of m.

Let x be any subset of m. Let V be the level of m. Then m is in V and so by #, m is a subset of V. So x is a subset of a subset of V; hence x is a subset of V. Now let V$^+$ be the next stage above V. As all the members *and* all the subsets of a stage are members of the next stage up, it follows that x is in V$^+$. So all the subsets of m are in V$^+$. So by Separation for Stages there is a set in the stage after V$^+$ whose members are exactly the subsets of m. That set is $\mathbb{P}m$.

This is the Union Set Axiom:

> For any set m, there is a set $\cup m$ whose members are exactly the objects that are members of a member of m.

Let y be any member of m and let x be any member of y. Let V be the level of m. Then m is in V and so by #, m is a subset of V. Therefore y is in V; so by #, y is a subset of V. So x is in V. So every member of a member of m is in V. So by Separation there is a set in V$^+$ whose members are just the members of members of m. That set is $\cup m$.

The Axiom of Choice

To deal with the Axiom of Choice it will help to recall the definition of a choice set. Let m be any non-empty set of non-empty sets no two of which have a common member. A set c is said to be a *choice set* for m if and only if (i) every member of c is in some member of m, and (ii) each member of m has exactly one member in common with c. Then the Axiom of Choice is:

> For any non-empty set m of non-empty sets, no two of which have a common member, there is a choice set c.

This involves just two controversial ideas. One is that there are no constraints on the kinds of selections from a stage that give us sets. In particular, there may be selections that are not the extension of any predicate. Call this AS, for 'arbitrary selection'. The other is that there are no constraints on the kinds of functions or assignments that exist, given that their domains are sets. In particular, there may be a function f that has no defining two-place predicate, that is, no φ such that $\varphi(x, y)$ if and only if $f(x) = y$. Call this AF, for 'arbitrary function'. The argument is as follows.

Let m be any non-empty set of non-empty sets no two of which have a common member. Let V be the level of m. So m is in V; so by #, m is a subset of V. Hence every p in m is in V. So, again by #, every p in m is a subset of V. Now for each p in m, let $f(p)$ be any one member of p. In assuming that there is such a function f, I am drawing on AF. As p is a subset of V, $f(p)$ is in V, for all p in m. So the objects $f(p)$ for p in m constitute a selection of members of V. Hence by AS there is a set c in the next stage above V whose members are precisely the objects $f(p)$ for p in m. It is easy to see that c is a choice set for m.

This argument is a justification for the Axiom of Choice only *given* that there are arbitrary selections and arbitrary functions. As anyone doubtful about the Axiom of Choice is likely to doubt this too, the argument is not really a justification. The point of the argument is to show that this axiom among others can be regarded as a partial articulation of an underlying conception of sets, functions, and universes of sets, as opposed to an opportunistically adopted crowbar.[12]

Where do doubts about the Axiom of Choice come from? Sometimes they issue from a constructivist view of mathematical entities.[13] But another source was confusion over the idea of a function. In the early nineteenth century the prevalent idea of function was a *rule* for calculating the value of a given input. Later, a function was thought of as the *set of input–output pairs determined by a rule*, where it is understood that each input has just one output. What distinguishes this concept from its predecessor is that rules that determine the same set of input–output pairs would, on this concept, determine the same function.[14] But this concept of a function was itself superseded by a concept of a function as a *set of input–output pairs*, each input having just one output. That is the concept now current, and it differs from its predecessor in that a function need not be determined by a rule. Some resistance to the Axiom of Choice can be explained in terms of adherence to the older concept of function. To those using the older concept, the idea of a set of arbitrary choices $f(p)$ from each set p (in a set of non-empty sets) is incoherent, as it implies both the presence of some rule determining choices and the absence of any rule as the choices are described as arbitrary. Once arbitrary choice is understood in terms of the current concept of function, no incoherence remains. A concept may lack instances even if coherent, and one might judge that this is precisely the situation with the concepts of arbitrary choice and arbitrary selection. But that judgement could be motivated only by viewing sets as intellectual artefacts, as far as I can see. Abandon that view and opposition to the Axiom of Choice becomes groundless.

The Axiom of Replacement

We have now covered all of Zermelo's original axioms plus the Axiom of Foundation. In his later work he added the Axiom of Replacement:

> For any set m and any functional relation F with domain m, there is a set whose members are exactly the objects assigned by F to members of m.[15]

Replacement is not implicit in the idea of a universe as a cumulative hierarchy. In the chapter on axiomatic set theory (Part IV, Chapter 1), it was pointed out that the Axiom of Replacement issues from Cantor's idea that a plurality is a set if and only if it has a cardinal number. Using the framework of a cumulative hierarchy, there is another way of viewing the axiom. What distinguishes a set from a proper class is that the collection of its members' levels is bounded, i.e. that there is a yet higher level than all of them. If we put '$L(y)$' for the level of y, L can be thought of as an operation that assigns to each object its level. We can then put the distinguishing condition on sets thus: for any set m, the collection of levels $L(y)$ for the members y of m is bounded. We can generalize this in the following way. For any operation $T(y)$ that assigns a unique stage to each object, and for any set m, the collection of stages $T(y)$ for y in m is bounded. Using a few of the axioms already mentioned, this generalization can be shown to be equivalent to the Axiom of Replacement. So Replacement tells us something about the hierarchy of stages: no unbounded class of stages can be indexed by a set, or, as set theorists might put it, no set is co-final with the hierarchy of stages. Although this is a structural claim, it also says that, relative to any set in a universe, the stages of that universe constitute an immeasurable multiplicity.

Reflection

In 1960, Lévy[16] articulated another strand of the iterative view of a universe of sets introduced three decades earlier by Zermelo. This is the idea of reflection. Explaining this will be simpler if we hold fixed the (possibly empty) collection of individuals that are members of the lowest stage of a universe. What remains unfixed by the iterative conception is the *upward extent* of a universe starting from the fixed collection of individuals. So we might ask: how extensive is the universe? It is easy to give a vacuous answer to this question. For example, one could say that a universe must be 'complete' or contain 'all' sets built up from the individuals of the universe. But the question cannot have a correct informative answer. For any such answer would have to specify some characteristic of the complete universe that would distinguish it from all its stages; but this is impossible on the iterative conception, as we can always take a cumulative hierarchy that has the specified characteristic as the starting point for further iterations of the 'set of' of operation; that is, one can treat it as another stage, and take all possible selections of its members as members of a yet higher stage.[17] This informal idea gives rise to a formal principle of set theory known as the Reflection Principle. Let $\langle V, \in_V \rangle$ be the interpretation of the language of set theory which has domain V and which assigns to '$\in$' the membership relation restricted to elements of V. Then reflection tells us that, for any sentence θ in the language of set theory, θ is true if and only if there is a stage V such that θ is true under the interpretation $\langle V, \in_V \rangle$. In short, θ is true if and only if θ is true in some stage V. Such a V is said to 'reflect the universe with respect to θ'. Call such a stage a θ-stage. Then allowing unlimited iteration of reflection leads to the proposition that θ is true if and only if the sequence of θ-stages is unbounded. That is the Reflection Principle.

As the idea underlying the Reflection Principle is a natural outgrowth of the iterative conception, some sufficiently precise formulation of it can be added as an axiom or axiom schema.[18] Lévy not only gave a precise formulation of the Reflection Principle but also showed how strengthened versions of it can be systematically generated using the very idea that underlies the principle; and he showed that these strengthenings are equivalent to successively stronger existential statements about infinite numbers.[19] The Reflection Principle can actually be derived from a few already mentioned axioms, including Infinity and Replacement. More significant from our point of view is that the Axioms of Infinity and Replacement can be derived from the Reflection Principle using just a few other axioms that fall within Zermelo's conception, namely Extensionality, Foundation, and Separation. Thus, the iterative conception extended to include iterated reflection allows us to dispense with the last trace of the 'limitation of size' idea, that trace being the idea of replacement, as a source of axioms.

The independence of the Continuum Hypothesis

Having an intuitive idea of sets distinct from the idea of concept-extensions, we do not have to fall back on the axioms as an implicit definition of 'set' and the relation '∈'. So Skolem's criticism of that position, that the axioms fail to fix the references of central notions of the theory of infinite cardinality, is no longer a threat to the value of set theory as a framework for the rigorous presentation of analysis. But later findings revived the worry that the theory of infinite cardinality and of infinite sets generally is vacuous, a mere formalism that fails to say anything true or false.

The main finding was the discovery that Cantor's Continuum Hypothesis is independent of the axioms of set theory. The Continuum Hypothesis (CH) is the hypothesis that there is no cardinal number between the first infinite cardinal, which is the number of natural numbers, and the number of real numbers. In terms of the alephs, the hypothesis is that $2^{\aleph_0} = \aleph_1$. By 1938 Gödel had discovered that, if first-order axiomatic set theory is consistent, so is the theory that results from adding CH.[20] In 1963 Cohen showed that, if first-order axiomatic set theory is consistent, so is the theory that results from adding the negation of CH.[21] These two results mean that CH is deductively independent of the first-order axioms of set theory, assuming their consistency. This discovery triggered a revival of Hilbert's formalist attitude towards statements about infinite sets. A few months after Cohen's findings were published, Robinson, the logician who developed a rigorous theory of infinitesimals, declared his view that 'the entire notion of sets is meaningless', mentioning the independence of CH as a factor.[22] Not long after, Cohen took up the formalist view about the infinite, on the basis of the independence results and the lack of satisfactory criteria for accepting axioms of infinity.[23]

Why should this discovery produce such a strong philosophical reaction? It was known from Gödel's First Underivability Theorem that there are statements about finite sets that are independent of the axioms of set theory, given that the axioms are consistent.[24] Why should the independence of a sentence about infinite sets lead to a formalist attitude to the transfinite parts of set theory, while the independence of sentences about finite sets leaves attitudes to finite set theory unchanged? Part of the answer is that the independence of CH was not a lone result. Cohen's work was quickly extended, in two ways. First, it was shown that CH remains independent of set theory even when the theory is extended by the addition of any of a number of increasingly strong axioms of infinity, given the consistency of those extensions.[25] Secondly, it was discovered that a very wide range of rival hypotheses about the cardinality of the continuum is consistent with set theory, if set theory is consistent; in fact, this is true also for general hypotheses about the cardinalities of power sets of infinite sets.[26] This means that the accepted axioms of set theory tell us next to nothing about the positions of power sets of infinite sets on the ladder of transfinite cardinals. These facts would not have had such an impact if we had some informal principle or principles beyond the axioms by means of which we could decide the truth of CH and related assertions. But we do not as yet have any idea how to decide the matter. This is why the independence of CH produced such a different response from the independence of the Gödel sentence for set theory, which expresses its own underivability in the theory. Informal reasoning establishes that the Gödel sentence is true if the theory is consistent. Hence that independence result gives no reason to suspect that there are sentences about finite sets that have no truth value.

The independence of CH is significant because CH is a fairly simple conjecture about the very thing that Cantor's transfinite set theory was devised to illuminate, namely, the continuum. Given the framework of Cantor's theory, and his findings about cardinalities of point sets, it was also a very natural conjecture. But until one conceives of the continuum, which is intuitively a geometrical line, as a set of points, and until one applies the theory of infinite cardinalities to point sets, the question of the cardinality of the continuum does not arise. Of course, CH can be expressed without reference to the continuum; it is equally a hypothesis about the cardinality of the power set of the natural numbers. But, however formulated, it remains a question that arises only within the theory of infinite sets and numbers. So, far from providing a means by which all questions about the continuum can be definitively settled, the theory actually produces questions that it cannot answer. In this context one is bound to ask whether the question really has an answer, whether 'the cardinality of the continuum' is not a mere artefact of the theory, whether the whole theory of infinite cardinality is not an illusion like the chromatic fringe produced by a faulty microscope.

One fact that has been cited in opposing the sceptical tide is that CH or its negation is a semantic consequence of second-order set theory.[27] So CH is true in every universe of sets that is a model of the second-order axioms or false in every such model.[28] It is very plausible that our conception of a universe of sets is really second-order, and so the first-order axioms are too weak to express the underlying ideas.[29] On these grounds one might conclude that CH does have a truth value and that the independence result is due to the inadequacy of first-order formalization. This inference would not be warranted, however, because neither CH nor its negation is derivable from the second-order axioms, given the consistency of the axioms.[30] That is, CH is second-order independent too, given the consistency of the axioms. Moreover, if one is sceptical about infinite set theory, that scepticism will transfer to the semantics of second-order theories (with infinite domains), or

211

at least to the clause stipulating that the range of second-order variables is the set of all subsets of the domain. Thus, one might take a formalist attitude to the claim that CH or its negation is a semantic consequence of second-order set theory.

Despite all this, the formalist response is unjustified. It depends on two contentious beliefs: (1) that neither CH nor its negation can be known to be true; (2) that there are no unknowable mathematical truths.[31] Belief (1) is based on the fact that at present we have no clue how to determine the cardinality of the continuum among the huge range of candidates. But this ignores the possibility that some completely new aspect of mathematics will be discovered in the future that will settle the question. However remote that possibility seems now, in a hundred years the matter may look very different. Belief (2) stems from the conviction that mathematical facts are in some way products of human intellect—idealism about mathematics. I am aware of no cogent argument for idealism about mathematics (though there are some interesting attempts), and I am not sure how (2) is deduced from it. In any case, without an inclination to idealism, it is not at all incredible there are unknowable mathematical facts.

Where does that leave us? There are two, perhaps three, possibilities. Let the word 'indeterminate' signify 'no fact of the matter'; so to say that the cardinality of the continuum is indeterminate is to say that the question of its cardinality has no unique correct answer. The possibilities are these: (i) there is no indeterminacy about these questions[32] of transfinite cardinality, just ignorance; (ii) there is indeterminacy arising from the variety of kinds of universe that conform to our conception of a universe of sets; (iii) there is indeterminacy arising from the absence of any reality that conforms to our conception of a universe of sets. Possibility (ii) is the hardest to maintain in light of the fact that the CH has the same truth value in all models of the second-order axioms (assuming that they have a model). If one takes this at face value, not just as a formal result, only possibility (i) remains open; if one takes it as a merely formal result (in set theory), grounds for that attitude would surely also be grounds for a formalist attitude to models of set theory in general, making possibility (iii) inescapable.[33] A decisive argument in favour of (i) or (iii) is not yet in currency. So these are the possibilities we have to face now.

How damaging is this situation? There is no doubt that the independence of CH and related independence facts dealt a severe blow to the original hopes for the theory of infinite cardinality.[34] Even so, the reliability of the theory is not at all under threat. Reliability (with respect to finitary statements) and consistency are equivalent for the customary systems of set theory, and the independence discoveries give no reason to doubt the consistency of the theory. That theory is the partial explication of a conception that gives no sign whatsoever of incoherence. If, as seems very likely, that conception is coherent, an expression of it (or any part of it) will be consistent, whether or not it is instantiated.

Conclusion

The main message of this chapter is that set theory is indeed a partial articulation of a conception that is complex yet, in all probability, coherent. Together with principles of extensionality and arbitrary choice, the axioms implicit in the extended iterative conception capture all of the set theory that is used in practice and standardly presented in textbooks.[35] It is fair to conclude then that axiomatic set theory is not just an agglomeration of statements opportunistically designed to avoid nasty consequences without sacrificing too much. Instead, it arises from a complex but quite natural conception of a universe of sets. Thus, we have a positive idea of a model of set theory, and because of this the fear that the theory is inconsistent has, quite reasonably, fallen away. A further source of confidence would be a convincing diagnosis and solution of the class paradoxes within the framework of the iterative conception. That is the topic of the next chapter.

Solving the Class Paradoxes 2

According to Zermelo's view of a universe of sets, there are many of them, as there is no restriction on the class of atoms that can constitute the initial stage of a universe. But even if we hold the initial stage fixed, there will be a plurality of universes, on Zermelo's view. There is no absolute all-inclusive universe (for a fixed initial stage), as any candidate for the title of 'universe' can be taken as a starting point for further iterations of the procedures by which higher stages are formed, so that the candidate universe is just an initial segment of a more extended universe. As stages are indexed by ordinal numbers, the idea can be expressed in terms of the series of ordinals: 'This series reaches no true completion in its unrestricted advance,' Zermelo wrote, 'but possesses only relative stopping-points.'[1] The proper classes of a universe U, such as the class of all its sets and the class of all its ordinals, are not sets in U but are sets in any universe that extends U, as the proper classes of U will be sets in the stage formed from U by adding to U all selections of members of U. In this Zermelo saw a solution of the class paradoxes. Thinking of a universe of set theory as a model of the theory, Zermelo wrote:

In this way the boundless extendability of the transfinite number series permits the presentation of set theory itself as an unlimited sequence of well-differentiated models. The sharp differentiation between these models of the (non-categorical!) axiom system yields a satisfactory clarification of the ultrafinite antinomies, for it is always the case that the non-sets of one model appear as sets both in the next model and in all subsequent ones.[2]

Let us look into Zermelo's idea more closely.

Zermelo's approach to the class paradoxes

Let us recall the paradoxes briefly. The Burali-Forti paradox is an argument to the effect that Ω, the class of all ordinals, has an ordinal that is strictly greater than itself. Cantor's paradox is this: the universal class U must contain all its subclasses, and so U must have at least as many members as subclasses; but, Cantor showed, any class has fewer members than subclasses. Russell's paradox is about the class R of things that are not members of themselves. A little reasoning leads to the conclusion that R is in R if and only if R is not in R.

To deal with the paradoxes of Cantor and Burali-Forti, Cantor drew a distinction between sets and Absolutely Infinite Multiplicities, later known as proper classes. The classes Ω, U, and R are not sets. The Burali-Forti paradox is blocked because Ω, being a proper class, has no ordinal number. The paradoxes of Cantor and Russell are blocked on the assumption, made explicit by von Neumann, that a proper class cannot be a member of a class. But this hardly *solves* those paradoxes. We need some independent reason for believing that a proper class cannot be a member of a class. At this point it is customary to say that a proper class is too big to be a member of a class. But this again is mysterious. Why should the size of a class bar it from membership of other classes?

Zermelo's proposal is different. Although Zermelo did not make this explicit, his idea entails that each of the troublesome class expressions has no absolute reference. What it refers to depends on which universe is the domain of discourse. When the context of use does not determine a universe, as often happens, the expression has no reference, like a noun phrase with an indexical element for which no value is supplied, such as 'the population of this village'. A universe, on Zermelo's conception, is a cumulative hierarchy in which all the axioms of second-order ZFC+AF are true. When the domain is a universe V, 'the class of all ordinals' refers to the class of all ordinals in V, which we might call Ω_V to make the relevant contextual parameter explicit. Ω_V is not a set in V, although it is a set in any universe that extends V and it has an ordinal greater than all those it contains. This greater ordinal is not in V, hence it is not in Ω_V, though it is in any universe extending V. So there is no implication that this new ordinal is greater than itself. That kind of trouble arises when we assume that the predicate 'is an ordinal' has a definite fixed extension regardless of context, an assumption to be rejected on Zermelo's approach.

When a universe V is the domain of discourse, the expression 'the class of all things' or 'the universal class' refers to the class of all things in V, which is V itself. V does not have all its subclasses as members and so we cannot conclude that the cardinality of V is at least as great as the cardinality of $\mathbb{P}V$; hence Cantor's theorem is not contradicted. The paradox arises from the assumption that the predicate 'is a thing' has a definite fixed extension regardless of context. Attention to pragmatic features of language shows that this is implausible.[3] The predicate 'is a thing' is to be construed as synonymous with 'is an entity' and as co-extensive with 'is self-identical'. On Zermelo's approach these predicates have no absolute fixed extension independent of context. It is a fair point that Cantor's paradox does not depend on the use of the word 'thing'. In place of 'the class of all things', we could use 'the class of all classes' and still arrive at a contradiction by the same route. But the solution is also the same. If V is the domain of discourse, 'the class of all classes' denotes the totality of classes in V, call it C_V. Not all subclasses of C_V are in C_V and so there is no reason think that the cardinality of C_V is at least as great as that of $\mathbb{P}C_V$; hence Cantor's theorem is not contradicted. What is rejected is the assumption that the predicate 'is a class' has an absolute extension regardless of context.

In a context with domain V, the expression 'the class of all things that are not members of themselves' refers to the class of all members of V that are not members of themselves. Let us call this class R_V. Actually R_V is identical with V, since nothing is a member of itself in a cumulative hierarchy. But we need not use that fact here. R_V is not a member of itself, although it is a member of all stages after V in any universe extending V. The fact that R_V is not a member of itself does *not* entail that it fulfils the condition for membership of R_V. For that is the condition of being a member of V but not of itself. As R_V is not a member of V, it does not fulfil the condition. So the argument of Russell's paradox does not go through. The argument would go through if it were correct to assume that the condition 'x is not a member of x' has a definite fixed extension independent of context. But this assumption is here being rejected. Parallel considerations apply if we use 'the class of all *classes* that are not members of themselves' in place of 'the class of all *things* that are not members of themselves'.

On Zermelo's approach to the paradoxes, there are no Absolutely Infinite Multiplicities and no classes that are too big to be members. There remains a notion of proper class *relative to* a universe. If V is a universe, any subclass of V that is not a subclass of some stage in V is not a set in V and it has no cardinal number in V. Those subclasses of V are proper classes relative to V. But they are sets with cardinal numbers in the first universe containing V as a stage and in all extensions thereof.

Completing the Zermelo solution

A solution must not only locate a fault in the argument leading to contradiction; it must also explain why it is a fault and why we failed to see it as a fault.

The fault lay in assuming certain predicates to have fixed extensions independent of context. That is wrong because it assumes the existence of an absolute all-inclusive universe of sets (for a fixed basis of atoms), when in fact there is no such total universe.

Why did we fail to see the fault as such? We do not always have difficulty in seeing that the extension of a predicate is context-sensitive when that is the case; consider, for instance, 'is large'. What, then, explains our failure to spot context sensitivity in the case of those predicates involved in the class paradoxes? I think that two factors combine to produce this result. One is that we do not become aware of the relevant contextual items, universes of set theory, until we begin to study models of set theory, which none of us does until a fairly late stage, whereas we make early acquaintance with the rudiments of set theory. The other factor is that the study and development of set theory is carried out mostly without fixing a universe, and the results are applicable whatever the universe, that is, whatever the base of individuals and whatever the extent of the hierarchy. So we do not feel the need to fix a domain. We do not think of our use of the set-theoretic language as missing a parameter value, there being no explicit indices for domains, and so we take the discourse to have a domain fixed by predicates used informally, a domain of 'all sets' or 'all individuals and all sets'. Then the extensions of the other predicates, such as 'is an ordinal' and 'is not a member of itself', are taken to be restrictions of that domain. So there is a ready explanation of the difficulty in coming to see this particular form of context dependence.

These remarks invite the question whether the predicate 'is a universe of set theory' has an absolute extension independent of context. Even when we fix what is meant by set theory, the answer has to be that the predicate has no absolute extension, on pain of re-introducing paradox. The talk of universes has a schematic character. It would become propositional discourse only if a universe U were specified or fixed by context as the domain of discourse. In that case the predicate 'is a universe of set theory' would apply to the sets in U that constitute universes of set theory, if there are any. In fact, Zermelo investigated universes that contain as stages an unbounded sequence of universes.[4] But without any universe fixed as the domain, talk about universes, including that used in completing Zermelo's solution of the paradoxes, does not consist of propositions strictly so-called.

This does not destroy the Zermelo solution. Discourse using language with a (hidden) parameter that has no value in the context of use need not be vacuous. It can be informative and truth-indicating without being true. As an example, consider:

> If an object x is to the left of an object y, y is not to the left of x.

The missing parameter value in this case is observer location and orientation, or viewpoint. The thought is truth-indicating, because were we to think it with a viewpoint in mind, thus supplying the hidden parameter with a value, the result would be a true thought. So here we have an example of an informative non-propositional thought, one that is truth-indicating but not strictly true. The only way of resisting this is to identify the thought with the following universally quantified proposition:

> For any viewpoint v, if an object x is to the left of an object y with respect to v, y is not to the left of x with respect to v.

Although these two thoughts are closely related, they are not the same. To think the thought expressed by the latter, one must possess a concept of viewpoint; to think the thought expressed by former, one need not possess a concept of viewpoint, though one's dispositions to apply a concept of 'left of' must be viewpoint-sensitive. The claims made in the solution of the paradoxes, e.g. that a proper class of one universe V is a set in any universe containing V, are like the first thought; they are informative non-propositional thoughts that are not true but are truth-indicating.[5]

The Liar paradox

An unexpected benefit of the Zermelo approach is a solution to the Liar paradox, given a 'levels' account of uses of the predicate 'is true', as is proposed in the otherwise divergent responses to the Liar paradox given by Tarski, Parsons, Kripke, and Burge.[6] On these approaches, the reasoning that leads to absurdity is supposed to be blocked once one pays attention to the levels. Levels may be properties of languages, or of parts of the extension and anti-extension of the predicate 'x is true', or of utterances, or some other thing depending on the favoured approach. In the absence of any indicator of level, we are led to conclude that the Liar statement is true if and only if it is not true, by applying the Tarski schema:

> [p] is true if and only if p,

where '[p]' stands for 'the proposition that p' (or 'sentence that p', or 'utterance that p'). The results of indicating levels explicitly depend on the particulars of the theory used to deal with the paradox. But an appropriately modified Tarski schema might look something like this:

[p] is $true_{\alpha+1}$ if and only if p, where [p] has level α.

Liar statements with indexed truth predicates would have this form:

(L) L is not $true_{\alpha}$.

These modifications yield anodyne conclusions of the form:

L is $true_{\alpha+1}$ if and only if L is not $true_{\alpha}$.

However, the problem for any such approach is that it always seems possible to reproduce the paradox by 'quantifying out' the index. That is, we can define a new predicate 'is TRUE' in the following way:

x is TRUE if and only if there is some level α such that x is $true_{\alpha}$.

Now let L be the statement: L is not TRUE. Absurdity again results, by the Tarski schema for 'TRUE' in place of 'true':

[p] is TRUE if and only if p.

So a levels approach needs supplementing. Assuming that the levels are well ordered, which is certainly consistent with a 'levels' approach, level indices are in effect ordinals. Here is where Zermelo's contribution applies. Unless the context of the definition determines some universe that delimits the class of ordinals, the attempt to define an absolute predicate 'is TRUE' has not succeeded. If a universe V is determined, the definition gives a notion of truth-in-V:

x is true-in-V if and only if there is some ordinal α in V such that x is $true_{\alpha}$.

Putting 'κ' for the first ordinal not in V, 'x is true-in-V' is equivalent to 'x is $true_{\kappa}$'. So

(L_V) L_V is not true-in-V

is a statement of level κ. A Tarski truth schema that is not relativized to level is inapplicable to L_V. Applying the truth schema with explicit level indices yields

L_V is $true_{\kappa+1}$ if and only if L_V is not true-in-V.

This is not self-contradictory, being equivalent to:

L_V is $true_{\kappa+1}$ if and only if L_V is not $true_{\kappa}$.

A definition of truth must be relative to a universe and therefore cannot succeed in escaping levels. In other words, there is no ultimate 'quantifying out', as that would require an ultimate class of all ordinals, hence an ultimate universe, which is impossible. Clearly, this is only a sketch of a solution. Also, it must be made clear that crucial statements of this solution do not have a level. Like statements in the Zermelo solution of the class paradoxes, they are schematic in character, in the sense that they express informative but not propositional thoughts, which are not true but truth-indicating.

Conclusion

The obscurities and inconsistencies that beset analysis seemed to be banished with the rigorous presentation and development of analysis within the framework of set theory in the latter half of the nineteenth century. That optimistic outlook was destroyed around the turn of the century by the discovery of paradoxes about transfinite sets. Zermelo produced an axiomatization of the theory in which those paradoxical arguments were clearly not reproducible. But the possibility that set theory harboured other paradoxes remained a serious worry, as the axioms did not seem to issue from any clear conception of a domain of sets, and the solutions of the class paradoxes then current were unconvincing. But a further development of our understanding of sets, the iterative conception, did produce a coherent picture partially articulated by the standard axioms. That I hope was shown in the previous chapter. This chapter has presented a solution of the class paradoxes based on an idea of Zermelo's that is a natural corollary of the iterative conception; it has no trace of the *ad hoc* character of the 'limitation of size' approach that has been the orthodoxy for so long.

We should not suffer a hangover from yesterday's paradoxes. Cantor introduced a new kind of entity, transfinite sets. The history of mathematics shows that the introduction of a new kind of entity is liable to give rise to paradoxes until we get clear about the restrictions on old methods and principles needed to make them applicable to the new entities. When these paradoxes are not easily solved, suspicion falls on the new entities. Recall that even the negative integers were regarded with suspicion at first, and paradoxes such as Arnauld's paradox no doubt contributed to the early resistance. We have no good reason to view the class paradoxes in a different way. They showed only that our early understanding of transfinite sets was incoherent. Although it is always possible to increase our understanding, our idea of sets is now sufficiently clear to banish any reasonable fear of incoherence. I conclude that we can have rational confidence in the coherence of set theory and, therefore, of the mathematics that can be modelled within it, which is all of classical mathematics.

Two elements of this conclusion are worth stressing, to avoid misunderstanding. Even if confidence in the *coherence* of set theory is rational, one can still rationally doubt that all of set theory is true. There may be nothing in reality that answers to a coherent conception. If, for example, ontological finitism is correct, there is no universe in which the axiom of infinity is true. Other considerations are needed to provide rational confidence in the truth of set theory. That fact is the source of much discussion in philosophy of mathematics over recent decades. Secondly, the conclusion is that *confidence*, rather than certainty, in the coherence of set theory is rational. On the contrary, though we may have rational confidence in the consistency of set theory, we cannot rationally have the kind of certainty that would come with a finitary consistency proof. What, then, *can* we rationally feel certain of concerning mathematics? That and related questions are considered in the next chapter.

The Search for Certainty: A Reckoning

Gödel's Underivability Theorems mark a watershed. Once they and related theorems were fully assimilated, Hilbert's Programme was not pursued, and no other foundational programme quite so ambitious replaced it. As the iterative conception of sets became more widely appreciated, the worry that set theory might be inconsistent quite reasonably abated, as did the sense of urgency that informed foundational work. None the less, basic epistemological questions remained. We cannot be certain of the reliability, regarding finitary consequences, of much mathematics. What *can* we be certain of? When we cannot be certain of the reliability, hence consistency, of some mathematics, can we none the less have a high degree of confidence in it?

Certainty, I take it, is belief without any doubt whatsoever. When we say that foundationalists want certainty, what we mean is that they want epistemologically rational certainty. Whether certainty about a given proposition is rational depends on the epistemic situation of the believer. Your lack of doubt that you are now looking at words on a page is rational; but it would be irrational if you had evidence that you were currently under the influence of a hallucinogen. The discovery of the class paradoxes altered our collective epistemic situation, effectively wiping out the increase in rational confidence in the coherence of analysis brought about by the nineteenth-century accounts of real analysis in terms of infinite classes and sequences. The foundationalist programmes were intended, at least in part, to alter our epistemic situation so as to reverse this setback. Rational certainty depends not only on the believer's epistemic situation, but also on the context of inquiry. In the context of an inquiry into scepticism about sensory evidence, some doubt about the existence of a page in front of you is mandatory, even if there is no reason to fear cognitive malfunction.[1] The context of foundational inquiry does not demand all-embracing Cartesian doubt. The aim is to overcome problems that arise with non-finitary reasoning about what is infinite and abstract; this means that we may find certainty in computation about what is finite and concrete, when that is spelled out.

Foundational programmes before Gödel's underivability theorems

Russell was keenly aware of the fallibility of our sense of intrinsic necessity, our sense of what is analytic, following his discovery that contradiction flows from Frege's Axiom V. From that time on, the aim of showing that we could be rationally certain of the truth of analysis and beyond was no longer on his agenda. But the aim of showing that we could be very confident about it was still alive. There are two ways in which Russell and Whitehead hoped to contribute to this. One was by showing how the relevant mathematics could be developed in a symbolic language with a syntactic framework so restrictive that no paradoxical argument in sight could be stated within it. What they came up with, the ramified theory of types, was too restrictive for the intended mathematics. The simple theory of types avoids this problem by being more permissive yet still strict enough to block the paradoxes that undermined earlier foundational work, while giving no sign of generating further contradictions. The second way of building rational confidence was by clarifying the relations of epistemic support. Russell had an interesting picture: laws about real numbers and analysis would receive support from the axioms from which they were deduced; the axioms would receive support from their most certain consequences, as long as those consequences were not shared with a rival set of axioms of greater or equal plausibility, and as long as the axioms were not known to have any false consequence. Whatever one thinks of Russell's epistemology of axioms, it is clear that no work was done by Russell or anyone else to show that the axioms of *Principia Mathematica* were well supported in this way. Whitehead and Russell never felt that their axioms of infinity and choice had sufficient support, and they eventually felt the same about reducibility. Of course, propositions of analysis receive scant gain in support by being deduced from axioms that have no greater credibility than those propositions to begin with. So the deduction of laws of analysis from the axioms of *Principia Mathematica* did not advance the moderate cause of showing analysis worthy of a high level of confidence. This holds even if the symbolic theory is interpreted as a simple theory of types. The end gain of the logicist programme was a demonstration that analysis and much of Cantor's theory of infinite classes can be developed in an apparently consistent system that blocks the class paradoxes.

That much was achievable by formalizing Zermelo's axiomatic set theory and its development. Hilbert's goal was different. Instead of aiming to show that we could be rationally confident that those bodies of mathematics are true, he aimed to show that we could be rationally certain that they are reliable with respect to finitary consequences. The goal is less ambitious in one way, focusing on reliability rather than truth, and more ambitious in another way, going for certainty rather than confidence. For certainty there would have to be a proof, with premises and modes of inference that we can be rationally certain of *ab initio*. These resources were to be drawn from finitary mathematics, the mathematics of explicit computation as applied to arrays of symbols. In the context, it was and remains rational to be certain about the correctness of this basis. A proof of reliability on this basis would have made its conclusion certain. Reliability clearly entails consistency. Thus, a finitary proof of the reliability of set theory would have put us in a position to be rationally certain that the theory is consistent. Reflection on this situation would reveal in addition that no possible future discovery could rationally undermine that certainty. Hilbert repeatedly said that he aimed to settle the foundational question 'once and for all'.[2] That kind of permanence would have been achieved had the hoped-for proof been forthcoming. The conception of this programme, in both goal and strategy, was immeasurably superior to the Whitehead–Russell programme. But it could not be done, for reasons given in Part IV, Chapter 2 that centre on Gödel's Second Underivability Theorem. A proof of the reliability of real analysis and beyond would have to use methods or premises beyond the secure basis of finitary reasoning.

Later foundational programmes

Since the demise of Hilbert's Programme, there have been several less ambitious programmes, some of these being scaled-down versions of Hilbert's Programme. Let us take a brief tour. Gentzen showed that the ordinal ε_0 is the least ordinal such that the consistency of arithmetic can be established by finitary methods plus induction up to that ordinal.[3] One programme of research follows Gentzen by trying to find the least ordinal α such that induction up to α together with finitary methods suffice for proving the consistency of a given formal theory that extends arithmetic.[4] This is a way of characterizing the extent beyond finitary reasoning to which we must go in order to establish the consistency of an accepted theory. The ordinal of the relevant induction principle may be thought of as a measure of this distance from finitary reasoning. But it is not clear what epistemological significance this has. As the uncertain aspect of the consistency proofs is confined to the inductive principle used, one might think of the ordinal as a measure of uncertainty. However, it is not plausible that uncertainty of the induction principle strictly increases as one ascends the ordinals, so some other considerations are needed to explain the foundational significance of the work in this programme.[5]

A way of gauging the strength of various parts of analysis is to find the weakest systems, classified by the strength of their set existence axioms, needed to prove given theorems of analysis. This is known as 'reverse mathematics'.[6] Using a formal system of analysis called Z_2, it has been found that for many important theorems τ of analysis there is a weakest natural subsystem of Z_2 in which τ is derivable. Investigation has settled on a small number of subsystems of varying strength. The foundational payoff comes from attempts to apply Hilbert's Programme to these subsystems. For example, the finitary reliability of one of these systems, called WKL_0, has been established by finitary means.[7] The interest of this comes from the fact that a significant portion of the non-finitary mathematics that is actually used, including some well known non-constructive theorems, is derivable within WKL_0.[8] Thus, we have a partial realization of Hilbert's Programme of foundational importance: much ordinary mathematics has been certified reliable by means that are secure from overthrow.

Aside from finitism, there are various foundational viewpoints, depending on what is regarded as certain and what as dubious. A more relaxed view, for example, accepts as certain the mathematics of enumerable sets and sequences, but nothing beyond. Another view counts as certain only predicative mathematics; another, only some version of constructive mathematics. Relative to each such restrictive viewpoint there is a potential programme analogous to Hilbert's Programme. This approach to foundational programmes has been explicated by Feferman.[9] Here is a slightly modified version of Feferman's account of what a programme of this sort aims at:

> A body of mathematics $\mathcal{M}$ is represented in a formal system T_1 that is not justified from restrictive viewpoint $\mathcal{F}$. The system T_1 is proof-theoretically reduced to a system T_2 that is justified from viewpoint $\mathcal{F}$.

Here $\mathcal{F}$ will typically be some version of a foundational 'ism' such as finitism, predicativism, constructivism, and so on. The central notion here is that of a proof-theoretic reduction. Informally put, the idea is that T_1 is *proof-theoretically reducible to* T_2 for a recursively defined set Φ of sentences in the languages of both T_1 and T_2 if and only if there is an effective operation $\mathbf{f}$ on T_1-derivations such that

(1) whenever x is a T_1-derivation of y and y is a sentence in Φ, then $\mathbf{f}(x)$ is a T_2-derivation of y, and
(2) a formal expression of (1) in code is derivable in T_2.[10]

The set Φ will be chosen so that its members are sentences which, on an intended reading, are regarded from foundational viewpoint $\mathscr{F}$ as having definite truth values. So if $\mathscr{F}$ is finitism and T_2 is PRA, Φ might be appropriately chosen to be the set of equations and inequations with primitive recursive terms.[11]

If T_1 is proof-theoretically reducible to T_2 for Φ, any sentence in Φ derivable in T_1 is also derivable in T_2, and a formalized expression of that fact is derivable in T_2. So for suitably chosen Φ a proof-theoretic reduction of T_1 to T_2 establishes that if T_2 is consistent so is T_1, as an absurdity (such as '$\mathbf{0} = \mathbf{1}$') would be T_1-derivable only if it were also T_2-derivable. But the main significance of proof-theoretic reduction lies in the following. Given that T_2 is justified from viewpoint $\mathscr{F}$, a proof-theoretic reduction of T_1 to T_2 for Φ establishes from viewpoint $\mathscr{F}$ that $\mathscr{M}$ is reliable with respect to the sentences in Φ. If from viewpoint $\mathscr{F}$ the set Φ contains all the formal sentences that have a truth value, what is established is that $\mathscr{M}$ is reliable from viewpoint $\mathscr{F}$.

The success of a Hilbert-style programme for part of analysis mentioned earlier fits into the framework: T_1 is the system WKL_0, T_2 is PRA, and Φ is the set of equations and inequations between closed terms in PRA. $\mathscr{M}$ comprises those theorems of analysis with formalizations derivable in WKL_0, and $\mathscr{F}$ is the finitist viewpoint. As finitary thinking (construed as primitive recursive arithmetic) does enjoy a quality of certainty denied to non-finitary thought, the finitary reliability of the significant portion of analysis and algebra represented in WKL_0 can be said to have been established with certainty.

Feferman's predicativist programme

Another programme that fits into this framework is Feferman's predicativist programme. Before saying more about the programme, a reminder about predicativism might be helpful. Impredicative definitions are those that purport to define an entity in terms of a totality to which that entity belongs. If the existence of a totality with a definite extent does not depend on any intellectual construction, such as the totality of planets in the solar system, there is no objection to defining an entity in that way. Thus, if one planet is larger than all other planets, we can single out an entity as 'the largest planet', even though this phrase alludes to the totality of planets.[12] But if the existence of the totality does depend on intellectual constructions, an attempt to single out one of its members in terms of that totality will fail, on the predicativist view. So, to illustrate, if the totality of sets of integers depends on intellectual constructions, we cannot single out a set of integers as 'the $\subseteq$-least set of natural numbers that has property P'.[13] That is the core of predicativist doctrine relevant here. What commitments this entails in practice depends on what totalities one takes to be intellectual constructions. Russell was inclined to think that any totality is an intellectual construction. But Poincaré and Weyl, following Kronecker,[14] regarded the sequence of natural numbers $\mathbb{N}$ as an independently given totality, while every totality that is built up by set-theoretic means from $\mathbb{N}$ is an intellectual construction. This view was taken up by Feferman. He has developed a formal type theory (named W in honour of Weyl) which has $\mathbb{N}$ as the base type and avoids impredicative definitions. Thus, it respects the Vicious Circle Principle. But it has the advantage of avoiding the syntactic complexities of *Principia Mathematica*.[15] Feferman's theory W is proof-theoretically reducible to first order Dedekind–Peano arithmetic (DPA) and is in fact a conservative extension of it.[16] So, assuming that first-order DPA is reliable with respect to finitary sentences, so is W. This and the fact that W introduces no vicious circles not already present in first-order DPA constitute very strong grounds for taking W to be as credible as first-order DPA.

The significance of this depends in part on how much of analysis can be done in W. Recall that Dedekind's Continuity Axiom was a major difficulty for the authors of *Principia Mathematica*. The Continuity Axiom is that every non-empty set of real numbers with an upper bound has a supremum, or least upper bound. The problem is that the concept of the supremum of a set of real numbers is impredicative. Adapting a move of Weyl's, Feferman replaces Dedekind's Continuity Axiom with the principle that every enumerable *sequence* of real numbers with an upper bound has a supremum.[17] This is admissible, since the concept of the supremum of a sequence can be defined predicatively.[18] With suitable reformulation, Feferman has found that a very large part of analysis can be developed within W, including almost all of the analysis that is currently applied in natural science.

Feferman further conjectures that all the mathematics that is actually indispensable to present-day natural science can be developed in W.[19]

The extensive mathematics that can be developed within W is just as reliable (with respect to finitary statements — I will drop this qualification henceforth) as first-order DPA, and we can rationally be as confident in that conclusion as we can be in the truth of first-order DPA. This may not be as great as the confidence we should have in the truth of finitary arithmetic, but it is still significant and greater than the confidence we should have in the truth of set theory. The mathematics of the finite integers, first-order DPA, has never been troubled with paradoxes, unlike analysis and set theory, and so one might think that there is no reason to harbour doubts about it. From the predicativist viewpoint, however, the matter is not so straightforward. Parsons has argued that our concept of the natural numbers is impredicative.[20] The following definition, for example, is obviously impredicative:

> The set of *natural numbers* is the $\subseteq$-least set that contains 0 and is closed under the successor operation.

Other definitions of the set of natural numbers that come readily to mind fare no better. Surely this shows that the predicativist viewpoint rules out taking the structure of natural numbers as given? If so, first-order DPA cannot coherently be taken on trust by predicativists. Feferman and Hellman have responded to this by showing that first-order DPA can be predicatively justified using the notion of a Dedekind-finite set, which does not involve a concept of natural numbers, together with a predicative second-order theory of finite sets.[21] With these resources, they show that (1) there is a predicatively acceptable definition of an N-structure, in effect the structure of natural numbers ordered by successor; (2) there exists such a structure; and (3) any two N-structures are isomorphic. Moreover, the predicative system used contains first-order DPA (and is a conservative extension of it). With this backing, predicativists can coherently take the reliability of W relative to first-order DPA as solid ground for taking W to be reliable absolutely.

Conclusion

We can be rationally certain of the reliability of WKL_0 and we can be rationally very confident that Feferman's system W is reliable. So a high degree of confidence in the reliability of a large amount of classical mathematics has already been justified by proof-theoretic reduction. This is still way short of

Hilbert's goal, which was to establish that we could be rationally certain that set theory, and therefore full analysis, are reliable.[22] However, we should not underestimate the extent of success in the search for certainty, and there is no reason to think that we have reached the limit of what can be achieved in this direction.[23]

Certainty about the reliability of set theory is not warranted. But a high degree of confidence in the reliability of set theory, hence of classical analysis, is warranted. Reliability and consistency for the normal set theories are equivalent. One reason for confidence in the consistency of set theory is that we have a positive conception of a model of the theory, namely, a universe of sets as a cumulative hierarchy, a conception that the axioms partially articulate. A secondary reason for confidence is that, after decades of work in set theory, no inconsistency in the theory has been found. Of course we do not have a rational basis for thinking that an inconsistency could not possibly be found in the future. Our confidence is rational but not indefeasible. Is this such a bad thing? It can be difficult, disturbing even, to have to accept that what we now firmly believe might later be found wrong. Conversely, belief in the invulnerability of our basic convictions brings solace. Russell's confession is telling: 'I wanted certainty in the kind of way people want religious faith.'[24] The desire for certainty of this infallibilist kind is deep-rooted, a natural reaction to past shocks. But it is an over-reaction. If we were to find an inconsistency, we would seek further clarification of the concepts involved, and opt for something clearer and more modest; we would still be able to retrench to a theory that includes much of applied mathematics.

The final balance, then, is positive. Though we cannot be *certain* of the reliability of *all* of classical mathematics, we can be certain of the reliability of a significant part of it, and we can be confident in the reliability of all of it.

Outlook 4

The central concern of this book is the epistemic status of non-finitary mathematics. Epistemology is not the only concern in foundational studies, though it has been dominant. The nature and intrinsic organization of mathematics has also been a major concern. Later developments in mathematics show that set theory is not the only basis for this kind of inquiry. Of course, those who think that true mathematics must be constructed will reject not only classical set theory but also the nineteenth-century mathematics out of which it grew. In this regard the development of constructive analysis can be regarded as partial fulfilment of an alternative foundational programme.[1] I am not able to evaluate the success and significance of this programme, and perhaps it is too early anyway. For those who accept classical mathematics, category theory has been offered as an alternative to set theory for its catholic reach. Mathematics is definitely not just logic, not just higher-order logic, not just set theory. The old picture of a single fundamental theory to which all else must be reduced has faded. If pure mathematics is the study of abstract structures, set theory is just one framework among others for thinking about that subject matter, and it may not be the best. Universes of sets are themselves structures, and these may be instances of something more general, as is suggested by topos theory. In addition, topos theory sheds new light on the intrinsic organization of mathematics, revealing a surprising unity between apparently disparate fields, topology and algebraic geometry on the one hand, and logic and set theory on the other.[2]

The initial impulse for foundational study was the need to clarify our understanding of the continuum and the basis of infinitesimal calculus. The standard set-theoretic account is an explication that has served well — witness the use made of it in classic textbooks on analysis.[3] But now there are other explications of the basic intuitions. Robinson's non-standard analysis rehabilitated infinitesimals.[4] Non-classical accounts include intuitionistic analysis and Bishop's constructive analysis. The development of synthetic differential geometry gives yet another perspective on the continuum and a novel theory of infinitesimals.[5] Thus we now have a plurality of mathematical ways of refining and abstracting from what are originally spatial intuitions. This too is a way in which foundational study has spread out and away from the monolithic view.

If new developments within mathematics advance our understanding of the nature and intrinsic organization of mathematics, epistemological advances are likely to come from developments outside. In the period covered by this book, the central epistemological concern has been to justify a body of mathematics. Another concern is to explain how it is possible for an individual to have mathematical knowledge and understanding. This inquiry needs fine-grained information about how we actually acquire our mathematical beliefs and abilities; then we can investigate how best to evaluate those modes of cognitive growth in epistemic terms. The empirical input must come primarily from cognitive sciences. Investigations of simple numerical abilities have already proved fruitful, aided by a recent confluence of evidence from different sources: experiments on healthy adults, children, and even infants, clinical tests on brain-damaged patients, brain imaging studies, and animal studies.[6] There is still a long way to go. The history of mathematics is another source of information. What we lack here is information about the messy initial period leading up to and beyond discovery, before arguments and results have been cleaned up and regimented for public presentation. Unfortunately, we all tend to throw away our jumbled scribblings and rough diagrams. To any mathematician reading this: please keep and file your notes! They are more precious than rubies, at least for epistemologists of mathematics. Perhaps mathematicians are slightly ashamed of the haphazard and non-systematic character of research. But this feeling is unwarranted. Fruitful research has to be that way: there is no programme for discovery. That is one of the lessons of foundational study.

Endnotes

PART I

Chapter 1

1. Mentioned in Kline (1972: 252).

2. Mancosu (1996: ch. 6), examines 17-cent. criticisms of Leibniz's infinitesimal calculus. These predate Berkeley's relatively famous criticism (Berkeley 1734) by several decades. See also Bos (1974).

3. Quoted in Kline (1980: 138–9).

4. Kline (1972: 466). In fact, there are notions to which the name 'sum' is given that are applicable to divergent series (Kline: 1972) ch. 47).

5. The expansion is found by re-expressing $1/(1 + x)$ as $(1 + x)^{-1}$ and then applying the binomial theorem for negative integer exponents.

6. A power series is a series whose nth term has the form $a_n(x - x_0)^n$ where x_0 is the same for all terms in the series while the coefficients a_n may differ.

7. Leibniz had shown that $\pi/4 = \int_0^1 1/[1 + x^2]dx$. Expanding the integrand as a power series, he obtained $1/(1 + x^2) = 1 - x^2 + x^4 - x^6 + \ldots$ Then integrating term by term and substituting 1 for x in the result gives $\pi/4 = 1 - 1/3 + 1/5 - 1/7 + \ldots$ (see Kitcher 1984: ch. 10).

8. Where l is the length of string and $0 < x < l$ and t is time elapsed, Daniel Bernouilli claimed that all solutions were of the form $y(t, x) = \sum_n^\infty a_n \sin(n\pi x/l).\cos(n\pi ct/l)$ (see Kline 1972: ch. 22).

9. These letters, extracts from which are cited in Kline (1972, 1980) and Kitcher (1984), were written in 1826 (Abel 1881: ii. 263–5 and ii. 267).

10. According to Kline (1980), such arguments were given by Ampère in 1806, by Bertrand in 1875, and by Lacroix in the second edition of his three-volume work *Traité du calcul différential et du calcul intégral* (1810–19).

11. The parallels postulate is that, for any line L and any point p not on L, exactly one line parallel to L in the plane of L and p runs through p. By 1829 Gauss, Lobachevsky, and Bolyai had independently discovered a non-Euclidean geometry known as *hyperbolic geometry*. This is the result of replacing Euclid's parallels postulate by the postulate that, for some line L and point p not on L, at least two lines parallel to L in the plane of L and p run through p. Gauss made clear in letters to Bessel his opinion that the geometry of space could not be established *a priori*. The relevant portions of these letters are translated in Ewald (1996). Another factor in loss of confidence in geometry *may* have been the discovery of flaws in Euclid's exposition.

12. Bolzano's example was found in his unpublished work of 1834. In 1860 Cellérier gave another example, though it was not published until much later. Weierstrass gave another example in 1872 that was published in 1875 (see Kline 1972: ch. 40, §3). For a mathematician's response to such counterintuitive findings, see Hahn (1933).

13. Peano (1890) and Hilbert (1891). For the full-story of the first century of space-filling curves with mathematical proofs, see the wonderful book by Sagan (1994).

14. By 'real numbers' I refer to those numbers we associate with points on the continuous number line, numbers that can be represented by an infinite decimal. (In fact, this definition of limit has much wider application, e.g. to complex numbers or, more generally, to the elements of any metric space.)

15. This definition can be applied more generally to functions defined on a subset of a metric space with values in a metric space. Examples are the space-filling curves mentioned earlier, which are continuous functions defined on the closed-unit interval (the set of real numbers between 0 and 1 inclusive) whose values are all the points $\langle x, y \rangle$ in the closed unit square, i.e. such that $0 \leqslant x, y \leqslant 1$, with distance between $\langle x_1, y_1 \rangle$ and $\langle x_2, y_2 \rangle$ defined as $\sqrt{[(x_2 - x_1)^2 + (y_2 - y_1)^2]}$.

16. The natural numbers are the non-negative integers.

17. An accessible account of Cauchy's error is given in Kitcher (1984: ch.10).

18. Why does the difference between pointwise and uniform convergence matter? Uniform convergence preserves continuity, in the sense that, if a sequence of continuous functions converges uniformly to a function, that function too is continuous. This is an advantage over pointwise convergence because there are sequences of continuous functions that converge pointwise to a discontinuous function. There are other advantages to uniform convergence.

19. An example is the function $\sin(1/x)$ for x between 0 and 2π. For discussion of this point, see Giaquinto (1994).

Chapter 2

1. Here is the standard argument by *reductio ad absurdum*. Suppose that $\sqrt{2}$ is the ratio of a pair of integers, say $\sqrt{2} = h/k$. Then we can cancel out all common factors greater than 1 in h/k. Let p/q be the result. So $\sqrt{2} = p/q$ where p and q have no common factors. As $\sqrt{2} = p/q$, $2 = (p/q)^2 = p^2/q^2$, and so $p^2 = 2q^2$. So p^2 is even. But the square of an odd number is odd: $(2m + 1)^2 = 4m^2 + 4m = 1$. Hence p is even: $p = 2m$, say. But $p^2 = 2q^2$, so $4m^2 = 2q^2$, so $2m^2 = q^2$. So q^2 is even. Hence q is even: $q = 2n$, say. So p and q have 2 as a common factor, contradicting the choice of p and q. Hence $\sqrt{2}$ is not the ratio of a pair of integers.

2. It suffices to show

(#) For any positive integers p and q, if p/q is not an integer neither is $(p/q)^2$.

For (#) entails that, for any positive integers n, p, q, if $n = (p/q)^2$, p/q is an integer; so, if for some positive integers p and q, $\sqrt{n} = p/q$, $\sqrt{n}$ is an integer; so if $\sqrt{n}$ is not an integer it is irrational.

Here is proof of (#). As in the previous note, assume that p and q have no common factor. If $q = 1$, p/q is an integer. So assume $q > 1$. If $p = 1$, $0 < (p/q)^2 < 1$, as required. So assume $p > 1$. Every integer > 1 has a unique prime factorization. So p^2 has the same prime factors as p but with each one occurring twice; similarly, q^2 has the same prime factors as q occurring twice. So p^2 and q^2 have no common prime factor, otherwise p and q would have a common prime factor. Clearly, two numbers have a common prime factor if and only if they have a common factor. Hence p^2 and q^2 have no common factor. Hence for no k is there an integer n such that $p^2 = n.k$ and $q^2 = 1.k$. Hence for all n, $p^2/q^2 \neq n$. Hence for all n, $(p/q)^2 \neq n$.

3. A real number x is an *upper bound* of a class C of real numbers if and only if, for every c in C, $c \leq x$. x is the *least upper bound* (or *supremum*) of C if and only if, for all upper bounds y of C, $x \leq y$.

4. Cantor's account was published in 1872. Cantor's attitude to the relation between fundamental sequences was not quite as simple as I have suggested; see Dauben (1979: 37–40).

5. Dedekind's account is given in Dedekind (1872). In the preface Dedekind says that his account stems from ideas he already had in 1858.

6. Rudin (1964) gives a concise yet thorough treatment of cuts. Note that he identifies a cut with its lower class.

7. The appendix to this chapter explains what this means.

8. $\{s_n\}$ is represented by the class of ordered pairs $\langle k, s_k \rangle$.

9. For Cantor's attitude, see Dauben (1979: 37–40). For Dedekind's attitude, see Kline (1972: 986).

10. See Dauben (1979: ch. 2).

11. Let me use the notation $\{x : \varphi(x)\}$ for the class of x satisfying the condition φ. An interval $(c, d) = \{x : c < x < d\}$ is open; an interval $(c, d) = \{x : c \leq x \leq d\}$ is closed.

12. Cantor had found that many classes of the second species have an important property, which he defined in 1879: C is *everywhere dense in* X if and only if every point of X is a limit point of C if not a point in C. This means that every neighbourhood of every point of X contains infinitely many points of C. This can happen even when C is much sparser than X. For example, the class of rationals is everywhere dense in the class of reals. Cantor had found a number of classes of the second species that were everywhere dense in a given interval. An obvious question then was whether every class of the second species that is a subclass of a given interval is everywhere dense in that interval. If so, classes of the second species might have a key role in explaining the nature of the continuum. But by 1880 Cantor had discovered that the generalization fails. However, in a series of papers on the theory of point classes (1879–84) he published many positive theorems involving his transfinite classification; see Dauben (1979: chs. 4, 5).

13. A relation $<$ on a class C is a *strict linear ordering* of C if and only if (i) for all x, y in C, exactly one of the following holds: $x < y$ or $x = y$ or $y < x$ (trichotomy), and (ii) for all x, y and z in C, if $x < y$ and $y < z$, then $x < z$ (transitivity).

14. If D is a non-empty subclass of C, x is <-least in D if and only if, for every y in D, $x \leq y$.

15. Cantor (1883, 1897).

16. Cantor (1883). I use 'infinite' and 'transfinite' interchangeably when qualifying ordinals and cardinals.

17. In a letter of 1873.

18. Cantor's first proof of this was published in 1874. The proof given here appears in Cantor (1895).

19. This was shown by Liouville in 1844.

20. Instead of 'enumerable', some people write 'denumerable' or 'countable'.

21. Cantor gave proofs that the rationals and algebraic numbers are enumerable in a paper of 1874. In the same paper he gave a proof of the non-enumerability of $\mathbb{R}$. The proof given here is from a paper of Cantor's published in 1891.

22. Given that any class can be well-ordered, this 'less-than' relation can be proved to be a strict linear ordering.

23. I use the terms 'infinite' and 'transfinite' interchangeably when applied to ordinal and cardinal numbers. The conclusion that there are at least two infinite numbers can be resisted by denying that the class of reals has a cardinal number.

24. Letter to Dedekind in Dedekind (1887).

25. Presented in the paper of 1891 mentioned in n. 21.

26. If an ordinal is identified with its predecessor class and $|x|$ is the cardinality of x, a more concise definition is: $\aleph_0 = |\omega|$; $\aleph_{\alpha+1} = |\{\beta : |\beta| = \aleph_\alpha\}|$; if λ is a limit ordinal, $\aleph_\lambda = |\{\beta : \text{for some } \alpha < \lambda, |\beta| = \aleph_\alpha\}|$.

27. At the meeting Hilbert presented only ten of the problems, but the published text of his lecture gives the full list (Hilbert 1900b). Hilbert's introduction and his exposition of the continuum problem is translated in Ewald (1996: vol. 2).

28. The section 'Personality, psychology, and depression' of Dauben (1979: ch. 12) explains how strongly affected Cantor was by Kronecker's opposition.

29. As to what Kronecker may have actually said, Jeremy Gray has told me, we have only Weber's obituary of him as evidence, in *Jahresberichte der Deutschen Mathematiker-Vereinigung* 2 (1893): 5–31, as follows: 'Mancher von Ihnen wird sich des Ausspruchs erinnern, den er in einem Vortrag bei der Berliner Naturforscher-Versammlung im Jahre 1886 tat "Die ganzen Zahlen hat der liebe Gott gemacht, alles andere ist Menschenwerk".' Also, Hilbert, who was acquainted with Kronecker's views through discussion with him, cites this maxim in presenting the Kroneckerian outlook in Hilbert (1920). For the extent of Kronecker's opposition to Cantor's work, see the section 'Leopold Kronecker (1823–1891): early opposition to Cantor's work' in Dauben (1979: ch. 3).

30. Dedekind (1888).

31. Some remarks of Dedekind might suggest that his concern in defining real numbers is merely a concern for rules and regimentation, for example his claim in part VI of Dedekind (1872) that the proposition that $\sqrt{2} \times \sqrt{3} = \sqrt{6}$ had never been established.

Endnotes

However, Jeremy Gray pointed out to me that Dedekind's remark can be taken as a rejection of the obvious geometric proof. (The square on the diagonal of a square S has twice the area of S. Hence a square of side 1 has a diagonal of $\sqrt{2}$ and a square of side $\sqrt{3}$ has a diagonal of $\sqrt{6}$. So $\sqrt{2}$ is to 1 as $\sqrt{6}$ is to $\sqrt{3}$; so ($\sqrt{3} \times \sqrt{2}$) is to 1 as ($\sqrt{3} \times \sqrt{6}$) is to $\sqrt{3}$ and therefore as $\sqrt{6}$ is to 1. So $\sqrt{3} \times \sqrt{2} = \sqrt{6}$.)

32. The general theory of classes in Cantor (1895, 1897) was much more extensive.

33. A class K is *closed under* s if and only if, for every x in K, $s(x)$ is in K.

34. This is 'second-order' induction (with quantifiers ranging over elements *and* a quantifier ranging over classes of elements). There is a first-order version of induction which goes by the same name. There are first-order and second-order versions of Dedekind–Peano arithmetic, depending on which version of induction is used.

35. This isomorphism theorem does not hold for the first-order version of Dedekind–Peano arithmetic.

36. Dedekind (1888: §73). In fact, he did not show that all simply infinite systems are isomorphic until §§132, 133.

37. Cantor (1895: §7).

38. §§135, 137. Dedekind has '$m + 1 = s(m)$' and '$m \times 1 = m$' instead of the equations with '0'. §155 defines exponentiation.

39. Frege's stated view is that the number n is the class of *concepts* that have extensions with exactly n members. A concept, on Frege's view, is what a predicate stands for, a predicate being what remains from a sentence when one or more names are removed; and a concept's *extension* is the class of entities satisfying a predicate that stands for the concept. However, concepts, according to Frege, are extensional: no two of them have the same extension; concepts are distinguished from classes only by being references of incomplete expressions, while classes are references of complete expressions. Thus, Fregean concepts are not what we normally have in mind when we use the term 'concept'. For our purposes it will be simpler and less misleading if we overlook the Fregean distinction and treat his 'concepts' as classes. See Furth's excellent introduction to Frege (1964) for elaboration and substantiation of this point.

40. The formal definitions are given in §§41–6 of Frege (1893) in Frege's symbolism. One will need to see earlier sections to understand the definitions. The informal account is in §§72–83 of Frege (1884).

41. Frege's endeavours, we noted, were exceptional in having a philosophical motivation.

PART II

Chapter 1

1. Here I follow Quine's 'The Ways of Paradox' (Quine 1962), where he gives a brief tour around some of the paradoxes that will be dealt with in this book.

2. Here is one. Let $a = b$ be given. Then (i) $a^2 = ab$, and so $a^2 - b^2 = ab - b^2$. Hence (ii)

$(a + b)(a - b) = b(a - b)$. Hence (iii) $a + b = b$. Hence (iv) $a + a = a$, and so $2a = a$. Hence (v) $2 = 1$. The fallacy comes in step (iii), where one divides both sides by $a - b$, which equals 0.

3. Cantor (1895); Burali-Forti (1897). They used the paradoxical argument to reach (different) conclusions by *reductio ad absurdum*. For its acceptance as a paradox, see Moore and Garciadiego (1981).

4. Cantor used the argument to show that there is no class of all classes in a letter to Dedekind dated 31 August, 1899 (Dauben 1979: p.242, n. 7).

5. Cantor (1891).

6. See Rang and Thomas (1981).

7. See Grattan-Guinness (1978).

Chapter 2

1. For a brief account see the sections 'Ordinal numbers' and 'Cardinal numbers' in Pt I, Ch. 2.

2. Cantor (1887–8); translations of relevant passages are given in Hallett (1984: 41).

3. Cantor (1883).

4. Cantor (1899).

5. See Hallett (1984: 165–6), and, for more on the Absolute , (1984: 39–48).

6. Cantor uses this criterion in his letter to Dedekind (Cantor 1899) to show that the cardinality of any infinite set is an aleph.

7. These are: (1) no AIM has cardinal number; (2) if there is a 1-to-1 correlation between two classes, both are sets or both are AIMs; (3) any subclass of a set is also a set.

8. Chapter 1 of pt VI below explains the idea of a cumulative hierarchy of sets.

9. The logician was P. Jourdain. I have no idea whether this was fair to Jourdain.

10. Russell (1906a: 153 in Russell (1973).

11. An injection from X to Y is 1-to-1 correlation of X with a subclass of Y.

12. This is the theorem that, if there is an injection from X to Y and an injection from Y to X, there is a bijection from one to the other.

13. To see that the class of all sets is an AIM, let f be the following bijection between the class of ordinals and a subclass of the class of all sets: for any ordinal α, $f(\alpha) =$ the class of ordinals preceding α. Using Cantor's criterion that a class C is an AIM if there is a bijection between the class of all ordinals and C or one of its subclasses, it follows that the class of all sets is an AIM (and, for the same reason, so is the class of all classes).

14. Cantor's theorem is compatible with the existence of a class of all *subsets* of U, as some subclasses of U will not be sets, hence not subsets of U. In particular, if c is any 1-to-1 mapping of sets to classes of sets, the class $\{x : x \in U \ \& \ x \notin c(x)\}$ need not be a set.

15. For each ordinal α the set of α's predecessors is not a member of itself. So f defined

Endnotes

in n. 13 is a bijection between the class of ordinals and a subclass of the class of things that are not members of themselves; hence that class is an AIM.

16. The argument for this is given in the previous note.

17. Hessenberg (1906), quoted in Hallett (1984: 168).

18. The mathematician Thomae concluded: 'Mathematics is the unclearest of all sciences' (Thomae 1906; quoted in Dauben 1979: 351). This was hyperbole, of course, as other sciences clearly depended on mathematics. But the remark indicates the uncertainty that typically followed awareness of the paradoxes.

Chapter 3

1. Frege (1893: §0).

2. Frege (1884: §14).

3. Consider, for example, Hilbert's first axiom of order, that if point b lies between points a and c, those points lie on a common line and b lies between c and a.

4. From a lecture given by Frege in 1885, 'Über formale Theorien der Arithmetik', quoted in Dummett (1991).

5. Frege (1903: §147).

6. In Frege's writing, a concept is what I have called a condition; to say of an object that it *falls under* a concept is to say that it satisfies a condition.

7. Frege (1893: §3).

8. Frege (1893: §9).

9. Frege (1893: §20). Michael Potter points out that Basic Law V is slightly more general than I have presented it, because it applies to any functions F and G, not just to concepts, which are functions whose value for any input is a truth-value.

10. Frege (1893: introduction).

11. ibid.

12. Frege (1879) was his initial attempt to give a language of the required kind, his *Begriffsschrift*. An improved version is set out in the first part of Frege (1893).

13. Frege (1893: introduction).

14. Frege (1893: §34).

15. The argument is: (1) $\forall x$ [F(x) $\leftrightarrow$ F(x)] (a logical truth); (2) $\{x : F(x)\} = \{x : F(x)\}$ (from (1) and (Va)); (3) $\exists z$ [$z = \{x : F(x)\}$] (from (2) by existential generalization).

16. The argument from the general formula to the contradiction is given in the appendix to Frege (1903).

17. The derivation is given in the appendix to Frege (1903).

18. Universal instantiation is the rule that permits inferences of the form: $\forall x$ F(x); $\therefore$ F(c). Existential generalization is the rule: F(c); $\therefore \exists x$ F(x). In both cases c is a singular term, such as a proper name or definite description.

19. Frege (1903: appendix). Another reason for Frege's aversion to this option may be his reluctance to allow that some functions are only partially defined. A first-level concept is a concept applicable to objects. Taking class abstraction as a function

238

from first-level concepts $\Gamma(x)$ to their extensions $\{x : \Gamma(x)\}$, this option entails that class abstraction is a partially defined function: 'we must take into account the possibility that there are concepts having no extension—at any rate, none in the ordinary sense of the word. Because of this, the justification of our second-level function $\{x : \Gamma(x)\}$ is shaken; yet such a function is indispensable for laying the foundation of arithmetic.'

20. ibid. In the introduction to the first volume of *Grundgesetze* (Frege 1893), Frege wrote: 'A dispute can arise, so far as I can see, only with regard to my Basic Law concerning courses-of-values (V), which logicians have not yet expressly enunciated, and yet is what people have in mind, for example, where they speak of the extensions of concepts. I hold that it is a law of pure logic. In any event the place is pointed out where a decision must be made.'

21. Resnik (1980) makes this point.

22. Lesniewski showed this, according to Sobocinski (1949); Resnik (1980: 215–19) also shows this.

23. See Dummett (1991: 6–7), and Parsons (1976); Resnik (1980) cites Frege (1969: 295–302).

Chapter 4

1. The extension of the concept expressed by a predicate '$F(x)$' is just $\{x: F(x)\}$, the class of satisfiers of the condition of being F.

2. Putting '$\varnothing$' for the empty class, $\varnothing \notin \varnothing$; so $\varnothing \in \{x : x \notin x\}$; hence $\exists y\, [y = \{x : x \notin x\}]$.

3. Here I am assuming that the variable marks a gap in an open sentence. This means that it is a 'free' variable rather than a variable 'bound' by a preceding quantifier. In the open sentence 'for every person x, x is no taller than y', the variable x is bound and the variable y is free.

4. Russell (1903: app. B).

5. There is a slight complication as the type of the extension of an n-place relation will need to store the types of its relata in appropriate order. An obvious way of doing this is to stipulate that the type of an n-place relation whose relata in order have types $t_1, \ldots, t_n$ is the sequence $\langle t_1, \ldots, t_n \rangle$. Now let the variables of a k-place predicate $F(x^1, \ldots, x^k)$ have types $t_1, \ldots, t_k$ respectively. The syntactic rule is: each x^i may be replaced by any term of type t_i but no other. The semantic rule is: the condition expressed by $F(x^1, \ldots, x^k)$ is true or false of each sequence of entities of types $t_1, \ldots, t_k$ respectively, but is neither true nor false of any other sequence.

6. The argument is this. Let C be a class of type $n + 1$. Then (a) for some condition $F(x_n)$, $C = \{x_n : F(x_n)\}$. So $e \in C \leftrightarrow e \in \{x_n : F(x_n)\}$. And (b) $e \in \{x_n : F(x_n)\} \leftrightarrow F(e)$. So $e \in C \leftrightarrow F(e)$. So '$e \in C$' has a truth value if and only if '$F(e)$' has a truth value. But '$F(e)$' has a truth value if and only if e is of type n, as only terms of type n can replace the variable in '$F(x_n)$'. So '$e \in C$' has a truth value if and only if e is of type n.

7. Whitehead and Russell (1910–13: the opening of ch. II of the introduction).

Endnotes

8. This may have been part of what troubled Russell in his discussion of 'Heine and the French' in his early formulation of the doctrine of types: Russell (1903: app. B).

9. The principle is expressed less directly in *Principia Mathematica*. Whitehead and Russell (1910–13: p I, §A, p. 95).

10. Gödel (1944).

PART III
Chapter 1

1. More precisely, a language L is semantically closed if the semantics of L can be stated in L. The semantics of L includes a definition of 'true-in-L' in the sense of Tarski (1932), but all that is needed here is that a concept of definability in L is expressible in L. Many natural languages are semantically closed.

2. A defining expression in this context is a description true of exactly one entity. Thus, 'the cube root of 8' defines 2, and 'Tolstoy's longest novel' defines *War and Peace*.

3. Given some assumptions about language that are true of most (perhaps all) fixed natural languages and typical formal languages, it can be proved that the total number of defining expressions in a language is $\aleph_0$, the number of natural numbers.

4. Versions of this were published by König (1905) and Dixon (1907), not as a paradox, but as part of arguments against Cantorian claims upheld by Zermelo. Russell (1908) appears to have been the first to see a paradox in the arguments. See Garciadiego (1985).

5. Berry's version is given in a letter to Russell of 1904. The version given here is closer to Berry's than Russell's presentation of it.

6. This is given in the section 'Cardinal numbers' in Pt I Ch. 2 above.

7. This is the same as saying that L has at most $\aleph_0$ expressions.

8. Richard (1905).

9. Poincaré (1906); Russell (1906*b*).

10. Russell (1906*b*, 1908, 1910); Whitehead and Russell (1910–13: vol. I, Introduction, ch. II, §I). Poincaré's formulation (Poincaré 1906, §xv) is no better.

11. Whitehead and Russell (1910–13: vol. I, Introduction, ch. II, §I).

12. Gödel (1944) claims that the three different formulations state three different principles. Chihara (1973) suggests that Russell had only one principle in mind.

13. A bound occurrence either is part of a quantifier phrase or is governed by a preceding quantifier phrase. For example, in the predicate 'for some integer x, $y = 2x$' the occurrence of 'y' is free, as we could intelligibly replace it by '4'. But the occurrences of 'x' are bound, as the first serves to indicate which variable-occurrences in the ensuing expression are governed by the quantifier 'for some integer x' and the second is governed by it, so that neither occurrence of 'x' marks a gap for a name.

Russell uses different terminology: free variables are called *real* variables and bound variables are called *apparent* variables.

14. Consider the predicate '$x > 0$ and for some y, $y = 1/x$'. If, in this predicate, the range of both the free variable 'x' and the bound variable 'y' is the class of rational numbers, the predicate expresses the condition of being a positive rational number with a rational inverse, which is satisfied by all positive rationals. If we alter the range of 'x' to the class of integers while the range of 'y' remains the class of rationals, the predicate expresses the condition of being a positive integer with a rational inverse, which is satisfied by just the positive integers. Finally, if the range of both of 'x' and 'y' is the class of integers, the predicate expresses yet another condition: that of being a positive integer with an integer inverse, which is satisfied only by 1. So the condition expressed by a predicate can be sensitive to the ranges of its free and bound variables.

15. There are two hidden variables if the basic language is the language of number theory. If the basic language is that of *Principia Mathematica*, 'x is an integer' is a defined predicate and so there will be more than two hidden variables.

16. In the notation of *Principia Mathematica* a circumflex over the free variable is used instead of a preceding lambda: $\lambda x[x$ is an integer] is $[\hat{x}$ is an integer]. The lambda notation is more common now.

17. Russell (1908); Whitehead and Russell (1910–13: vol. I, Introduction, ch. II, §I).

18. A class y is said to *include* x when x is a subclass of y; it is said to *contain* x when x is a member of y.

19. In fact, the relation '$\leq$' need not be a well-ordering. It suffices if it is a partial ordering such that one element precedes all others.

20. This is the principle that, for any predicate $F(x)$ in a semantically closed language L, there is a class $\{x: F(x)\}$ such that, for any object y, $y \in \{x: F(x)\} \leftrightarrow F(y)$.

21. Chihara (1973) shows that Cantor's paradox also has a hypothetical definition whose reference would be in the range of one of its *bound* variables.

22. The device is von Neumann's. A class x is defined to be an ordinal if and only if it is well ordered by the $\in$ -relation and every member of it is a subclass of it. This entails that an ordinal is identical with the class of ordinals that precede it. In the context of a distinction between sets and other classes, this definition is intended to apply only to sets. But if no such distinction is made, this identification ensures that, if there were a class of all ordinals, that class would itself be an ordinal.

23. This is adapted from an example Russell invented for a different purpose.

24. We get the same paradox by considering whether the condition of not being true of itself is a condition true of itself. This is one of several paradoxes of truth set out in Pt III Ch. 4.

25. See Goldfarb (1989).

26. In reaching this conclusion, I assume that a complex entity constitutively depends on its constituents and I am using the interpretation of 'defines in terms of' given earlier that counts variable ranges as crucial.

27. Define $z \in^1 y \leftrightarrow z \in y$, and $z \in^{n+1} y \leftrightarrow \exists w[z \in w \ \& \ w \in^n y]$. Then x is an element of c's membership tree if and only if, for some positive integer n, $x \in^n c$. The membership tree of a set is also known as its *transitive closure*. I visualize a membership tree as growing downwards, like a root system; hence x lies below y when, for some positive integer n, $x \in^n y$.

28. The Cantor set is obtained as follows. Let I_1 be the class of closed intervals $\{[0, 1/3], [2/3, 1]\}$ left after removing the open middle third from the interval $[0, 1]$, and let I_{n+1} be the class of intervals left after removing the open middle thirds from all the intervals that are members of I_n. Now define E_n as the union of the members of I_n, i.e. $[0, 1/3^n] \cup [(2/3^n, 3/3^n] \cup \ldots \cup [(3^n-1)/3^n, 1]$. The Cantor set is the intersection of all the sets E_n. It can be defined thus: $\{x : \exists a \forall n[a_n = 0 \text{ or } 2, \ \& \ x = \sum_{n=1}^{\infty} a_n 3^{-n}]\}$. This set is notable for being non-enumerably infinite but of measure zero.

29. It is also guaranteed by the Axiom of Foundation: every non-empty class x has a member y such that y has no member in common with x. If a class c occurred in its own membership tree, the class of elements of the branch from c down to and including c would be a counterinstance of the axiom. However, no one had any inkling of this axiom in the 1910s, when Russell was working on the paradoxes; nor was there any need for such an axiom in the context of type theory.

30. Mathematical functions in the modern sense are extensional, as they are identical if they have the same inputs (arguments) and the same output (value) for each input, regardless of how they are defined. A mathematical function can be identified with the class of its ordered input–output pairs.

31. Whitehead and Russell (1910–13: vol. I, p. 65).

32. ibid. 75.

33. Though Whitehead and Russell co-authored *Principia Mathematica*, Russell was responsible for the underlying philosophy of logic. The philosophical material in *Principia Mathematica* was published in earlier papers by Russell alone. Russell (1948) counters the impression that Whitehead's contribution was not significant.

Chapter 2

1. Whitehead and Russell (1910–13: preface and Introduction).

2. Russell (1911).

3. According to Russell, a propositional function presupposes all its values, and those are propositions. If the domain of *PM* contains everything presupposed by an entity in its domain, it must contain propositions.

4. Strictly speaking, I should say 'classes or relations-in-extension'. Some mathematical objects are presented as the extensions of predicates of two or more variables. Today we treat these as classes whose members are ordered n-tuples, for $n > 1$. Whitehead and Russell called them *relations-in-extension* (or simply *relations*) and treated them as distinct from classes. But the difference is insignificant: an n-place relation is to a propositional function with exactly n free variables in its defining predicate as a

class is to a propositional function with exactly 1 free variable in its defining predicate. I will continue to talk as though relations are classes.

5. '. . . we have avoided the decision as to whether a class of things has in any sense an existence as one object' (Whitehead and Russell 1910–13: Introduction, ch. I; see also the start of the summary of ∗20).

6. See ibid. ∗20 for details. Here is a brief indication using modern notation. Sentences having forms on the left are replaceable by sentences having forms on the right:

$\{x : G(x)\} = \{x : H(x)\}$ $\forall x [G(x) \leftrightarrow H(x)]$;

$y \in \{x : G(x)\}$ $G(y)$;

$\Phi(\{x : G(x)\})$ $\exists H [\forall x [G(x) \leftrightarrow H!(x)] \ \& \ \Phi(\lambda x.H!(x))]$.

Roughly speaking, the first translates 'the class of Gs is the same as the class of Hs' as 'a thing is a G if and only if it is an H'; the second translates 'y is a member of the class of Gs' as 'y is a G'; and the last translates 'Φ is true of the class of Gs' as 'Φ is true of some flat propositional function H that is coextensive with G.' Flatness (indicated by '!') is explained in the section to come on the Axiom of Reducibility.

7. Whitehead and Russell (1910–13: Introduction, ch. III). Class terms are said to be *incomplete* because the translations of sentences containing them—see previous note—have no constituents that refer to a class. Assuming that anything referred to in a sentence is referred to in every translation of that sentence, we can say that incomplete symbols are non-referring name-like constituents of the surface syntax of sentences in which they occur.

8. Russell (1903: ch. 6).

9. Russell (1903) mentions those of Frege (1893) and Peano (1895).

10. How can it be that wherever there is nothing there is one thing, namely the class of nothing? How can it be that wherever there is exactly one thing there are two things, namely the one thing and the unit class containing it?

11. Russell writes about his paradox and others in *The Principles of Mathematics* (Russell 1903).

12. The argument appears in the introduction to the 2nd edn of *The Principles of Mathematics*, published in 1937.

13. On route to *PM*, Russell argues that class talk must be regarded as a *façon de parler* if vicious circles are to be avoided, but the argument assumes that variables have unrestricted range, an assumption rejected in *PM* (Russell 1906b).

14. In fact, the 1st edn of *PM* has two different accounts of the hierarchy, and the account in the 2nd edn is different again. Michael Potter goes into the matter in Potter (2000). The account given here is faithful to the basic ideas.

15. A predicate $\varphi(x)$ is the defining predicate of the propositional function $\lambda x \varphi(x)$ and of the class $\{x : \varphi(x)\}$.

16. Whitehead and Russell (1910–13: Introduction, ch. II, §v and the summary at the end of ∗12).

17. Using variables with superscripts indicating order, these second and third-order propositional functions can be presented thus:

$\lambda x^0[\forall \varphi^1 \, (\varphi^1$ is required of a great general $\rightarrow x^0$ has $\varphi^1)]$.

$\lambda x^0[\exists \varphi^2 \, (\varphi^2$ is required of a great general & x^0 has $\varphi^2)]$.

18. In *PM* both expressions 'type' and 'order' are used, but the usage of 'type' is not uniform. For the most part, the usage in *PM* is the now standard usage given here.

19. Again using superscripts to indicate order, these functions can be presented thus:

$\lambda \varphi^1 \, [\varphi^1$ is required of a great general].

$\lambda \varphi^1 \, [\forall x^0 \, (\exists \eta^2 \, (\eta^2$ is required of a great general & x^0 has $\eta^2) \rightarrow x^0$ has $\varphi^1)]$.

20. In the preface to the 1st edn of *PM* the authors allow that other versions of the theory of types and orders might do as well as theirs; so, whatever their precise intention for the substitution rule, the alternative would probably have been acceptable.

21. Let θ be any propositional function (p.f.). Let the type of θ be 1. Then trivially the order of θ is ≥ 1. Let us assume by way of inductive hypothesis, that for all $k \leq n$, a p.f. of type k has order $\geq k$. Let the type of θ be $n + 1$, where $n \geq 1$. The free variable in θ has type n and so ranges only over p.f.s of type n. By the hypothesis, those p.f.s have order $\geq n$; so the free variable in θ has order $\geq n$; so the maximum order of variables in θ is $\geq n$; as the order of θ is one above that maximum, the order of θ is $\geq n + 1$. Hence by mathematical induction, the order of a p.f. is never less than its type.

22. Whitehead and Russell (1910–13: Introduction, ch. II, §§iv, v).

23. For a presentation of formal systems that deals with the details omitted here, see Hatcher's systems PT and RT in Hatcher (1982: ch. 4).

24. 'Real analysis' is a customary abbreviation for 'real-number analysis'. The point holds also for complex analysis, which is an extension of real analysis.

25. A real number r is an *upper bound* of a class c of real numbers when, for all x in c, $x \leq r$; a real number s is the *least upper bound* of c when s is an upper bound of c such that, for all upper bounds u of c, $s \leq u$. The definition of 'greatest lower bound' is parallel.

26. To illustrate this, recall that Dedekind cuts are ordered pairs (A_1, A_2) of non-empty classes of rationals such that (a) for any rationals p and q, if $p < q$ and $q \in A_1$, then $p \in A_1$, (b) A_2 is the class of rationals not in A_1, and (c) A_1 has no greatest member. Let us follow common practice by defining real numbers to be the first elements of cuts (known as *lower* or *left* cuts) and let c be a class of reals defined: $c = \{r : \varphi(r)\}$, where the range of 'r' contains all reals. Then, if c has upper bounds, the least upper bound of c is defined as the union of the members of c; that is,

l.u.b.$(c) = \{q : q$ is a rational & $\exists r \, [\varphi(r) \, \& \, q \in r]\}$.

This definition of the least upper bound of c is impredicative, as it falls in the range of the bound variable r.

27. The treatment of real numbers in *PM* is to be found in *310, but the definitions of some of the concepts involved are scattered in earlier parts. Reals are effectively defined as lower cuts. For an accessible introduction to the axioms of the theory of real numbers, see Apostol (1967: introd., p 3).

28. At the time of writing *PM* and revising it for the 2nd edn, it looked very likely that real analysis within ramified type theory without the Axiom of Reducibility would be weaker than classical real analysis. This was later proved. (A technical note: the proof

is an application of Gödel's Second Underivability Theorem to classical analysis on the assumption that it is consistent; for the consistency of ramified analysis is provable in classical analysis, provable even in primitive recursive arithmetic according to Burgess and Hazen 1998.)

29. Myhill (1974). Appendix B of vol. I of the 2nd edn of *PM* (Whitehead and Russell 1925–7) gives an argument for induction over the natural numbers on the basis of a claim about orders that is not conclusively proved. See Gödel (1944).

30. Gödel (1944).

31. In *PM* the word 'predicative' is used instead of 'flat'. The *PM* usage is confusing, since 'not predicative' and 'impredicative' (in its current use) are quite different. While the universe of *PM* contains no impredicative propositional functions (as none is defined in terms of a class to which it belongs), it contains many that are not 'predicative' (as many have order more than one above the order of entities to which they apply).

32. Whitehead and Russell (1910–13: *12.1, *12.11).

33. This is true for reasoning involved in the project of developing classical mathematics within the system of *PM*. It is not true in *opaque* or *intensional* contexts, that is, contexts requiring us to distinguish between co-extensive propositional functions. In particular, it is not true in reasoning about certain paradoxes, as Church (1976) points out.

34. To illustrate this, let c be a non-empty class of reals bounded above, defined $c = \{r : \varphi(r)\}$. Then taking reals to be left cuts, the least upper bound of c is defined to be the class $\{q : q$ is a rational $\& \exists r [\varphi(r) \& q \in r]\}$. The Axiom of Reducibility allows us to assume that there is a propositional function $\lambda q.\psi(q)$ of order one plus the order of q such that, for all q, $\psi(q)$ if and only if q is rational $\& \exists r [\varphi(r) \& q \in r]$. Thus, the least upper bound of c is $\{q : \psi(q)\}$, and the latter has order one plus the order of its members q (as the order of a class is the order of the corresponding propositional function), which we can see is the order of the members r of c. So the least upper bound of a class of reals can be assumed to be a real of the same order as the reals in the class.

35. 'x is closed under f' means 'for any member w of x, $f(w)$ is also a member of x' and one way of symbolizing this is '$f[x] \subseteq x$'. The smallest class having property F is the class that has property F and is a subclass of every class having property F.

36. The class $\{x : \forall y [(c \subseteq y \& f[y] \subseteq y) \rightarrow x \in y]\}$ falls in the range of the variable 'y'.

37. Let the order of the xs in '$\forall y [(c \subseteq y \& f[y] \subseteq y) \rightarrow x \in y]$' be $n - 1$. Reducibility allows us to assume, first, that the order of the ys is n and, second, that there is a function $\lambda x.\psi(x)$ such that $\{x : \psi(x)\} = \{x : \forall y [(c \subseteq y \& f[y] \subseteq y) \rightarrow x \in y]\}$, where $\{x : \psi(x)\}$ has order one above the order of its members, $1+(n-1)$. The identity shows that this nth order class is what was intended.

38. Whitehead and Russell (1910–13: Introduction, ch. II, §vii). Cf. Russell (1910: §vii), and Russell (1907).

39. Here I mean the quasi-empirical induction described by Russell, not the principle of mathematical induction.

40. Whitehead and Russell (1910–13: Introduction, ch. II, §vii). I am not sure when Russell first took this lesson to heart. He was still writing as though certainty was attainable in *The Principles of Mathematics* (Russell 1903: ch. 1, §II), but he had already discovered the contradiction in Frege's system. Perhaps the sections in which his asseverations of certainty occur are unrevised parts of the manuscript written before he discovered the contradiction.

41. 'That the axiom of reducibility is self-evident is a proposition which can hardly be maintained' (ibid.).

42. This was first publicly articulated in Russell (1907), where he introduces the Axiom of Reducibility but not by name.

43. I have large doubts about it. Gödel (1947) endorses the *possibility* of knowing an axiom in a quasi-inductive way, but he draws back from Russell's claim that the basis for accepting an axiom is 'always largely inductive'. It is an interesting question whether any axiom has been widely accepted as a truth (as opposed to a hypothesis for deduction) without a significant degree of intrinsic plausibility.

44. But Whitehead and Russell did not know that there are instances of mathematical induction not derivable in ramified type theory: see n. 29. This was established only much later by Myhill (1974).

45. The induced property is that expressed by the predicate substituted for '$\varphi(x)$' in the formula 'If $\varphi(0)$ and $\varphi(n + 1)$ for every n such that $\varphi(n)$, then for every m $\varphi(m)$.'

46. Let me refine this slightly. Let *elementary arithmetic* be arithmetic with the standard axioms for the successor function, and the defining equations for addition, multiplication, and exponentiation, plus the (mathematical) induction axiom where the induced property contains no unbounded quantifiers. Burgess and Hazen (1998) have shown that elementary arithmetic is interpretable within ramified type theory without the Axiom of Reducibility. I think that elementary arithmetic contains the bulk of what we can properly describe as nearly indubitable and all or almost all the arithmetic that we can count as data. Elementary arithmetic falls short of primitive recursive arithmetic, which is not interpretable in ramified type theory without reducibility.

47. Whitehead and Russell (1925–7: Introduction to the 2nd edn). Michael Potter points out that Whitehead had no part in the changes to the 2nd edn, so perhaps only Russell changed his mind. But I presume that the 2nd edn had Whitehead's imprimatur, and on that basis I refer to both authors.

48. ibid.

49. This would be a step back from the claim that 'self-evidence is never indispensable', but it is suggested by the implication that the axiom is objectionable in the introduction to the 2nd edn of *PM*: 'Also Cantor's proof that $2^n > n$ breaks down unless n is finite. Perhaps some further axiom, less objectionable than the axiom of reducibility, might give these results, but we have not succeeded in finding such an axiom.'

50. Whitehead and Russell (1910–13: *88.03). See the summary of *88 for the informal exposition. The axiom is only needed in cases where the class c is infinite. Classes are 'pairwise disjoint' when no two of them have a common member.

51. The matter will be discussed further in Pt V, Ch. 1.
52. For examples, see theorems in Whitehead and Russell (1910–13: *112 and *114).
53. Whitehead and Russell (1910–13: *120.03).
54. Whitehead and Russell (1910–13: vol. II, summary of §C).
55. Russell (1919: 141).
56. After the critical number they are all identical with the empty class. This is pointed out in the second paragraph after *120.03 in Whitehead and Russell (1910–13).
57. Russell (1956*b*).
58. Russell (1959). Robin Gandy records a remark made by Russell in conversation illustrating the sloppiness of his Cambridge tutors. Russell recalled that, though they proved the binomial theorem only for a positive-integral exponent, they stated and used it with a real exponent. 'I asked them how the general case could be proved. "We prove it", they replied, "by the principle of permanence of form"!' (Gandy 1973).

Chapter 3

1. Russell (1903: ch. VI, §78; ch. X, §101). Russell uses 'predicable of' for 'true of'.
2. Grelling and Nelson (1908).
3. A reminder: '$\forall c$' means 'for every c'; '$\neg$' means 'it is not the case that'.
4. The generalized argument runs thus. First, suppose r_n is true of r_n, i.e. $r_n T r_n$. Then for $c_i = r_n$, $(1 \leq i \leq n)$, $r_n T c_1$ & $c_1 T c_2$ & ... & $c_{n-1} T c_n$ & $c_n T r_n$. So r_n is not true of r_n. Hence if r_n is true of r_n, r_n is not true of r_n. Then by the law that $(P \rightarrow \neg P) \rightarrow \neg P$, (i) r_n is not true of r_n. Secondly, suppose that r_n is not true of r_n. Then for some $c_1, c_2, \ldots,$ c_{n-1}, c_n, $r_n T c_1$ & $c_1 T c_2$ & ... & $c_{n-1} T c_n$ & $c_n T r_n$. Let $d_1, d_2, \ldots, d_{n-1}, d_n$ be such:

$$(\$) \, r_n T d_1 \, \& \, d_1 T d_2 \, \& \ldots \& \, d_{n-1} T d_n \, \& \, d_n T r_n.$$

The first conjunct says that r_n is true of d_1, i.e.

$$(\pounds) \, \forall c_1 \, \forall c_2 \ldots \forall c_{n-1} \, \forall c_n \, \neg [d_1 T c_1 \, \& \, c_1 T c_2 \, \& \ldots \& \, c_{n-1} T c_n \, \& \, c_n T d_1].$$

But if we put $c_n = r_n$ and $c_i = d_{i+1}$ when $1 \leq i \leq n-1$, we obtain a counterexample to ($\pounds$) from ($\$$) by moving the first conjunct of ($\$$) to the end. Thus, the supposition that r_n is not true of r_n entails a contradiction. Hence, by *reductio ad absurdum*, it is not the case that r_n is not true of r_n. That is, (ii) r_n is true of r_n. Finally, combine (i) and (ii) to get the contradiction.
5. The basis for this is Diogenes Laertius (1925: II. 108). Diogenes Laertius lived *c.* AD230. He compiled his work from sources of varying reliability (Robert Sharples, personal communication). See Hamblin (1970: 89–91).
6. Diogenes Laertius (1925: V. 49).
7. This is because the result of inserting any sequence of endorsements (i.e. statements of the form 'Y is true') in a chain is contradictory if the original chain is.
8. The same must hold for sentences in place of propositions, in order to deal with versions of the Liar paradox such as 'This sentence does not express a true proposition'.

9. According to Russell, a definite description does not stand for a constituent of the proposition expressed by a sentence containing it, and so it cannot be used to mention something, on a narrow use of the word 'mention'. But here I use the word broadly, so that the unique satisfier of the condition 'x is such-&-such' is what is mentioned by use of the definite description 'the such-&-such.' This is needed if the proposed solution is to deal with versions of the Liar paradox based on e.g. 'The statement I am now making is not true.'

10. Kripke (1975).

Chapter 4

1. Ramsey died in 1930 at the age of 26, (see the introduction to Ramsey 1990 by D. Mellor). By then he had already published important philosophical papers, and in his work in mathematical logic he had proved two theorems that later gave rise to a branch of combinatorics known as Ramsey theory.

2. Ramsey (1925).

3. Ramsey cites Peano as an earlier proponent of this view of the second group of paradoxes. The ascription 'linguistic' is Peano's. Ramsey said that he regarded it as a matter of epistemology, but that does not square with his diagnosis of those paradoxes.

4. Ramsey attributes this paradox to Weyl.

5. Ramsey (1925: end of §i).

6. Russell (1903: ch. X, §101). Russell's identification of these paradoxes may also have been based on an inclination to regard statements about classes as statements about propositional functions.

7. Hart (1983); Feferman (1984a). Parsons (1974) comments on the parallels between Russell's paradox and the Liar paradox.

8. In formal language, the relation is $\lambda\varphi\lambda x[\varphi Rx]$ and the propositional function obtained from it by universal quantification is $\lambda x[\forall\varphi[\varphi Rx]]$.

9. Ramsey (1925: §ii).

10. ibid. §iv.

11. Russell (1919: 202). 'We may take the axiom of infinity as an example of a proposition which, though it may be enunciated in logical terms, cannot be asserted by logic to be true'. The publication dates of these works are, in order, 1903, 1910, and 1919.

12. Ramsey (1925: §i). I take it that a tautology is *completely general* when a symbolic expression for it contains no symbol for an individual constant. The question whether there are logical truths other than tautologies is not addressed. Ramsey cites Wittgenstein (1922) as the source of the account of tautology he presents.

13. Strictly speaking, type indices would have to be supplied to get tautologies.

14. Ramsey (1925: §v).

15. Bacon is necessarily distinct from Shakespeare, and it is impossible that Hesperus is distinct from Phosphorus. However, people who deny that Bacon is distinct from

Shakespeare are not making a logical mistake, as they would be if they were denying a tautology; similarly, people who said that Hesperus is distinct from Phosphorus were not contradicting themselves. The same point can be made about distinctness claims using demonstratives.

16. Russell (1903: §111). The view was preserved in *Principia Mathematica*, with the qualification that the definition in terms of classes is shorthand for a definition in terms of propositional functions.

17. In *Principia Mathematica* the empty class of things of type i is distinct from the empty class of things of type h when $i \neq h$ because $\{x_i : x_i \neq x_i\}$ is of type $i + 1$ while $\{x_h : x_h \neq x_h\}$ is of type $h + 1$. On Ramsey's account they are distinct because they are functions with distinct domains, the class of things of type i and the class of things of type h, each assigning a contradiction to everything in its domain.

18. Arguments for this claim are presented in Pt II, Ch. 4.

19. An *a priori* truth is one knowable without the use of experience as evidence for it or for premises from which it is inferred.

PART IV

Chapter 1

1. Zermelo (1908).

2. Cantor was exceptional in having a view, prior to the discovery of the class paradoxes, that is not compatible with the Comprehension Principle.

3. Notably Lebesgue, in Baire *et al*. (1905). For discussion see Monna (1972), Moore (1982), and Ch. 1 of Pt V above. In *Principia Mathematica* the Axiom of Choice is referred to as the Multiplicative Axiom. The reservations of Whitehead and Russell about this axiom discussed in Pt III Ch. 2 are essentially those of Lebesgue.

4. In most expositions of axiomatic set theory, this is built into the underlying logic.

5. Bolzano (1851: §13), and Dedekind (1888: §v, th. 66).

6. For a reminder, see the subsection on ordinals in Pt I Ch. 2.

7. There is one exception—the set whose sole member is the empty set. The empty set is trivially well ordered by the empty relation.

8. Von Neumann (1923).

9. This is ensured by the following set-theoretic definition: x is an *ordinal* if and only if x is well ordered by the membership relation and every member of x is a subset of x.

10. Hilbert (1925).

11. '$\{\aleph_\beta : \beta < \lambda\}$' abbreviates '$\{x : x = \aleph_\beta \ \& \ \beta < \lambda\}$'.

12. Cantor (1899), where he also states versions of the Separation Axiom and Union Set Axiom.

13. Why 'Replacement'? We can think of a 1-to-1 correlation in terms of members of one set being replaced by their correlates, as Fraenkel did, instead of being paired with them Fraenkel (1922a). The version of Replacement now used is due to Skolem (1922).

Endnotes

14. The Axiom of Replacement entails the Cantorian principle as a 1-to-1 correlation is just a functional relation $F(x, y)$ such that $F(w, y)$ and $F(x, y)$ only if $w = y$. Conversely, assume the Cantorian principle and let F be a functional relation with a set m as domain. We just need to deduce from this that $F[m]$ is a set. For each y in $F[m]$, let '$F^{-1}(y)$' denote $\{x : x \in m \,\&\, F(x, y)\}$. For each y in $F[m]$, $F^{-1}(y)$ is a subclass of m and so is a set (by Separation). So for each y in $F[m]$, $F^{-1}(y)$ is in $\mathbb{P}(m)$, which is a set (by the Power Set Axiom). Put $d = \{z : \exists y \,[y \in F[m] \,\&\, z = F^{-1}(y)]\}$. It follows that d is a subclass of $\mathbb{P}(m)$; hence d is a set (by Separation). Now let $R(z, y)$ be the relation with domain d such that $R(z, y)$ if and only if $z = F^{-1}(y)$. It is clear that R correlates d 1-to-1 with $F[m]$; as d is a set, it follows by the Cantorian Principle that $F[m]$ is a set. The fact that the Axiom of Replacement is equivalent to the Cantorian principle undermines the idea in Boolos (1971) that the only reason for adopting the axiom is opportunistic: it has many desirable consequences and, as far as is known, no undesirable ones. That view was dropped in Boolos (1984), but the Cantorian basis of the axiom is not given in that article.

15. Von Neumann (1925). Von Neumann's terminology is quite different and was not adopted elsewhere.

16. It is not difficult to show that the Axiom of Separation is entailed by the Axiom of Replacement. (Hint: let F be the class of ordered pairs $\{\langle x, x \rangle : x \in B\}$.) In fact, von Neumann used a yet more general principle from which the Axioms of Replacement and Choice are derivable.

17. Von Neumann (1925). The idea is already present in Fraenkel (1922a).

18. See Pt II Ch. 2 above.

19. Von Neumann (1925: §2, §§3.iii, 3.iv). I have simplified. Von Neumman's theory allows individuals (non-classes) in the domain. The criterion for being a proper class, equivalent to the one given above, is that the class is the domain of a function whose range is the class of all arguments, where an *argument* is a set or an individual.

20. This, of course, requires that the axiom schema is itself presented with sufficient formality, for example as follows: $\forall m \exists y [S(y) \,\&\, \forall x [(x \in y) \leftrightarrow (x \in m \,\&\, \psi(x))]]$, where '$y$' does not occur in $\psi(x)$.

21. Skolem (1922). In this remarkable paper Skolem not only solves Zermelo's problem but also proves the need for the Axiom (schema) of Replacement: Where 'w' does not occur in open sentence $\psi(xy)$, $\forall x \forall y \forall z ([\psi(xy) \,\&\, \psi(xz)] \rightarrow y{=}z) \rightarrow \forall m \exists w (S(w) \,\&\, \forall y [(y \in w) \leftrightarrow \exists x (x \in m \,\&\, \psi(xy))])$. It is not difficult to show that any instance of the Axiom schema of Separation follows from an instance of the Axiom schema of Replacement.

Chapter 2

1. Hausdorff (1914) is the classic reference.

2. 'No one shall be able to drive us from the paradise that Cantor created for us' (Hilbert 1926).

3. Von Neumann (1925).

4. Or: ZFC with individuals. In some contexts one wants to exclude individuals. ZF is ZFC minus the Axiom of Choice. NBG is a version of von Neumann's axiomatization as reformulated by Bernays and Gödel. Skolem's findings apply in all these cases.

5. Skolem (1922: §6), where he also suggests that the Continuum Hypothesis is probably independent of the axioms (assuming their consistency), a fact not established until some four decades later.

6. Zermelo (1930) did just that. The axiom is known as the Axiom of Foundation.

7. The extension of an n-ary function on D is a class of ordered pairs whose first is an n-tuple of members of D and whose second is a member of D, no two pairs having the same first element. For unary functions this is just a class of ordered pairs no two of which have the same first element.

8. Löwenheim (1915); Skolem (1920, 1922).

9. Skolem (1922).

10. This assumption is legitimized by Mostowski's Collapsing Theorem, which was not proved until many years after LS.

11. In set theory a function d is identified with the set of ordered pairs $\langle n, x \rangle$ such that $d(n) = x$. A function d *enumerates* a set c if and only if d is a function from (an initial segment of) ω such that, for every x in c, there is exactly one n in ω for which $d(n) = x$. (ω is the set of finite ordinals, which are the representatives in set theory of the natural numbers.)

12. Hasenjaegar (1967).

13. Bolder conclusions, some quite extravagant, have been drawn from LS and related facts. But the arguments given are often quite sketchy.

14. Dedekind (1872).

15. A sequence $\{r_n\}$ of rationals satisfies the *Cauchy condition* just when, for any integer $n > 0$ there is integer $m > 0$ such that for all integers $k > m$, $|r_m - r_k| < 1/2^n$.

16. Brouwer (1929: §iii) gives an intuitionist counterexample.

17. Although the (translated) title of one of Brouwer's major papers is 'Foundations of Set Theory Independent of the Logical Principle of the Excluded Middle', its content is clearly revisionary (Brouwer 1918, 1919); in later work he explicitly contrasts 'Formalist refoundation' with 'Intuitionist reconstruction' (Brouwer 1928). For an exposition of Brouwer's views and their development, see van Stigt (1990).

18. Weyl (1918).

19. A *left Dedekind cut* is a non-empty set C of rationals such that (a) there are rationals greater than every member of C; (b) for any rationals p and q, if $p < q$ and $q \in C$, then $p \in C$; and (c) C has no greatest member.

20. A reminder: r is an *upper bound* of a set S of reals if and only if each member of S is less than or equal to r, r is the *least upper bound* of S if and only if r is least among the upper bounds of S.

21. For Weyl's theory of orders (or levels), see Mancosu (1998b). Weyl did not follow

Whitehead and Russell in proposing that distinctions of order be built into the syntax of mathematical language.

22. Weyl (1920); see the helpful account in Mancosu (1998*b*).

23. Weyl (1925).

24. Hilbert (1922).

Chapter 3

1. Hilbert (1926).

2. Hilbert (1929); cf. Bernays (1930*b*). Bernays was Hilbert's main co-worker. Others who played a significant role in the foundational programme were Ackermann and von Neumann.

3. This law is also known as the Principle of Limited Omniscience.

4. The conjecture was made in a letter of 1742 to the mathematician Euler. The conjecture has not, as I write, been decided.

5. Non-transparent contexts include indirect speech, belief attributions, modal statements, and others. These are not relevant for ordinary mathematical discourse.

6. For the same reason, finitism does not accept the Law of Negation Transfer: Not every x has Goldbach's property if and only if some x does not have it.

7. Here I mean Dedekind–Peano arithmetic with quantifiers for members of the domain but not for subsets of the domain, i.e. first-order Dedekind–Peano arithmetic.

8. Hilbert (1926).

9. Following Smorynski (1989).

10. Something slightly stronger than a mere disposition may be required here—I am not sure exactly what.

11. However, I would not say that the thought could have a truth value, though it is truth-indicating in the sense that all the strictly finitary information that can be drawn from it is true. This is a matter of theoretical semantics to be pursued elsewhere. I will here ignore the difference between being true and being truth-indicating.

12. Hilbert (1926), in van Heijenoort (1967: 376).

13. Interdefinability: $[\forall x \varphi(x) \leftrightarrow \neg \exists x \neg \varphi(x)]$ and $[\exists x \varphi(x) \leftrightarrow \neg \forall x \neg \varphi(x)]$. Negation transfer: $[\forall x \neg \varphi(x) \leftrightarrow \neg \exists x \varphi(x)]$ and $[\neg \forall x \varphi(x) \leftrightarrow \exists x \neg \varphi(x)]$.

14. The result of interchanging 'line' and 'point' in a theorem is again a theorem.

15. It is understood that the theories would have to be used in conjunction with other theories linking theoretical variables with observable states in order to obtain directly testable predictions.

16. Hilbert (1928*a*), in van Heijenoort (1967: 457).

17. Hilbert (1922), repeated in (1926, 1928*a*); see van Heijenoort (1967: 367, 464).

18. Here I have oversimplified slightly. If the marks we are considering include handwritten ones, there may be some for which it is not perceptually decidable whether

they are instances of a given symbol. But this can be remedied by restricting marks to those produced by normal mechanical printing.

19. For some idea of PRA, see Cutland (1980: ch. 3, §3).

20. Skolem (1923); Hilbert and Bernays (1934: 307–46). This identification may be pragmatic. There has been some dispute about the extent of finitary reasoning, some taking it to amount to PRA (Tait 1981), some requiring something narrower (Niebergall and Schirn 1998), and others requiring something broader (M. Detlefsen, personal communication).

21. See Tait (1981: §§ii–vi).

22. For the classic account see Turing (1936: §8, i and iii), in Davis (1965: 135–40). Many mathematical logic textbooks include an account of computability and some give more than one account, e.g. Boolos and Jeffrey (1974).

23. Schematically: $\tau = \sigma \rightarrow [\varphi(\tau) \rightarrow \varphi(\sigma)]$, where $\varphi(\tau)$ is a formula containing τ and $\varphi(\sigma)$ is the result of replacing all occurrences of τ by occurrences of σ.

24. This is free-variable induction over the positive integers. We could just as well have used free-variable induction over the natural numbers, using '$\varphi(0)$' in place of '$\varphi(1)$'.

25. Cf. Hilbert and Bernays (1934: 298).

26. So-called 'strict finitists' would constitute an exception.

Chapter 4

1. By 'arithmetic', I mean first-order Dedekind–Peano arithmetic, not primitive recursive arithmetic (which does not need justifying).

2. Perhaps the right word is 'abduction' rather than 'induction', but sometimes the latter is used broadly, so as to include the former. Let that be the convention here.

3. Russell (1907). Russell uses the expressions 'empirical premisses' and 'logical premisses' to mark the distinction.

4. The Axiom of Choice is called the Multiplicative Axiom in *Principia Mathematica*.

5. This is the philosophically important goal Hilbert came to eventually; his conception of his programmatic goals evolved.

6. But be careful: it does not follow that there is an effective way of deciding, for any given formula of the language, whether or not it is a theorem.

7. It is also known as *ex contradictione quodlibet* and sometimes *ex falso quodlibet*.

8. Universal instantiation covers inferences from $\forall x \varphi(x)$ to $\varphi(\tau)$, for terms τ not containing any free variable that would be bound in some occurrence of τ in $\varphi(\tau)$ (by falling within the scope of a quantifier in $\varphi(x)$).

9. Brouwer (1912); see also Poincaré (1905). These objections were voiced more than a decade before the methods of Hilbert's finitist proof theory were worked out.

10. Brouwer (1928).

Endnotes

11. Smorynski (1989) suggests that Brouwer had neither read the paper (Hilbert 1928a), nor heard the lecture on which it was based.

12. Weyl (1925, 1928).

PART V

Chapter 1

1. Let R be a formal relation on k-tuples of syntactic objects in the language of a system T. Let S be a theory in the language of arithmetic.

> R is *represented* in S by a k-place predicate $\varphi(x_1, \ldots, x_k)$ in the language of S if and only if, for any k numerals $\mathbf{n}_1, \ldots, \mathbf{n}_k$ in the language of S, (i) if $\mathbf{n}_1, \ldots, \mathbf{n}_k$ code objects $\alpha_1, \ldots, \alpha_k$ respectively such that $R(\alpha_1, \ldots, \alpha_k)$, then $\varphi(\mathbf{n}_1, \ldots, \mathbf{n}_k)$ is a theorem of S, and (ii) if not, $\neg\varphi(\mathbf{n}_1, \ldots, \mathbf{n}_k)$ is a theorem of S.

Representation in S is usually defined for relations on the natural numbers, rather than syntactic relations. (A relation on the natural numbers is a set of n-tuples of natural numbers.) A syntactic relation R is representable (in the sense given above) in S by φ if and only if the set of n-tuples of code numbers of syntactic objects that stand in the relation R is representable (in the normal sense) in S by φ. Other expressions for 'represented' are 'strongly represented', 'binumerated', 'syntactically defined'.

2. For discussion of this matter and its implications, see Auerbach (1985, 1992).

3. Many quite different arithmetical predicates may represent a given formal property in a true formal system of arithmetic, and yet their numerical equivalence may not be derivable in the system.

4. To simplify exposition, I have assumed that the infinitely many variables—an unbounded number of variables are needed—are *primitive* symbols. But this is not essential, for we can have **v** as a primitive symbol and then we can define numerals and variables thus: α is a *numeral* if and only if α is **0** or for some numeral **n** α is **sn**; α is a *variable* if and only if for some numeral **n** α is $\mathbf{v_n}$.

5. Let $\langle n \rangle$ = the expression coded by n. Decoding the numerical expressions yields:

> $\tau(x)$ if and only if $x = \lceil \mathbf{0} \rceil$ or, for some $u < x$, $x = \lceil \mathbf{v}_u \rceil$ or, for some $u < x$ and some $v < x$, $\tau(u)$ and $\tau(v)$ and $[x = \lceil \mathbf{s}\langle u \rangle \rceil$, or $x = \lceil +\langle u \rangle\langle v \rangle \rceil$, or $x = \lceil \times\langle u \rangle\langle v \rangle \rceil]$.

The quantifiers here are bounded, e.g. 'for some $u < x$' rather than just 'for some u'. This is needed to keep the definition primitive-recursive. But it has no significance for the syntactic meaning of the arithmetical predicate, as the code of an expression is greater than the code of any of its parts. When this simple fact about coding is borne in mind, the parallel between the definition of 'term' and the definition of τ is obvious.

6. See the section 'Finitary reasoning: methods' in Pt IV Ch. 3 for further remarks on PRA and a reference.

7. Definability in arithmetic is representability in the theory whose theorems are all sentences of $\mathscr{L}$ that are true under the intended arithmetical interpretation.

254

8. Also known as Gödel's First Incompleteness Theorem, it was discovered in 1930 and its proof published in Gödel (1931). Tarski's theorem was published in Tarski (1932).

9. It is assumed that T has the resources of propositional logic, so that if A and A↔B are derivable in T so is B; and it is assumed that T has inference by universal instantiation.

10. A formal system T is ω-consistent when, if all formulas of the form φ(**n**) are derivable in T, ¬∀xφ(x) is not derivable in T. ω-consistency entails consistency. Actually, Gödel's argument only needs a subspecies of ω-consistency known as 1-consistency.

11. This property of incompleteness is syntactic. It is to be distinguished from semantic incompleteness, which holds of a theory T when there is a sentence α in the language of T which is true in some but not all models of T. The semantic notion, unlike the syntactic notion, presupposes set theory. Moreover, semantic and syntactic in completeness do not coincide for second-order theories. (There is still another notion of incompleteness that applies to a derivation relation ⊢_L for the logic of a given language L; cf. n. 21.)

12. Rosser (1936). The Rosser sentence δ says that there is no T-derivation of δ unless there is an earlier T-derivation of ¬δ (in the enumeration of T-derivations by their codes).

13. He mentioned the link at the end of §1 of Gödel (1931), in Gödel (1986: 149, 151); and he spelled it out in §7 of Gödel (1934), in Gödel (1986: 362, 363).

14. If T is a consistent system of arithmetic containing PRA, the system T + ¬γ (the system whose axioms are T's axioms plus the negation of a Gödel sentence for T) is consistent but unsound. So consistency does not entail soundness. But soundness does entail consistency, as no arithmetical sentence and its negation are both true.

15. See Wang (1981: 654); Feferman (1984a). Gödel pointed out that the weaker incompleteness theorem is similarly provable using other semantic antinomies in place of the Liar. Gödel (1931: n.14), in Gödel (1986: 149). Boolos (1989) uses Berry's paradox in this way.

16. This is a heady topic with its own literature. Webb (1968) is a sober appraisal.

17. For the process of diagonalizing, see the exposition of Richard's paradox in Pt III Ch. 1 above.

18. Hilbert (1900b). The same is said in Hilbert (1900a). His most famous expression of the view is in a letter to Frege in 1899: 'If the arbitrarily chosen axioms do not contradict each other with all their consequences, then they are true and the things defined by them exist' (trans. in Frege (1980)). Hilbert is assuming that an axiom system can define its subject matter; this requires that the axiom system is *categorical*, in the sense that any structured domain about which the axioms, when appropriately interpreted, are true is isomorphic to any other such structured domain. Hilbert did point out that his axioms for real numbers are categorical—I take this from Hallett (1995). But not all axiom systems of interest are categorical, e.g. axiom systems for set theory. However, the question of existence can be separated from the question of definition. For we can

ask: is there *any* structured domain about which all the axioms of the given system are true when appropriately interpreted? The turn-of-century Hilbert answers: yes, if the axiom system is consistent.

19. The definition of truth of sentences goes by way of a recursive definition of the relation that holds between a formula (with free variables) and a sequence of members of the domain when the formula is *true of* (or *satisfied by*) the sequence. The truth definition gives the semantic roles of the logical symbols (e.g. '¬', '→', '∀', '∃'). A truth definition will be found in any formal logic textbook.

20. Hilbert and Ackermann (1928). An $\mathscr{L}$-sentence α is a *semantic consequence* of a set of $\mathscr{L}$-sentences Γ if and only if α is true under any interpretation of $\mathscr{L}$ under which all the sentences of Γ are true. Semantic consequence is to be distinguished from syntactic consequence: α is a *syntactic consequence* of Γ if and only if α is derivable from Γ. The expression 'theorem' is ambiguous in the same way as 'consequence' when unqualified.

21. This was Gödel's first major discovery (Gödel 1929), his doctoral thesis. The result is easily seen to be equivalent to the completeness of first-order logic: α is derivable from Γ whenever α is a semantic consequence of Γ. Thus, the derivability relation 'completely' captures first-order semantic consequence. Gödel drew this conclusion in his thesis and his result is known the Completeness Theorem for first order logic.

22. A *model* of a theory T is an interpretation of T's language under which all the axioms of T are true. For the sense of 'interpretation', see the section 'The downward Löwenheim–Skolem Theorem' in Pt IV Ch. 2. 'There exists a model M of T', 'T has a model M', and 'T is true under interpretation M' are here used synonymously.

23. The proof assumes some non-finitary set theory, in particular the Axiom of Choice. Also, a model of formal arithmetic, analysis, or set theory will be an infinitary object. Though all this might have been acceptable to Hilbert around 1900, when he was claiming that consistency entails existence, it does not square with the finitism that Hilbert espoused 25 years later.

24. For an account of DPA, see the section 'The natural numbers' in Pt I Ch. 2. Dedekind–Peano arithmetic is often called Peano arithmetic and denoted 'PA'. I depart from convention to avoid confusion (of PA with PRA) as well as to give Dedekind due credit.

25. Sets of natural numbers are subsets of the domain of the intended interpretation; so 'R' ranges over subsets of the domain, as required of a second-order variable. We need not insist that the theory is intended to be about the natural numbers as opposed to the positive integers. Historically speaking, DPA was a theory of positive integer arithmetic. See Dedekind (1888) and Peano (1889).

26. Dedekind (1888). This is known as the *categoricity* of second-order DPA. Two models are isomorphic when there is a structure-preserving bijective mapping from one to the other. There is no corresponding theorem for first-order theories. On the contrary, if a theory in a first-order enumerable language has a model with an infinite domain, it has models with domains of every infinite cardinality—that is the full

Löwehnheim–Skolem theorem. So no first-order theory with an infinite model is categorical.

27. In fact, T is ω-consistent, on the assumption that $\mathfrak{N}$ is a model of T, because a formula of the form $\neg\forall x\varphi(x)$ will be false in $\mathfrak{N}$ if all formulas of the form $\varphi(\mathbf{n})$ are true in $\mathfrak{N}$.

28. Suppose T+$\neg\gamma$ were inconsistent. This means that there is a derivation of a contradiction χ & $\neg\chi$ from T+$\neg\gamma$. Then applying the law of propositional logic (which is part of the logic of T) known as *reductio ad absurdum*, we could obtain a derivation of $\neg\neg\gamma$ from T; then by the double-negation law of propositional logic we could obtain a derivation of γ from T.

29. The second-order theory of real numbers, like second-order DPA, is categorical and incorporates PRA. So, assuming that that theory has an intended model $\mathfrak{R}$, the same argument can be run using that theory in place of second order DPA, and $\mathfrak{R}$ in place of $\mathfrak{N}$. Canvassing the possibility of incompleteness in the introduction to his doctoral thesis, Gödel hinted at such an argument using the categoricity of second-order real-number theory (without, however, alluding to the crucial distinction between first and second-order theories).

30. See Shapiro (1991) for a defence of this claim.

31. It is assumed that finitary arithmetic is true. Hence S is consistent. Tait (1981) argues that finitary arithmetic *is* PRA. If so, S will be formal PRA.

32. If, as suggested in Pt IV Ch. 3, the correctness of a finitary general statement consists not in its being true but in its indicating truth, in the sense that all its instances are true, this needs restating. What the First Underivability Theorem shows is that being a correct finitary statement, where that consists in being a true strictly finitary statement or a truth-indicating finitary general statement, does not have the unproblematic syntactic character of derivability.

33. Kreisel (1976) and Smorynski (1989) argue for this.

34. In fact there are infinitely many finitary general truths underivable in S. For if we add δ to S as an axiom we get a new formal system S + δ which is consistent, since δ is unrefutable in S; so the Gödel sentence δ^1 for S + δ is underivable in S + δ, hence underivable in S. Similarly, the Gödel sentence δ^{n+1} for S + δ +. . .+ δ^n is underivable in S. The generalization follows by induction.

35. Detlefsen (1990).

36. Finitary sentences include finitary general formulas. In other contexts the word 'sentence' is used for formulas without free variables, and so excludes finitary general formulas.

37. S is consistent, being true. It is then trivially ω-consistent, as no string of symbols of the form $\neg\forall x\varphi(x)$ is a finitistic formula.

Chapter 2

1. From here on I will omit the qualification 'in code'.

2. $neg(x)$ is a primitive recursive function, hence representable in T, as T contains PRA.

Endnotes

3. The systems of interest all contain PRA. So all true equations between numerals or terms built up from numerals and basic arithmetical operations, and the negations of all false ones, are derivable in them. Also, the laws of classical propositional and quantifier logic hold in them. This is enough to ensure the equivalence of the various explications of consistency of the system.

4. See e.g. Boolos and Jeffrey (1974: 187); Smorynski (1977: 827). Bernays, I am told, was the first to actually prove the Second Underivability Theorem (Hilbert and Bernays 1939); Gödel gave only a sketch without formulating derivability conditions. Jeroslow (1973) shows that, if in place of a sentence expressing its own underivability one uses a sentence expressing that its negation is derivable, two of Bernays's derivability conditions can be dropped, for T with quantifiers. The neatest formulation of derivability conditions and the most convenient for the general study of formal provability, is due to Löb (1955).

5. Some mathematical logic texts do not give any proof that their version of the T-derivability formula satisfies the derivability conditions; Monk (1976: ch. 17) does.

6. Modus Ponens, also known Detachment, is the rule that permits the inference from {A, A → B} to B.

7. In some mathematical logic texts, e.g. Monk (1976) and Boolos and Jeffrey (1974), there is a different argument for the Second Underivability Theorem, one that uses Löb's theorem (Löb 1955).

8. Feferman (1989).

9. For elaboration, see the appendix to this chapter. Feferman (1960) distinguishes between extensional and intensional theorems, and shows the intensionality of the Second Underivability Theorem. The extensional/intensional distinction in relation to the Underivability Theorems is discussed at length by Auerbach (1985).

10. Detlefsen (1986). I (and probably others) uncritically accepted the orthodox view, until Detlefsen forced me to take a closer look at the matter.

11. The idea goes back to Rosser (1936). For an update on consistency-guaranteed systems, see Visser (1989).

12. See n. 4.

13. This is the one derivability condition that is still needed in Jeroslow's modification of the proof.

14. A sentence α is consistent with a set of sentences Γ when no contradictory pair of sentences can both be derived from premisses drawn from $\Gamma \cup \{\alpha\}$ using T's inference rules.

15. Feferman (1960) contrived a predicate $A^*_T(x)$ that represents in T, but does not express, the property of being an axiom of T. A Feferman system is a system T^* such that $A^*_T(x)$ expresses the property of being an axiom in T^*, but is otherwise like T.

16. This holds for sentences in first-order languages not restricted to one-place predicates. This fact follows from Church's Theorem that there is no effective decision procedure for validity in first-order predicate logic, and from the fact that for first-order predicate logic validity and derivability coincide.

17. Feferman (1960) points this out. He shows that the study of improper formal systems can be rewarding, e.g. in giving information about relations between theories (deductively closed sets of sentences). Also, Feferman used the idea behind T^F to show that the possibility of an internal consistency proof of a theory depends crucially on the *presentation* of the theory. Having shown how important is the way in which a body of mathematics is formally presented, Feferman (1982, 1989) led the way in developing an account of what we might call standard presentations of formal theories.

18. T^R is a modification of a way of presenting a formal system due to Rosser (1936).

19. Even if β is derivable from $\{\delta_1, \ldots, \delta_n\}$, and each of $\delta_1, \delta_2, \ldots, \delta_n$ is derivable from the axioms before one of its contradictories, β may not be derivable from the axioms before one of *its* contradictories.

20. It might be thought that Rosser systems formalize actual or ideal practice when that includes responding to discovery of a contradiction in our theories: if derivations are enumerated in order of increasing epistemic vulnerability, we discard those that conflict with earlier ones (see Detlefsen 1986: 120–3). Whatever the merits of this suggestion, I regard it as changing the subject. Hilbert's Programme was aimed at showing our actual theories of arithmetic, analysis, and set theory to be consistent (among other things); it was not concerned with what we would or should do if we found one of those theories to be inconsistent. On the side issue, I doubt that there is a formalizable procedure for the right way of responding to discovery of contradictions. Certainly Rosser systems will not do. For if we discovered an inconsistency in one of our theories by finding apparent proofs with contradictory conclusions, we would not and should not proceed simply by discarding one of the candidate proofs and then sail on, leaving the logic and the axioms of the theory unchanged.

21. In fairness to their originators, it should be said that such non-standard systems were not invented for the purposes of rescuing Hilbert's Programme.

22. Gödel (1972b); see also Feferman's introduction in Gödel (1990: 282–7).

23. T is *outer consistent* if and only if no T-derivable equation between primitive recursive terms can be shown to be false or to have a false numerical instance by applying the rules of the equational calculus: (i) substituting primitive recursive terms for free-variables, and (ii) substituting one primitive recursive term for another when their equality has been derived in T. A primitive recursive term is, roughly, a numeral or a term whose value expressed as a numeral can be computed, when numerals have been substituted for all its free-variables.

24. This principle is also known as Π_1^0 reflection for T, Π_1^0 sentences and finitary sentences being the same.

25. The technical change means that the proof dispenses with the derivability condition $\mathrm{Prov}_T(\ulcorner \alpha \urcorner) \to \mathrm{Prov}_T(\ulcorner \mathrm{Prov}_T(\ulcorner \alpha \urcorner) \urcorner)$. This condition (roughly) is essential to the proof of the Second Underivability Theorem but does not hold for non-standard systems.

26. Gödel (1931); see Gödel (1986: 195).

Endnotes

27. Gödel's views can be traced in an evolving series of talks and articles: Gödel (*1933o, *1938b, *1941, 1958, 1972a). (Starred items are from the *Nachlass*.)

28. Gödel (1972a), in Gödel (1990: 273); cf. Gödel (1958), in Gödel (1990: 241, 242).

29. Gentzen (1936, 1938). Justification for the claim that the methods used in the consistency proof apart from induction up to ε_0 are finitary is given in Gentzen (1936: §§7–11, 16).

30. Hilbert and Bernays (1939: §§5, 3c). Gentzen (1943: §2) shows how a proof of induction up to α (where $\omega \leq \alpha < \varepsilon_0$) can be formalized in formal number theory.

31. Gentzen (1938: §4.4).

32. Gödel (1972a), in Gödel (1990: 273).

33. Further evidence in this direction is Gentzen's direct proof that induction up to ε_0 is not provable in number theory (Gentzen 1943).

34. Tait (1981).

35. This is reliability with respect to *finitary* claims, i.e. no false finitary theorems.

36. Heyting (1930).

37. Gödel (1933). The same theorem was proved, independently of Gödel, by Gentzen and Bernays in 1933.

38. Perceiving here must be sensory; it is not clear whether sensory imaging is excluded.

39. See Gödel (*1933o, *1941) for this.

40. Martin-Löf (1984). These are notes by G. Sambin of lectures given in Padua in June 1980. Intuitionistic type theory originated with work by Martin-Löf in the 1970s and has been adopted by computer scientists. I do not know to what extent it fulfils the needs of intuitionist philosophy of mathematics.

41. 'D' for *Dialectica*, as it is commonly known as Gödel's *Dialectica* interpretation of intuitionist arithmetic (after the journal in which it was first published) (Gödel (1958)); Gödel (1972a) is the same thing with extensive additional footnotes, in which he refines and explains his ideas in the main text. For the original idea, see Gödel (*1941). For a similar consistency proof of classical arithmetic bypassing intuitionist arithmetic, see Shoenfield (1967): ch. 8, §3. For consistency proofs of analysis by extensions of Gödel's methods, see Spector (1962) and Luckhardt (1973).

42. That is, the consistency of classical arithmetic is made more certain by its proof relative to D than by its proof relative to intuitionistic arithmetic.

43. It is doubtful whether Hilbert ever accepted this fact, but his chief co-worker Bernays certainly did. In the preface of Hilbert and Bernays (1934), Hilbert said that Gödel's results showed that sharper methods were needed to obtain finitary consistency proofs of more extensive systems. For Bernays's attitude, see Bernays (1935, 1941, 1954). Bernays saw that a non-finitary consistency proof could have epistemic value, and in 1935 he considered finitary proofs of a non-finitary system's consistency relative to a more evident non-finitary system as a way forward.

44. Mostowski (1966: 24).

PART V

Chapter 1

1. Zermelo (1930).
2. Compare Gödel (*1933o) with Gödel (1947) for this difference in attitude.
3. A sequence S of stages is a sequence of *consecutive* stages when, for any V, W in S, W immediately follows V in S if and only if W is the next stage above V.
4. The idea of a cumulative hierarchy was also formulated by von Neumann (1929).
5. At this point Gödel had the following footnote: 'This phrase ["iterated application"] is meant to include transfinite iteration; i.e., the totality of sets obtained by finite iteration is considered to be itself a set and a basis for further applications of the operation "set of".' This is fn. 12 of Gödel (1947) and fn. 13 of Gödel (1964) as reprinted in Gödel (1990: 254–70). Gödel (1964) is a revised and expanded version of Gödel (1947). Another footnote, which I omit, is marked a few words later in the quotation.
6. Gödel (1947, 1964).
7. Scott (1974).
8. If V is not lower than W, W is V or is lower than V; then W = V or W ∈ V; then V ∉ W, otherwise there would be a circular membership chain: V ∈ V or V ∈ W ∈ V. Hence if V ∈ W, V is lower than W.
9. A proof of well-foundedness that does not use the axiom of Accumulation is given in Potter (1991: ch. 1).
10. Mirimanoff (1917) was the first to study the sets with no infinite descending membership chains (the well-founded sets). He did not claim that all sets are well founded, but deemed non-well-founded sets to be extraordinary.
11. As the stages are well ordered, they can be indexed by the ordinals. The *rank* of a set m is the ordinal index of the lowest stage of which m is a subset. So if α is the rank of m, the level of m is $V\alpha+1$. Rank is defined by transfinite recursion as follows: $\text{rank}(m) = \cup\{\text{rank}(p) + 1 : p \in m\}$.
12. For an opposing view, see Cohen (1971).
13. However, one version of constructivism, Brouwer's intuitionism, admits an axiom of choice. But, owing to the intuitionistic meaning of quantifier expressions, the intuitionistic axiom is a constructive principle quite different from the classical Axiom of Choice. See Dummett (1977: Ch. 2 §4).
14. To illustrate, let $f(n)$ be $[(n + 1)!/2 \times (n-1)!]$ and let $g(n)$ be $1 + 2 + \ldots + n$, for each positive integer n; as $[(n + 1)!/2 \times (n - 1)!] = 1 + 2 + \ldots + n$ for every positive integer n, the functions f and g are one and the same, on this view.
15. Zermelo (1930). Versions of the axiom had been proposed ealier by Fraenkel (1922) and Skolem (1922a). Hallett (1984) credits von Neumann for the axiom.
16. Lévy (1960a, b). See also Bernays (1961).
17. See Wang (1974: 189) for a report of Gödel's statement of informal reflection. See also Lear (1977).

18. To state the schema, we use a device known as relativization of a formula θ to a set Y. If Y is a set, θ^Y (the relativization of θ to Y) is the result of replacing every existential subformula $\exists x\varphi$ of θ by $\exists x\,(x \in Y\ \&\ \varphi)$ and every universal subformula $\forall x\varphi$ by $\forall x\,(x \in Y \to \varphi)$, working from innermost subformulas outwards. Then θ^Y is true if and only if θ is true in the model with domain Y and which assigns to '$\in$' the membership relation restricted to members of Y. Now let θ have at most n free variables $x_1, x_2, \ldots, x_n$. The Reflection Schema is:

$$\forall\alpha\,\exists\beta\,[\beta > \alpha\ \&\ \forall x_1 \ldots \forall x_n (x_1 \in V\beta\ \&\ \ldots x_n \in V\beta \to [\theta \leftrightarrow \theta^{V\beta}])].$$

Lower-case Greek letters are variables for ordinals, and $V\beta$ is the βth stage. There is a version of the Reflection Principle that does not mention ordinals and stages. Let '$S(y)$' mean 'y is a set' and let '$St(x)$' abbreviate '$\forall y \in x[S(y) \to (y \subseteq x\ \&\ \forall z[z \subseteq y \to z \in x])]$' (read: x is supertransitive). Then we can express the Reflection Principle thus:

$$\forall a\exists b[a \in b\ \&\ St(b)\ \&\ \forall x_1 \ldots \forall x_n(x_1 \in b\ \&\ \ldots x_n \in b \to [\theta \leftrightarrow \theta^b])].$$

19. Lévy (1960*a*, *b*, 1962).

20. Gödel (1938). The proof was published in Gödel (1940). In this work Gödel also proved the consistency of adding the Axiom of Choice (AC) and the Generalized Continuum Hypothesis (GCH) to the axioms, given that those axioms form a consistent set. GCH is: $2^{\aleph_\alpha} = \aleph_{\alpha+1}$. The method is to show that any universe of sets in which the axioms are true has an inner model, the constructible hierarchy, in which also AC and GCH are true. The axiom system used is known as NBG, which is equivalent to ZF with respect to sentences in the language of set theory. The axioms of ZF are: Extensionality, Union Set, Power Set, Replacement, Infinity. NBG is an acronym for von Neumann, Bernays, and Gödel; ZF is for Zermelo–Fraenkel.

21. Cohen (1963). Cohen (1966) is a full exposition. Cohen showed how to expand a countable model of the axioms of set theory to a model of those axioms in which AC and CH is false. This entails that AC and GCH are independent of the axioms of set theory, assuming the axioms are consistent.

22. Robinson (1965). See also Robinson (1969).

23. Cohen (1971). This is the text of a talk given in 1967.

24. The coding of syntax of the language of set theory can be done using hereditarily finite sets instead of numbers. (The hereditarily finite sets are the sets of level Vn for $n \in \omega$. They can be thought of as sets with a finite membership tree.) So a sentence about hereditarily finite sets can be constructed according to the recipe of Gödel or Rosser that is independent of the axioms of set theory, given their (ω-)consistency.

25. These axioms assert the existence of inaccessible cardinals, hyper-inaccessible cardinals, Mahlo cardinals, hyper-Mahlo cardinals, etc. These all follow from ZFC plus the statement M that there exists a measurable cardinal, and it was shown in Lévy and Solovay (1967) that CH is independent of ZFC + M, given that ZFC + M

is consistent. ZFC is ZF plus the Axiom of Choice. (For ZF see n. 18.) By contrast, the statement that there is a model of ZF, which can be expressed as a sentence of set theory, is independent of ZF (assuming consistency of ZF) but is derivable from ZF plus the statement that there is an inaccessible cardinal. For definitions of the types of cardinal mentioned here, see Drake (1974: chs. 4, 6).

26. Easton (1970) shows that, for any increasing function $G(\alpha)$ from regular ordinals to ordinals satisfying the sole condition that $\aleph_{G(\alpha)} > \aleph_\alpha$, the hypothesis that $\forall \alpha \, [2^{\aleph_\alpha} = \aleph_{G(\alpha)}]$ can be consistently added to ZFC, if ZFC is consistent.

27. A sentence φ in the language of a theory T is a *semantic consequence* of T if and only if φ is true in every model of T.

28. Here we are assuming that second-order ZF has a model. Zermelo's universes of set theory are of the form $V\alpha$, where α is inaccessible. All models of second-order ZF are isomorphic to one or another of these 'inaccessible' $V\alpha$, and CH is already decided in the least such $V\alpha$. There is a corresponding theorem about models of NBG; see Zermelo (1930) and Shepherdson (1952). An ordinal α is inaccessible when it is infinite and is greater than any sum of fewer than α ordinals less than α and greater than (the ordinal of) $2^{|\beta|}$ for any lesser ordinal β.

29. See Scott's introduction to Bell (1985) for an expression of this view, and Shapiro (1991: ch. 5).

30. Weston (1977). There is no conflict here: in second-order logic not all the semantic consequences of a second-order theory are derivable from it.

31. Robinson (1965) claims that 'only a small minority of mathematicians, even those with platonist views, accept the idea that there may be mathematical facts which are true but unknowable.' It is clear that he did not accept that idea.

32. Anyone who accepts Zermelo's view must accept that *some* questions of cardinality have different answers in different universes; e.g., are there inaccessible cardinals? But the cardinality questions under discussion here, such as the continuum question, have a more local character, in that their possible answers can be formulated with bounded quantifiers. One might expect that *these* questions have a determinate answer, even on Zermelo's view.

33. Mostowski (1972) takes position (ii) and is roundly criticized by Kreisel for it. Mostowski's article, Kreisel's critique, and Mostowski's reply appear in Lakatos (1972), which is part of the proceedings of a conference held in 1965. See also the remarks by Robinson, the article by Bernays (1972), and the ensuing discussion on these matters, all in the same collection.

34. See Scott's introduction to Bell (1985) for a perspective on the matter.

35. The system {Extensionality, Foundation, Separation, Reflection, Choice} is equivalent to the system known as ZFC + AF. (For ZFC, see n. 23.) AF is the Axiom of Foundation. In first-order versions of these theories Separation, Reflection, and Replacement are formulated as schemas and their instances are axioms. A useful exposition of the provability relations between reflection principles and other axioms is given by Gloede (1976).

Endnotes

Chapter 2

1. Zermelo (1930).
2. Zermelo (1930). The 'ultrafinite antinomies' are the class paradoxes and 'nonsets' of a model are its proper classes. When Zermelo says that we can present 'set theory itself' as an unlimited sequence of models, I take it he meant that the *subject matter* of set theory can be presented that way.
3. Following a theft, one might claim 'Everything that was in that box was taken.' This would not be refuted by finding some old dust particles in the box. But if the forensic investigator reports that 'Everything in the box has an inorganic origin', the report would be refuted by finding some dead skin cells among the dust particles. Whether the dust particles count as 'things', then, is context-dependent.
4. Zermelo (1930). V is a universe if and only if $\langle V, \in _V\rangle$ is a model of the second-order version of ZFC + AF. Such a universe has the form of a stage V_α where α is a strongly inaccessible ordinal. (An ordinal α is *strongly inaccessible* if and only if α is infinite, and α is not the sum of fewer than $|\alpha|$ ordinals before α, and for any β before α, $2^{|\beta|} < |\alpha|$. Here '$|\delta|$' denotes the cardinal number of predecessors of δ.) So a universe has a universe among its members if and only if it contains an inaccessible ordinal, hence an inaccessible stage. The Axiom of Inaccessibles is: For every β there is an α after β such that α is inaccessible. A universe in which the Axiom of Inaccessibles is true contains an unbounded sequence of universes.
5. There is a general phenomenon here that has not received due attention, in my judgement. (Russell's 'typically ambiguity' may be an instance.) Clearly, it needs a proper basis in semantic theory. I think that this can be supplied, but pursuing it here would take us too far afield.
6. Tarski (1944); Parsons (1974); Kripke (1975); Burge (1979).

Chapter 3

1. It is possible for someone to have very different degrees of rational confidence in the same proposition at the same time relative to different contexts. In the context of ongoing inquiry into scepticism, one must doubt the existence of material objects distributed in accord with appearances, but in the context of simultaneous inquiry into ways of reducing current discomfort, such doubts are normally irrational.
2. Hilbert (1929, 1931).
3. A reminder: ε_0 is the least ordinal α such that $\omega^\alpha = \alpha$. Induction up to α is the rule

$$\forall\beta<\alpha\,[\,[\forall\delta<\beta\,P(\delta)\,]\to P(\beta)] \qquad \therefore\ \forall\beta<\alpha\,P(\beta).$$

In the present context P is restricted to decidable quantifier-free predicates. For an explanation without symbols, see 'The question of finitary reasoning' in Pt IV Ch. 3.
4. Expositions of this work are Schütte (1977), Takeuti (1987), and Pohlers (1989).
5. See also Feferman's critical remarks on this matter in Feferman (1988*a*, 1993*a*).

6. Reverse mathematics was initiated by Friedman and pursued by Simpson and others; see Simpson (1985). Simpson (1988) explains the relation of reverse mathematics to Hilbert's Programme.

7. Friedman obtained a stronger result (viz., that WKL_0 is conservative over PRA for Π_2^0–sentences) by non-finitary means, and Sieg (1985) obtained a finitary proof. Simpson (1988) reports that the same has been shown for a strengthening of WKL_0.

8. These discoveries are largely due to Simpson and his co-workers. Simpson (1988) gives examples and references.

9. Feferman (1988a, 1993a).

10. Feferman (1988a) gives the technically precise definitions.

11. These are numerals or terms built from numerals and symbols for functions on numerals with a primitive recursive definition.

12. Logically unpacking this phrase reveals an allusion to the totality in the form of a quantifier phrase: the planet x such that *for all planets y* if $y \neq x$, x is larger than y.

13. Unpacking gives: the set x of natural numbers such that x has P and *for all sets y of natural numbers* if y has P then x is included in y.

14. Poincaré (1913); Weyl (1918). Kronecker is reported to have said that God made the integers but all else is the work of man; see Pt I Ch. 2, n. 28.

15. See Feferman (1988b) for an exposition of W.

16. Feferman and Jäger (1993, 1996).

17. Weyl (1918).

18. This is outlined in the subsection on Weyl in Pt IV Ch. 2. Here it is given in more detail, as presented by Feferman (1988b). Let real numbers be identified with left Dedekind cuts. Let S be a non-empty set of reals bounded above, given by a property P. Then the supremum of S is defined: $\mathrm{Sup}(S) = \{q : q \in \mathbb{Q} \,\&\, \exists r(P(r) \,\&\, q \in r)\}$ where $\mathbb{Q}$ is the set of rationals and 'r' is a variable ranging over reals. This is impredicative as the supremum of S falls within the range of 'r'. Now let $\mathbf{r}$ be a non-empty sequence of reals bounded above, given by a relation R: for all $n \in \mathbb{N}$, $q \in \mathbf{r}_n$ if and only if $R(q, n)$. The supremum of $\mathbf{r}$ is defined: $\mathrm{Sup}(\mathbf{r}) = \{q : q \in \mathbb{Q} \,\&\, \exists n R(q, n)\}$. This is predicative, as $\mathrm{Sup}(\mathbf{r})$ is real while no variable in the definition ranges over reals. Using an enumeration q_m ($m \in \mathbb{N}$) of the rational numbers and identifying each q_m with m, this can be reduced to a purely arithmetical definition of the form $\mathrm{Sup}(\mathbf{r}) = \{m : \exists n R^*(m, n)\}$. The existence of this set follows from W's arithmetical comprehension axiom: $\exists a \forall n[n \in a \leftrightarrow \varphi(n)]$, where $\varphi(x)$ is an arithmetical sentence with only 'x' free, and 'n' is a variable ranging over natural numbers.

19. Feferman (1988a, 1993b). In Feferman (1998a) a postscript is added to the reprint of 1988b (= ch. 13) which further discusses the conjecture.

20. Parsons (1983).

21. Feferman and Hellman (1995).

22. Hilbert's official attitude to these bodies of mathematics was instrumentalist. Detlefsen points out that a thorough instrumentalist does not need to establish the

Endnotes

reliability of full analysis and set theory, but only as much as could be instrumentally gainful, thus excluding proofs that are too long, complex, or abstruse for us to discover. So Detlefsen proposes another programme: find a mathematical criterion for instrumentally gainful proof and show by finitary means that the parts of our non-finitary mathematics satisfying the criterion are finitary-reliable (Detlefsen 1986: ch. 5; 1990: n. 24). (Detlefsen implies that this is Hilbert's Programme, but the credit should go to Detlefsen himself.) I do not know whether this programme has been pursued, or whether it is feasible. Any proposal as to the limits of what is instrumentally gainful must rest on empirical grounds, and so some uncertainty is unavoidable; but this may be negligible, and it may be possible to establish reliability for parts of analysis beyond the reach of theories already known to be reducible to finitary arithmetic.
23. I have not mentioned reductions of non-constructive to constructive mathematics. This is largely because I am not able to gauge how much has been achieved in this area. There have been reductions of formalizations of analysis and set theory to formalizations of counterparts with intuitionistic logic, by extending Gödel's 'double-negation' translation of classical arithmetic into intuitionistic arithmetic. But even if we take intuitionistic logic to be constructively justified, these counterparts are not. See Troelstra (1986) for discussion and references. Feferman (1988*a*: §8) mentions reductions to the constructive not achieved by translation and gives references.
24. Russell (1956*b*).

Chapter 4

1. Bishop (1967), Bishop and Bridges (1985); see also Beeson (1985). For philosophical underpinnings of constructivism, see Dummett (1975); Tennant (1987); and Wright (1986).
2. McLarty (1992) and MacLane and Moerdijk (1992) are introductions.
3. e.g. Apostol (1957) and Rudin (1964). Not all analysis texts define the real numbers, but basic point-set theory is indispensable in standard approaches.
4. Robinson (1966). Machover and Hirschfeld (1969) and Bell and Machover (1977: ch. 11) are expositions with further material; Keisler (1976) is a useful primer.
5. Kock (1981) and Bell (1985) are expositions.
6. For recent accounts, see Butterworth (1999) and Dehaene (1997).

Bibliography

Abel, N. (1881). *Oeuvres complètes*, 2 vols, ed. L. Sylow and S. Lie. Christiana: Grøndahl.

Apostol, T. (1957). *Mathematical Analysis*. Reading, Mass: Addison-Wesley.

—— (1967). *Calculus*, 2nd edn. New York: John Wiley.

Auerbach, D. (1985). Intensionality and the Gödel theorems. *Philosophical Studies* **48**, 337–51.

—— (1992). How to say things with formalisms. In Detlefsen (1992).

Baire, R., Borel, E., Hadamard, J., and Lebesgue, H. (1905). Cinq lettres sur la théorie des ensembles. *Bulletin de la Société Mathématique de France* **33**, 261–73; trans. by G. Moore in an appendix of Moore (1982) and reprinted in Ewald (1996).

Beeson, M. (1985). *Foundations of Constructive Mathematics: Metamathematical Studies*. Berlin: Springer-Verlag.

Bell, J. (1985). *Boolean-Valued Models and Independence Proofs in Set Theory*, 2nd edn. Oxford: Clarendon Press.

—— (1998). *A Primer of Infinitesimal Analysis*. Cambridge: Cambridge University Press.

—— and Machover, M. (1977). *A Course in Mathematical Logic*. Amsterdam: North-Holland.

Benacerraf, P. and Putnam, H. (eds.) (1964) *Philosophy of Mathematics: Selected Readings*. Englewood Cliffs, NJ: Prentice-Hall; 2nd edn. Cambridge: Cambridge University Press, 1983.

Berkeley, G. (1734). *The Analyst; or A Discourse Addressed to an Infidel Mathematician*. In A. Luce and T. Jessop (eds.), *The Works of George Berkeley Bishop of Cloyne*, vol. 4. London: Nelson, 1948–57.

Bernays, P. (1930a). Die Grundgedanken der Fries'schen Philosophie in ihrem Verhältnis zum heutigen Stand der Wissenschaft. *Abhandlungen der Fries'schen Schule* **5**, 99–113.

—— (1930b). Die Philosophie der Mathematik und die Hilbertsche Beweistheorie. *Blätter für Deutsche Philosophie* **4**, 326–67; trans. in Mancosu (1998a).

—— (1935). Sur le platonisme dans les mathématiques. *L'Enseignement mathématiques* **34**, 52–69; trans. in Benacerraf and Putnam (1964).

—— (1941). Sur les questions méthodologiques actuelle de la théorie hilbertienne de la démonstration. In F. Gonseth (ed.), *Les Entretiens de Zurich, 6–9 Décembre 1938*. Zurich: Leeman.

Bibliography

—— (1954). Zur Beurteilung der Situation in der beweistheoretischen Forschung. *Revue internationale de philosophie* **8**, 9–13.

—— (1961). Zur Frage der Unendlichkeitsschemata in der axiomatischen Mengenlehre. In Y. Bar-Hillel, E. Poznanski, M. Rabin, and A. Robinson (eds.), *Essays on the Foundations of Mathematics*. Jerusalem: Magnes Press.

—— (1972). What do some recent results in set theory suggest? In Lakatos (1972).

—— (1976). *Abhandlungen zur Philosophie der Mathematik*. Darmstadt: Wissenschaftliche Buchgesellshcaft.

Bishop, E. (1967). *Foundations of Constructive Analysis*. New York: McGraw-Hill.

—— and Bridges, D. (1985). *Constructive Analysis*. Berlin: Springer-Verlag.

Bolzano, B. (1851). *Paradoxien des Unendlichen*. Liepzig: Reclam; trans. by D. Steele as *Paradoxes of the Infinite*. London: Routledge & Kegan Paul; partially reprinted in translation in Ewald (1996).

Boolos, G. (1971). The iterative conception of set. *Journal of Philosophy* **68**, 215–32; reprinted in Benacerraf and Putnam (1964), 2nd edn. 1983.

—— (1984). Iteration again. *Philosophical Topics* **17**, 5–12.

—— (1989). New proof of the Gödel Incompleteness Theorem. *Notices of the American Mathematical Society* **36**, 388–90.

—— and Jeffrey, R. (1974). *Computability and Logic*. Cambridge: Cambridge University Press.

Bos, H. (1974). Differentials, higher-order differentials and the derivative in the Leibnizian calculus. *Archive for History of the Exact Sciences* **14**, 1–90.

Brouwer, L. (1912). *Intuitionisme en formalisme*. Groningen: Noordhoff; trans. in Benacerraf and Putnam (1964).

—— (1918). Begründung der Mengenlehre unabhängig vom logischen satz vom ausgeschlossenen Dritten: Erster Teil, Allgemeine Mengenlehre. *Koninklijke Akademie van wetenschappen te Amsterdam*, Proceedings of the Section of Sciences **12**, no. 5, 1–43.

—— (1919). Begründung der Mengenlehre unabhängig vom logischen satz vom ausgeschlossenen Dritten: Zweiter Teil, Theorie der Punktmengen. *Koninklijke Akademie van wetenschappen te Amsterdam*, Proceedings of the Section of Sciences **12**, no. 7, 1–33.

—— (1928). Intuitionistische Betrachtungen über den Formalismus. *Koninklijke Akademie van wetenschappen te Amsterdam*, Proceedings of the Section of Sciences **31**, 374–9; trans. in van Heijenoort (1967).

—— (1929). Mathematik, Wissenschaft und Sprache. *Monatshefte für Mathematik und Physik* **36**, 153–64; trans. as 'Mathematics, science and language' in Mancosu (1998*a*).

—— (1952). Historical background, principles and methods of intuitionism. *South African Journal of Science* **49**, 139–46; reprinted in *L. E. J. Brouwer: Collected Works*, vol. 1, ed. A. Heyting. Amsterdam: North-Holland, 1975.

Browder, F. (ed.) (1976). *Mathematical Developments Arising from Hilbert Problems*.

Proceedings of Symposia in Pure Mathematics, **28**. Providence, RI: American Mathematical Society.

Burali-Forti, C. (1897). Una questione sui numeri transfiniti. *Circolo Matematico di Palermo, Rendiconti* **11**, 154–64; trans. in van Heijenoort (1967).

Burge, T. (1979). Semantical paradox. *Journal of Philosophy* **76**, 269–98; reprinted with a postscript in Martin (1984).

Burgess, J. and Hazen, A. (1998). Predicative logic and formal arithmetic. *Notre Dame Journal of Formal Logic* **39**, 1–17.

Butterworth, B. (1999). *The Mathematical Brain*. London: Macmillan.

Cantor, G. (1883). *Grundlagen einer allgemeinen Mannigfaltigkeitslehre: Ein mathematisch-philosophischer Versuch in der Lehre des Unendlichen*. Leipzig: Teubner.

—— (1887–8). Mittheilungen zur Lehre vom Transfiniten, I, II. *Zeitschrift für Philosophie und philosophische Kritik* **91**, 81–125; **92**, 240–65.

—— (1891). Über eine elementare Frage der Manngifaltigkeitslehre. *Jahresbericht der Deutschen Mathematiker-Vereinigung*, **1**, 75–8.

—— (1895). Beiträge zur Begründung der transfiniten Mengenlehre, 1. *Mathematische Annalen*, vol. 46; trans. in Cantor (1952).

—— (1897) Beiträge zur Begründung der transfiniten Mengenlehre, 2. *Mathematische Annalen*, 49; trans. in Cantor (1952).

—— (1899). Letter to Dedekind of 28 July, 1899; trans. in van Heijenoort (1967).

—— (1932). *Gesammelte Abhandlungen*, ed. E. Zermelo. Berlin: Springer.

—— (1952). *Contributions to the Founding of the Theory of Transfinite Numbers*, trans. by P. Jourdain, 1915. New York: Dover.

Chihara, C. (1973). *Ontology and the Vicious Circle Principle*. Ithaca, NY: Cornell University Press.

——(1990). *Constructibility and Mathematical Existence*. Oxford: Oxford University Press.

Church. A. (1976). Comparison of Russell's resolution of the semantical antinomies with that of Tarski. *Journal of Symbolic Logic* **41**, 747–60.

Cohen, P. (1963). The independence of the continuum hypothesis, I. *Proceedings of the National Academy of Sciences USA*, **50**, 1143–8.

—— (1966). *Set Theory and the Continuum Hypothesis*. New York: Benjamin Press.

—— (1971). Comments on the foundations of set theory. In D. Scott (ed.), *Axiomatic Set Theory*. Proccedings of Symposia in Pure Mathematics, **13**(1). Providence, RI: American Mathematical Society.

Cutland, N. (1980). *Computability*. Cambridge: Cambridge University Press.

Dauben, J. (1979). *Georg Cantor: His Mathematics and Philosophy of the Infinite*. Cambridge, Mass.: Harvard University Press.

Davis, M. (ed.) (1965). *The Undecidable*. New York: Raven Press.

Dedekind, R. (1872). *Stetigkeit und irrationale Zahlen*. Braunschweig: Vieweg; trans. as 'Continuity and irrational numbers' in Dedekind (1963); this translation is reprinted, with corrections, in Ewald (1996), vol. 2.

Bibliography

—— (1888). *Was sind und was sollen die Zahlen?* Braunschweig: Vieweg; trans. as 'The nature and meaning of numbers' in Dedekind (1963).

—— (1963). *Essays on the Theory of Numbers*, trans. by W. Beman, 1901. New York: Dover.

Dehaene, S. (1997). *The Number Sense*. Oxford: Oxford University Press.

Detlefsen. M. (1986). *Hilbert's Program: An Essay on Mathematical Instrumentalism*. Dordrecht: D. Reidel.

—— (1990). On an alleged refutation of Hilbert's Program using Gödel's First Incompleteness Theorem. *Journal of Philosophical Logic* **19**, 343–77; reprinted in Detlefsen (1992).

—— (ed.) (1992). *Proof, Logic and Formalization*. London: Routledge.

Diogenes Laertius (1925). *Diogenes Laertius: Lives of Eminent Philosophers*, with a translation by R. Hicks. London: Heinemann.

Dixon, A. (1907). On well-ordered aggregates. *Proceedings of the London Mathematical Society* **4**(2), 18–20.

Drake, F. (1974). *Set Theory: An Introduction to Large Cardinals*. Amsterdam: North-Holland.

Dummett, M (1975). The philosophical basis of intuitionist logic. In H. Rose and J. Shepherdson (eds.), *Proceedings of the Logic Colloquium, Bristol, July 1973*. Amsterdam: North-Holland; reprinted in Benacerraf and Putnam (1964), 2nd edn 1984.

—— (1977). *Elements of Intuitionism*. Oxford: Clarendon Press.

—— (1991). *Frege: Philosophy of Mathematics*. London: Duckworth.

Easton, W. (1970). Powers of regular cardinals. *Annals of Mathematical Logic* **1**, 139–78.

Ewald, W. (1996). *From Kant to Hilbert*. Oxford: Clarendon Press.

Feferman, S. (1960). Arithmetization of metamathematics in a general setting. *Fundamenta Mathematicae* **49**, 35–92.

—— (1964). Systems of predicative analysis. *Journal of Symbolic Logic* **29**, 1–30; reprinted in Hintikka (1969).

—— (1982). Inductively presented systems and the formalization of metamathematics. In D. van Dalen, D. Lascar, and T. Smiley (eds.), *Logic Colloquium '80*. Amsterdam: North-Holland.

—— (1984*a*). Toward useful type-free theories, I. *Journal of Symbolic Logic* **49**, 75–111; reprinted in Martin (1984).

—— (1984*b*). Kurt Gödel: conviction and caution. *Philosophia naturalis* **21**, 546–62; reprinted in Feferman (1998).

—— (1986). Introductory note to *1931c*. In Gödel (1986).

—— (1987). Infinity in mathematics: is Cantor necessary? In *L'infinito nella scienza*, ed. G. Francia. Rome: Instituto della Enciclopedia Italiana; reprinted with minor corrections and additions in Feferman (1998).

—— (1988*a*). Hilbert's Program relativized: proof-theoretical and foundational reductions. *Journal of Symbolic Logic* **53**, 364–84.

—— (1988*b*). Weyl vindicated: *Das Kontinuum* seventy years later. In C. Celluci and G. Sambin (eds.), *Temi e prospettive della logica e della scienza contemporanee*, vol. I. Bologna: Cooperative Libraria Universitaria Editrice; reprinted with minor corrections and additions in Feferman (1998).

—— (1989). Finitary inductively presented logics. In R. Ferro *et al.* (eds.), *Logic Colloquium '88*. Amsterdam: North-Holland; reprinted with minor corrections and additions in D. Gabbay (ed.)*What Is a Logical System?* Oxford: Clarendon Press, 1994.

—— (1993*a*). What rests on what? The proof-theoretic analysis of mathematics. In J. Czermak (ed.), *Philosophy of Mathematics*. Proceedings of the Fifteenth Intternational Wittgenstein Symposium, Part 1. Vienna: Verlag Hölder-Pichler-Tempsky; reprinted in Feferman (1998).

—— (1993*b*). Why a little bit goes a long way: logical foundations of scientifically applicable mathematics. In *PSA 1992*, vol. 2. East Lansing, Mich.: Philosophy of Science Association; reprinted in Feferman (1998).

—— (1998). *In the Light of Logic*. Oxford: Oxford University Press.

—— and Hellman, G. (1995). Predicative foundations of arithmetic. *Journal of Philosophical Logic* **24**, 1–17.

—— and Jäger, G. (1993). Systems of explicit mathematics with non-constructive μ-operator, I. *Annals of Pure and Applied Logic* **65**, 243–63.

—— —— (1996). Systems of explicit mathematics with non-constructive μ-operator, II. *Annals of Pure and Applied Logic* **79**, 37–52.

Fraenkel, A. (1922*a*). Zu den Grundlagen der Cantor-Zermeloschen Mengenlehre. *Mathematische Annalen* **86**, 230–7.

—— (1922*b*). Über den Begriff 'definit' und die Unabhängigkeit des Auswahlaxioms. *Sitzungsberichte der Preusischen Akademie der Wissenschaften, Physickalische–mathematische Klasse*, 253–7; trans. in van Heijenoort (1967).

—— Bar-Hillel, Y., and Lévy, A. (1973). *Foundations of Set Theory*. Amsterdam: North-Holland.

Frege, G. (1879). *Begriffsschrift, eine der arithmetischen nachgebildete Formelsprache des reinen Denkens*. Halle: Nebert; trans. in van Heijenoort (1967).

—— (1884). *Die Grundlagen der Arithmetic*. Breslau: Koebner; trans. as Frege (1950).

—— (1893). *Grundgesetze der Arithmetic*, vol. 1. Jena: Pohle; partial trans. in Frege (1964).

—— (1903). *Grundgesetze der Arithmetic*, vol. 2. Jena: Pohle; partial trans. in Frege (1952).

—— (1950). *The Foundations of Arithmetic*, trans. of Frege (1884) by J. Austin. Oxford: Blackwell.

—— (1952). *Translations from the Philosophical Writings of Gottlob Frege*, trans. by P. Geach and M. Black. Oxford: Blackwell.

—— (1964). *The Basic Laws of Arithmetic*, trans. by M. Furth. Berkeley and Los Angeles: University of California Press.

Bibliography

—— (1969). *Nachgelassene Schriften*, ed. H. Hermes, F. Kambartel, and F. Kaulbach. Hamburg: Felix Meiner.

—— (1980). *Philosophical and Mathematical Correspondence*. Oxford: Blackwell.

Friedman, H. (1973). The consistency of classical set theory relative to a set theory with intuitionistic logic. *Journal of Symbolic Logic* **38**, 315–19.

Gandy, R. (1973). Bertrand Russell as mathematician. *Bulletin of the London Mathematical Society* **5**, 342–8.

Garciadiego, A. (1985). The emergence of some of the nonlogical paradoxes of the theory of sets, 1903–1908. *Historia Mathematica* **12**, 337–51.

Gentzen, G. (1936). Die Widerspruchsfreiheit der reinen Zahlentheorie. *Mathematische Annalen* **112**, 493–565; trans. by M. Szabo in Gentzen (1969).

—— (1938). Neue Fassung des Widerspruchsfreiheitbeweises für die reine Zahlentheorie. *Forschungen zur Logik und zur Grundlegung der exakten Wissenschaften*, n.s. no. 4, 19–44. Leipzig: Hirzel; trans. by M. Szabo in Gentzen (1969).

—— (1943). Beweisbarkeit und Unbeweisbarkeit von Anfangsfällen der transfiniten Induktion in der reinen Zahlentheorie. *Mathematische Annalen* **119** no.1, 140–61; trans. by M. Szabo in Gentzen (1969).

—— (1969). *The Collected Papers of Gerhard Gentzen*, trans. and ed. M. Szabo. Amsterdam: North Holland.

Giaquinto, M. (1994). Epistemology of visual thinking in elementary real analysis. *British Journal for the Philosophy of Science* **45**, 789–831.

—— (1999). Review of Resnik (1997). *Mind* **108**, 783–8.

Gloede, K. (1976). Reflection principles and indescribability. In *Sets and Classes: On the Work of Paul Bernays*. Amsterdam: North-Holland.

Gödel, K. (1929). *Über die Vollstandigkeit des Logikkalküls*; reprinted with a translation in Gödel (1986).

—— (1931). Über formal unentscheidbare Sätze der *Principia Mathematica* und verwandter Systeme, I. *Monatshefte für Mathematik und Physik* **38**, 173–98; reprinted in Gödel (1986) and trans. in van Heijenoort (1967) and Gödel (1986).

—— (1933). Zur intuitionistischen Arithmetik und Zahlentheorie. *Ergebnisse eines mathemati-schen Kolloquiums* **4**, 34–8; trans. in Gödel (1986).

—— (*1933o). The present situation in the foundations of mathematics. In Gödel (1995).

—— (1934). On undecidable propositions of formal mathematical systems (mimeographied lecture notes taken by S. Kleene and J. Rosser); reprinted with Gödel's revisions in Davis (1965) and Gödel (1986).

—— (1938a). The consistency of the generalized continuum hypothesis. *Proceedings of the National Academy of Sciences, USA* **24**, 556–7; reprinted in Gödel (1990).

—— (*1938b). Lecture at Zilsel's. In Gödel (1995).

—— (1940). *The Consistency of the Continuum Hypothesis*. Annals of Mathematics

*Asterisked items are from the *Nachlass*.

Studies, 3. Princeton: Princeton University Press; reprinted as 'The consistency of the axiom of choice and the generalized continuum hypothesis with the axioms of set theory' in Gödel (1990).

—— (*1941). In what sense is intuitionistic logic constructive? In Gödel (1995).

—— (1944). Russell's mathematical logic. In P. Schilpp (ed.), *The Philosophy of Bertrand Russell*. Evanston and Chicago: Northwestern University Press; reprinted with revisions in Benacerraf and Putnam (1964).

—— (1947). What is Cantor's continuum problem? *American Mathematical Monthly* **54**, 515–25; errata **55**, 151. Gödel (1964) is revised and expanded version.

—— (1958). Über eine bisher noch nicht benützte Erweiterung des finiten Standpunktes. *Dialectica* **12**, 280–7; trans. in Gödel (1990).

—— (1964). What is Cantor's continuum problem? In Benacerraf and Putnam (1964). This is a revised and expanded version of Gödel (1947); both versions are reprinted in Gödel (1990).

—— (1972*a*). On an extension of finitary mathematics which has not yet been used (revised and expanded translation of Gödel 1958). In Gödel (1990).

—— (1972*b*). Some remarks on the undecidability results. In Gödel (1990).

—— (1986). *Collected Works*, vol. I. Oxford: Oxford University Press.

—— (1990). *Collected Works*, vol. II. Oxford: Oxford University Press.

—— (1995). *Collected Works*, vol. III. Oxford: Oxford University Press.

Goldfarb, W. (1979). Logic in the twenties: the nature of the quantifier. *Journal of Symbolic Logic* **44**, 351–68.

—— (1989). Russell's reasons for ramification. In C. Savage and C. Anderson (eds.), *Rereading Russell: Essays on Bertrand Russell's Metaphysics and Epistemology*. Minneapolis: University of Minnesota Press.

Goldman, A. (1986). *Epistemology and Cognition*. Cambridge, Mass.: Harvard University Press.

Grattan-Guinness, I. (1978). How Bertrand Russell discovered his paradox. *Historia Mathematica* **5**, 127–37.

—— (1996). How did Bertrand Russell write *The Principles of Mathematics* (1903)? Lecture in the Philosophy of Mathematics series of the King's College Centre for Philosophical Studies, 30 October.

Grelling, K. and Nelson, L. (1908). Bemerkungen zu den Paradoxien von Russell und Burali-Forti. *Abhandlungen der Frieschen Schule*, n.s. **2**.

Hahn, H. (1933). The Crisis in Intuition. In *Krise und Neuaufbau in den exakten Wissenschaften*. Leipzig: Fünf Wiener Vorträge; trans. in *Hans Hahn: Empricism, Logic, and Mathematics. Philosophical Papers*, ed. B. McGuinness . Dordrecht: Reidel, 1980.

Hallett, M. (1984). *Cantorian Set Theory and Limitation of Size*. Oxford: Oxford University Press.

—— (1995). Hilbert and Logic. In M. Marion and R. Cohen (eds.), *Québec Studies in Philosophy of Science I*. Dordrecht: Kluwer.

Bibliography

—— (1996). Introduction to the translation of Zermelo (1930). In Ewald (1996).

Hamblin, C. (1970). *Fallacies*. London: Methuen.

Hart, W. (1983). Russell and Ramsey. *Pacific Philosophical Quarterly* **64**, 193–210.

Hasenjaegar, G. (1967). On Löwenheim–Skolem type insufficiencies of second-order logic. In J. Crossley (ed.), *Sets, Models and Recursion Theory*. Amsterdam: North-Holland.

Hatcher, W. (1982). *The Logical Foundations of Mathematics*. Oxford: Pergamon Press.

Hausdorff, F. (1914). *Grundzüge der Mengenlehre*. Leipzig: De Gruyter.

van Heijenoort J. (ed.) (1967). *From Frege to Gödel*. Cambridge, Mass.: Harvard University Press.

Hessenberg, G. (1906). Grundbegriffe der Mengenlehre. *Abhandlungen der Fries'schen Schule*, n.s. **1**, 479–706.

Heyting, A. (1930). Die formalen Regeln der intuitionistichen Mathematik. In *Sitzungsberichte der Preussischen Akademie der Wissenschaften, physikalische-mathematische Klasse*, pp. 57–71, 158–69.

Hilbert, D. (1891). Über die stetige Abbildung einer linie auf ein Flächenstück. *Mathematische Annalen* **38**, 450–60.

—— (1900*a*). Über den Zahlbegriff. *Jahrensbericht der Deutschen Mathematiker-Vereinigung* **8**, 180–94; trans. in Ewald (1996).

—— (1900*b*). Mathematische probleme. *Nachrichten der Königlichen Gesellshaft der Wissenshaften zu Göttingen* 253–97; trans. in Browder (1976); excerpts trans. in Ewald (1996).

—— (1920). *Probleme der mathematischen Logik*. Transcription of lectures given in Göttingen; excerpts trans. in Ewald (1996).

—— (1922). Neubegründung der Mathematik: Erste Mitteilung. *Abhandlungen aus dem mathematischen Seminar der Hamburgischen Universität* **1**, 157–77; trans. in Mancosu (1998*a*).

—— (1926). Über das Unendliche. *Mathematische Annalen* **95**, 161–90; trans. in van Heijenoort (1967).

—— (1928*a*). Die Grundlagen der Mathematik. *Abhandlungen aus dem mathematischen Seminar der Hamburgischen Universität* **6**, 65–85; reprinted in Hilbert (1928); trans. in van Heijenoort (1967).

—— (1928*b*). *Die Grundlagen der Mathematik, mit Zusätzen von Hermann Weyl und Paul Bernays*. Hamburger Mathematische Einzelschriften **5**, Leipzig: Teubner.

—— (1929). Probleme der Grundlegung der Mathematik. *Mathematische Annalen* **102**, 1–9; trans. in Mancosu (1998*a*).

—— (1931). Die Grundlegung der elementaren Zahlentheorie. *Mathematische Annalen* **104**, 485–94; trans. in Mancosu (1998).

—— and Ackermann, W. (1928). *Grundzüge der theoretischen Logic*. Berlin: Springer.

—— and Bernays, P. (1934). *Grundlagen der Mathematik*, vol. I. Berlin: Springer.

—— —— (1939). *Grundlagen der Mathematik*, vol. II. Berlin: Springer.

Hintikka, J. (ed.) (1969). *The Philosophy of Mathematics*. Oxford: Oxford University Press.

Jeroslow, R. (1973). Redundancies in the Hilbert–Bernays derivability conditions for Gödel's Second Incompleteness Theorem. *Journal of Symbolic Logic* **38**, 359–67.

Keisler, H. (1976). *Foundations of Infinitesimal Calculus*. Boston, Mass.: Prindle, Weber & Schmidt.

Kitcher, P. (1984). *The Nature of Mathematical Knowledge*. Oxford: Oxford University Press.

Kline, M. (1972). *Mathematical Thought from Ancient to Modern Times*. New York: Oxford University Press.

—— (1980). *Mathematics: The Loss of Certainty*. Oxford: Oxford University Press.

Kock, A. (1981). *Synthetic Differential Geometry*. London Mathematical Society Lecture Note Series 51. Cambridge: Cambridge University Press.

Kolmogorov, A. (1925). On the principle of the excluded middle (in Russian). *Matematicheskii sbornik* **32**, 646–67; trans. in van Heijenoort (1967).

König, J. (1965). Über die Grundlagen der Mengenlehre und das Kontinuumproblem. *Mathematische Annalen* **61**, 217–21; trans. in van Heijenoort (1967).

Kreisel, G. (1965). Mathematical logic. In T. Saaty (ed.), *Lectures in Modern Mathematics*, vol. 3. New York: John Wiley.

—— (1976). What have we learnt from Hilbert's Second Problem? In F. Browder (ed.), *Mathematical Developments arising from Hilbert Problems*, Proceedings of Symposia in Pure Mathematics, 28. Providence, RI: American Mathematical Society.

—— (1980). Kurt Gödel, 28 April 1906—14 January 1978. *Biographical Memoirs of Fellows of the Royal Society* **26**, 148–224; corrections, **27**, 697, and **28**, 718.

Kripke, S. (1975) Outline of a theory of truth. *Journal of Philosophy* **72**, 690–716; reprinted in Martin (1984).

Lakatos, I. (ed.) (1972). *Problems in the Philosophy of Mathematics*. Proceedings of the International Colloquium in the Philosophy of Science, London, 1965, vol. 1. Amsterdam: North-Holland.

Lear, J. (1977). Sets and semantics. *Journal of Philosophy* **74**, 86–102.

Lévy, A. (1960*a*). Axiom schemata of strong infinity in axiomatic set theory. *Pacific Journal of Mathematics* **10**, 223–38.

—— (1960*b*). Principles of reflection in axiomatic set theory. *Fundamenta Mathematicae* **49**, 110.

—— (1962). On the principles of reflection in axiomatic set theory. In E. Nagel, P. Suppes, and A. Tarski (eds.), *Logic, Methodology and Philosophy of Science*. Stanford: Stanford University Press.

—— (1979). *Basic Set Theory*. Berlin: Springer.

—— and Solovay, R. (1967). Measurable cardinals and the continuum hypothesis. *Israel Journal of Mathematics* **5**, 234–48.

Löb, M. (1955). Solution of a problem of Leon Henkin. *Journal of Symbolic Logic* **20**, 115–18.

Bibliography

Löwenheim, L. (1915). Über Möglichkeiten im Relativkalkül. *Mathematische Annalen* **76**; trans. in van Heijenoort (1967).

Luckhardt, H. (1973). *Extensional Gödel Functional Interpretation: A Consistency Proof of Classical Analysis*. Springer Lecture Notes in Mathematics, no. 306. Berlin: Springer.

Machover, M. and Hirschfeld, J. (1969). *Lectures on Non-standard Analysis*. Springer Lecture Notes in Mathematics, pp. 94. Berlin: Springer.

MacLane, S. and Moerdijk, I. (1992). *Sheaves in Geometry and Logic: A First Introduction to Topos Theory*. New York: Springer-Verlag.

McLarty, C. (1992). *Elementary Categories, Elementary Toposes*. Oxford: Clarendon Press.

Mancosu, P. (1996). *Philosophy of Mathematics and Mathematical Practice in the Seventeenth Century*. Oxford: Oxford University Press.

—— (ed.) (1998a). *From Brouwer to Hilbert: The Debate on the Foundations of Mathematics in the 1920s*. Oxford: Oxford University Press.

—— (1998b). *Hermann Weyl: Predicativity and an Intuitionistic Excursion*. In Mancosu (1998a).

Martin, R. (ed.) (1984). *Recent Essays on Truth and the Liar Paradox*. Oxford: Oxford University Press.

Martin-Löf, P. (1984). *Intuitionistic Type Theory*. Naples: Bibliopolis.

Mirimanoff, D. (1917). Les Antinomies de Russell et de Burali-Forti et le problème fondamental de la théorie des ensembles. *L'Enseignement Mathématique* **19**, 37–52.

Monk, J. (1976). *Mathematical Logic*. New York: Springer Verlag.

Monna, A. (1972). The concept of function in the nineteenth and twentieth centuries, in particular with regard to the discussions between Baire, Borel, and Lebesgue. *Archive for History of Exact Sciences* **9**, 57–84.

Montague, R. and Vaught, R. (1959). Natural models of set theories. *Fundamenta Mathematicae* **47**, 219–42.

Moore, G. (1980). Beyond first-order logic: the historical interplay between mathematical logic and axiomatic set theory. *History and Philosophy of Logic* **1**, 95–137.

—— (1982). *Zermelo's Axiom of Choice: Its Origins, Development, and Influence*. New York: Springer-Verlag.

—— and Garciadiego, A. (1981). Burali-Forti's Paradox: a reappraisal of its origins. *Historia Mathematica* **8**, 319–50.

Mostowski, A. (1966). *Thirty Years of Foundational Studies*. Oxford: Basil Blackwell.

—— (1972). Recent results in set theory. In Lakatos (1972).

Myhill, J. (1974). The undefinability of the set of natural numbers in the ramified *Principia*. In G. Nakhnikian (ed.), *Bertrand Russell's Philosophy*. London: Duckworth.

von Neumann, J. (1923). Zur Einführung der transfiniten Zahlen. *Acta Litterarum ac Scientiarum Regiae Universitatis Hungaricae Francisco-Josephinae: Sectio Sci-Math*. **1**, 199–208; reprinted in von Neumann (1961); trans. in van Heijenoort (1967).

—— (1925). Eine Axiomatisierung der Mengenlehre. *Journal für die reine und angewandte*

Mathematik **154**, 219–540; (correction in **155**, 128); reprinted in von Neumann (1961); trans. in van Heijenoort (1967).

—— (1929). Über eine Widerspruchsfreiheitsfrage in der axiomatischen Mengenlehre. *Journal für die reine unde angewandte Mathematik* **160**, 227–41.

—— (1961). *John von Neumann: Collected Works*, vol. 1. Oxford: Pergamon.

Niebergall, K., and Schirn, M. (1998). Hilbert's finitism and the notion of infinity. In M. Schirn (ed.), *The Philosophy of Mathematics Today*. Oxford: Clarendon Press.

Parsons, C. (1974). The Liar Paradox. *Journal of Philosophical Logic* **3**, 381–412; reprinted with a postscript in Martin (1984).

—— (1976) Some remarks on Frege's conception of extension. In Schirn (1976).

—— (1983). The impredicativity of induction. In *How Many Questions: Essays in Honor of S. Morgenbesser*. Indianapolis: Hackett.

Peano, G. (1889). *Arithmetices principia, novo methodo exposita*. Turin: Bocca; reprinted in Peano (1957–9), vol. 2; extracts trans. by van Heijenoort as 'The principles of arithmetic, presented by a new method' in van Heijenoort (1967).

—— (1890). Sur une courbe qui remplit toute un aire plane. *Mathematische Annalen* **36**, 157–60.

—— (1895–1908). *Formulaire de mathématique*, 5 vols. Turin: Bocca.

—— (1957–9). *Opere Scelte*. Rome: Edizione Cremonese.

Pohlers, W. (1989). *Proof Theory: An Introduction*. Springer Lecture Notes in Mathematics, no. 1407. Berlin: Springer-Verlag.

Poincaré, H. (1905). Les mathématiques et la logique, I. *Revue de Métaphysique et Morale* **13**, 815–35; trans. by W. Ewald in Ewald (1996).

—— (1906). Les mathématiques et la logique, II, III. *Revue de Métaphysique et Morale*, **14**, 17–34, 294–317; trans. in Ewald (1996).

—— (1913). *Dernière Pensées*. Paris: Flammarion; trans. by J. Bolduc as *Mathematics and Science: Last Essays*. New York: Dover Press, 1963.

Potter, M. (1991). *Sets: An Introduction*. Oxford: Clarendon Press.

—— (2000). *Reason's Nearest Kin: Philosophies of Arithmetic from Kant to Carnap*. Oxford: Oxford University Press.

Powell, W. (1975). Extending Gödel's negative interpretation to ZF. *Journal of Symbolic Logic* **40**, 221–9.

Quine, W. (1951). Two dogmas of empiricism. *Philosophical Review* **60**, 20–43; reprinted in W. Quine, *From a Logical Point of View*. Cambridge, Mass.: Harvard University Press, 1980.

—— (1960). Carnap and Logical Truth. *Synthèse* **12**, 350–74; reprinted in Benaceraff and Putnam (1964).

—— (1962). The ways of paradox. In *The Ways of Paradox and Other Essays*. Cambridge, Mass.: Harvard University Press 1976; first published as 'Paradox' in *Scientific American* **206**, no. 4, 84–96, 1962.

—— (1969). Epistemology naturalized. In *Ontological Relativity and Other Essays*. New York: Columbia University Press.

Bibliography

Ramsey, F. (1925). The foundations of mathematics. *Proceedings of the London Mathematical Society*, 2nd series, **25**(5); reprinted in Ramsey (1990).

—— (1990). *Philosophical Papers*, ed. D. Mellor. Cambridge: Cambridge University Press.

Rang, B. and Thomas, W. (1981). Zermelo's discovery of the 'Russell Paradox'. *Historia Mathematica* **8**, 15–22.

Resnik, M. (1980). *Frege and the Philosophy of Mathematics*. Ithaca, NY: Cornell University Press.

—— (1997). *Mathematics as a Science of Patterns*. Oxford: Clarendon Press.

Richard, J. (1905). Les principes des mathématiques et le problème des ensembles. *Revue générale des sciences pures et appliquées* **16**, 541; trans. in van Heijenoort (1967).

Robinson, A. (1965). Formalism 64. In Y. Bar-Hillel (ed.), *Logic, Methodology and Philosophy of Science*. Proceedings of the 1964 International Congress at Jerusalem. Amsterdam: North-Holland.

—— (1966). *Non-standard Analysis*. Amsterdam: North-Holland.

—— (1969). From a formalist's point of view. *Dialectica* **23**, 45–9.

Rosser, J. (1936). Extensions of some theorems of Gödel and Church. *Journal of Symbolic Logic* **1**, 87–91; reprinted in Davis (1965).

Rudin, W. (1964). *Principles of Mathematical Analysis*, 2nd edn. New York: McGraw-Hill.

Russell, B. (1903). *The Principles of Mathematics*. London: George Allen & Unwin.

—— (1906). On some difficulties in the theory of transfinite numbers and order types. *Proceedings of the London Mathematical Society*, series 2(4); reprinted in Russell (1973).

—— (1906b). Les Paradoxes de la logique. *Revue de Métaphysique et Morale* **14**, 627–50; the English version, 'On "insolubilia" and their Solution by symbolic logic', is reprinted in Russell (1973).

—— (1907). The regressive method of discovering the premises of mathematics. In Russell (1973).

—— (1908). Mathematical logic as based on the theory of types. *American Journal of Mathematics* **30**; reprinted in Russell (1956a).

—— (1910). La Théorie des types logiques. *Revue de Métaphysique et de Morale*, **18**; Eng. lang. version, 'The theory of logical types', reprinted in Russell (1973).

—— (1911). L'Importance philosophique de la logistique. *Revue de Métaphysique et Morale* **19**, 281–91; trans. by P. Jourdain as 'The philosophical implications of mathematical logic' in *The Monist* **23**, 481–93, 1913; and in Russell (1973).

—— (1919). *Introduction to Mathematical Philosophy*. London: George Allen & Unwin.

—— (1948). Whitehead and 'Principia Mathematica'. *Mind* **57**, 137–8.

—— (1952). Is mathematics purely linguistic? In Russell (1973).

—— (1956a). *Logic and Knowledge*, ed. R. Marsh London: George Allen & Unwin.

—— (1956b). Reflections on my eightieth birthday. In *Portraits from Memory*. London: George Allen & Unwin; reprinted as 'Postscript' in the paperback edn of Russell's *Autobiography*. London: Routledge, 1991.

—— (1959). *My Philosophical Development*. London: George Allen & Unwin.

—— (1967–9). *Autobiography*. London: George Allen & Unwin; paperback edn London: Routledge, 1991.

—— (1973). *Essays in Analysis*, ed. D. Lackey. London: George Allen & Unwin.

Sagan, H. (1994). *Space-Filling Curves*. New York: Springer-Verlag.

Schirn, M. (ed.) (1976). *Studies on Frege, I: Logic and Philosophy of Mathematics*. Stuttgart: Friedrich Frommann Verlag.

Schütte, K. (1977). *Proof Theory*. Berlin: Springer.

Scott, D. (1974). Axiomatising set theory. In Jech (ed.), *Axiomatic Set Theory*. Proccedings of Symposia in Pure Mathematics, **13**(2). Providence, RI: American Mathematical Society.

Shapiro, S. (1991). *Foundations with Foundationalism: A Case for Second Order Logic*. Oxford: Oxford University Press.

Shepherdson, J. (1952). Inner models for set theory, II. *Journal of Symbolic Logic* **17**, 225–37.

Shoenfield, J. (1967). *Mathematical Logic*. Reading, Mass.: Addison-Wesley.

Sieg, W. (1985). Fragments of arithmetic. *Annals of Pure and Applied Logic* **28**, 33–71.

Simpson, S. (1985). Reverse mathematics. In A. Nerode and R. Shore (eds.), *Recursion Theory*. Proceedings of Symposia in Pure Mathematics, 42. Providence, RI: American Mathematical Society.

—— (1988). Partial realizations of Hilbert's Programme. *Journal of Symbolic Logic* **53**, 349–63.

Skolem, T. (1920). Logisch-kombinatorische Untersuchungen über die Erfüllbarkeit oder Beweisbarkeit mathematischer Sätze nebst einem Theoreme über dichte Mengen. *Videnskapsselskapets skrifter, I: Matematisk-naturvidenskabelig klasse,* no. 4; trans. in van Heijenoort (1967).

—— (1922). Einige Bemerkungen zur axiomatischen Begründung der Mengenlehre. *Matematikerkongressen I Helsingfors den 4–7 Juli 1922, Den femte skandinaviska matematikerkongressen, Redogörelse*. Helsinki: Akademiska Bokhandeln, 1923; trans. in van Heijenoort (1967).

—— (1923). Begründung der elementaren Arithmetik durch die rekurrierende Denkweise ohne Anwendung scheinbarer Veränderlichen mit unendlichen Ausdehnungsbereich. *Videnskapsselskapets skrifter, I. Matematisk-naturvidenskabelig klasse,* no. 6; trans. in van Heijenoort (1967).

Smorynski, C. (1977). The incompleteness theorems. In J. Barwise (ed.), *Handbook of Mathematical Logic*. Amsterdam: North-Holland.

—— (1989). Hilbert's Programme. *Centrum voor Wiskunde en Informatica Quarterly* **1**, 3–59.

Sobocinski (1949). L'Analyse de l'antinomie russellienne par Lesniewski. *Methodos* **1**, 220–8.

Spector, C. (1962). Provably recursive functionals of analysis: a consistency proof of analysis by an extension of principles formulated in current intuitionistic mathematics. In J. Dekker (ed.), *Recursive Function Theory*. Proceedings of Symposia in Pure Mathematics, 5. Providence, RI: American Mathematical Society.

van Stigt, W. (1990). *Brouwer's Intuitionism*. Amsterdam: North-Holland.

Tait, W. (1981). Finitism. *Journal of Philosophy* **77**, 524–46.

Takeuti, G. (1987). *Proof Theory*, 2nd edn. Amsterdam: North-Holland.

Tarski, A. (1932). Der Wahrheitsbegriff in den Sprachen der deduktiven Disziplinen. *Anzeiger der Akademie der Wissenschaften in Wein* **69**, 23–5; trans. by J. Woodger in Tarski (1956).

—— (1944). The semantic conception of truth. *Philosophy and Phenomenological Research* **4**, 341–76.

—— (1956). *Logic, Semantics and Metamathematics: Papers from 1923 to 1938*, ed. and trans. by J. Woodger. Oxford: Clarendon Press.

Tennant, N. (1987). *Anti-Realism and Logic*. Oxford: Clarendon Press.

Thomae, J. (1906). Gedankenlose Denker: Eine Ferienplauderei. *Jahresbericht der Deutschen Mathematiker-Vereinigung* **15**, 434–38.

Troelstra, A. (1986). Introductory note to *1933e*. In Gödel (1986).

Turing, A. (1936). On computable numbers, with an application to the Entscheidungsproblem. *Proceedings of the London Mathematical Society*; reprinted in Davis (1965).

Visser, A. (1989). Peano's smart children: a provability logical study of systems with built-in consistency. *Notre Dame Journal of Formal Logic* **30**, 161–96.

Wang, H. (1974). *From Mathematics to Philosophy*. London: Routledge & Kegan Paul.

—— (1981). Some facts about Kurt Gödel. *Journal of Symbolic Logic* **46**, 653–9.

Webb, J. (1968). Metamathematics and the philosophy of mind. *Philosophy of Science* **35**, 156–78.

Weston, T. (1977). The continuum hypothesis is independent of second-order ZF. *Notre Dame Journal of Formal Logic* **18**, 499–503.

Weyl, H. (1918). *Das Kontinuum: Kritische Untersuchungen über die Grundlagen der Analysis*. Leipzig: Veit.

—— (1920). Über die neuen Grundlagenkrise der Mathematik. *Mathematische Zeitschrift* **10**, 39–79; trans. in Mancosu (1998*a*).

—— (1925). Die heutige Erkentnisslage in der Mathematik, *Symposion* **1**, 1–23; trans. in Mancosu (1998*a*).

—— (1928). Diskusssionsbemerkungen zu dem zweiten Hilbertschen Vortrag über die Grundlagen der Mathematik. *Abhandlungen aus dem Mathematischen Seminar der Hamburgischen Universität* **6**, 86–8; trans. in van Heijenoort (1967).

Whitehead, A. and Russell, B. (1910–13). *Principia Mathematica*, vols. I, II, and III. Cambridge: Cambridge University Press.

—— —— (1925–27). *Principia Mathematica*, vols. I, II, and III, 2nd edn. Cambridge: Cambridge University Press.

Wittgenstein, L. (1922). *Tractatus Logico-Philosophicus*. London: Routledge & Kegan Paul.

Wright, C. (1986). *Realism, Meaning and Truth*. Oxford: Blackwell.

Zermelo, E. (1908). Untersuchungen über die Grundlagen der Mengenlehre, I. *Mathematische Annalen* 261–81; trans. in van Heijenoort (1967).

—— (1930). Über Grenzzahlen und Mengenbereiche: Neue Untersuchungen über die Grundlagen der Mengenlehre. *Fundamenta Mathematicae* **16**, 29–47; trans. by M. Hallett in Ewald (1996).

Index

The notes are not indexed.

Index

Index